DATE DUE			
S77/96			

201-9500   PRINTED IN U.S.A.

Camosun College
Learning & Teaching Centre

FIFTH FLOOR
1483 DOUGLAS STREET   VICT
NA

TELEPHONE: 604-387-60

D1020303

Teaching in Practice

Andy Farquharson

· ·

Teaching in Practice

How Professionals Can Work Effectively with Clients, Patients, and Colleagues

Jossey-Bass Publishers
San Francisco

Substantial discounts on bulk quantities of Jossey-Bass books are available to corporations, professional associations, and other organizations. For details and discount information, contact the special sales department at Jossey-Bass Inc., Publishers. (415) 433–1740; Fax (800) 605–2665.

For sales outside the United States, please contact your local Paramount Publishing International Office.

 Manufactured in the United States of America on Lyons Falls Pathfinder Tradebook. This paper is acid-free and 100 percent totally chlorine-free.

Library of Congress Cataloging-in-Publication Data

Farquharson, Andy.
   Teaching in practice : how professionals can work effectively with clients, patients, and colleagues / Andy Farquharson. — 1st ed.
     p. cm. —(The Jossey-Bass higher and adult education, health, and social and behavioral science series)
   Includes bibliographical references and index.
   ISBN 0-7879-0128-8
   1. Communication in human services. 2. Human services personnel. 3. Counselor and client. 4. Teaching. 5. Adult learning. I. Title. II. Series: Jossey-Bass higher and adult education series. III. Series: Jossey-Bass social and behavioral science series.
HV29.7.F37 1995
361.3'2—dc20   95-17001

FIRST EDITION
HB Printing 10 9 8 7 6 5 4 3 2 1

Contents

Preface

T he origins of this book can be traced back to my experience as the director of a family counseling organization. At that time I was fortunate enough to have an experienced staff, which allowed me the freedom to explore how the agency might play a more preventive role in the community. It quickly became apparent that my training as a clinical social worker had not prepared me to become involved in community development activities. Therefore I enrolled in some additional graduate-level social work courses in an effort to upgrade my knowledge and skills for working at the community level. These courses did not, however, do much to clarify my confusion. In due course this led me to share my frustration with a colleague who was involved in community education. His advice was that I shift my part-time studies from conventional social work courses to the unfamiliar field of adult education. I have since lost contact with the person who gave me this advice, but his suggestion has profoundly changed my career.

Enrolling in my first course in adult education I quite abruptly experienced what I can only describe as a transformation of perspective. Not only did I find a new paradigm to guide my community development activities, but I also reframed many of my other activities in social work as well.

Quite simply, I came to understand that my role in community development was to help community members learn—and for me to learn from them. In helping the community learn, I at times engaged in direct teaching and on other occasions was involved in the facilitation of learning. One way in which I facilitated learning was to work toward removing internal barriers, such as a lack of self-confidence, and external barriers that blocked people in the community from gaining access to educational resources. Reframing my community development role in this way also clarified other aspects of my practice. I was able to use my new understanding to look at my counseling practice with individuals and families. My overall conclusion was that my practice was replete with teaching and learning interventions.

This shift in my practice eventually led me to acquire two further graduate degrees in adult education and to pursue a career in teaching and community development. Throughout my career I have maintained an active engagement with what are commonly known as self-help or mutual aid groups. These I regard as a particular example of one kind of autonomous adult learning, and I have come to believe that self-help groups have much to teach us about effective methods and about the limitations of professional paradigms of practice. Thus my understanding of both adult learning and mutual aid techniques have had a considerable influence on my approach to teaching.

This is the context for this book, which is constructed on the perspective that a good deal of practice in the human service professions, including social work, nursing, and medicine, is intimately concerned with teaching and the facilitation of learning. Reframed in this way, practice roles can be clarified and teaching interventions become more purposeful and more influential. My own experience is that some of my most effective and creative work has been done in situations in which I was consciously involved in teaching or the facilitation of learning. This has been particularly true of situations in which I was able to build partnership relationships with people functioning as learners rather than people fulfilling learned and constricted roles as clients, patients, or students.

My aim in this book is to infect you with some of my own enthusiasm for teaching as a practice intervention and to encourage other helping professionals to view the continuous development of teaching and facilitation skills as a career-long challenge. In my own case I was not a naturally gifted teacher, but I believe I have continued to improve through teaching praxis—the blend of action and reflection.

Intended Audience

This book is addressed to people who work or plan to work in a wide range of human service professions. These people include nurses and physicians, social workers, probation officers, psychologists and occupational therapists, pharmacists, and community workers. The common characteristic of all of these people is that they occupy strategic helping roles that give them the opportunity to teach and to facilitate learning. True, some of these opportunities may be subtle and fleeting, but nonetheless these professionals are positioned to teach when people may be most open to learning. A second audience for this book consists of people who are engaged in preprofessional training for these same helping professions. Professional schools and faculties provide an important opportunity to influence the operational paradigms of future human service practitioners, by giving them a perspective that enables them to detect teaching opportunities. This is also a time when the process of developing knowledge, attitudes, and skills for effective teaching and facilitation can commence.

In some programs—notably nursing schools—there are already courses exclusively devoted to teaching as a part of professional practice. However, in many programs teaching receives only scant attention, either because it is not yet accepted as a core skill or because it has been squeezed out by other topics in crowded curricula. This may change in the future: two current trends that may promote a higher priority for teaching are an increasing emphasis on promoting preventive health measures and technologies that support distance education. These changing patterns of service delivery may eventually produce more courses devoted exclusively to teaching and learning. Alternatively, these trends may result in programs in which content dealing with teaching and learning becomes interwoven throughout the curricula. In this latter case, teaching may come to be seen not as a discrete intervention, but rather as an integral component of many other methods. In either case this book can serve as an introductory text for those who will teach in their human service practice. This book does not presume to be the single definitive text on this subject—rather, it represents a springboard into including teaching as an important facet of one's practice. In this spirit the book is replete with examples drawn from practices in the helping professions and full of references to some stimulating reading in the adult education literature.

Overview of the Text

The first part of this book is concerned with recognizing some of the ways teaching is evident in human services practices and with the nature of the processes of teaching and learning. The opening chapter begins by offering a wide range of examples of the formal and informal, explicit and implicit teaching activities of helping professionals. These activities are directed at many different types of learners: individuals, families, groups, and communities. Helping professionals also become involved in teaching their colleagues through continuing education programs.

Chapter Two begins to focus on the development of an understanding of the learning process; this includes a consideration of the impact of learning styles on the process of both learning and teaching. An important distinction is made between professional and experiential ways of knowing, and between knowledge that is produced through technical/rational inquiry and know-how that is the product of life experience. The latter part of the chapter deals with some general considerations for working with adults as learners.

The focus of the book then shifts to the theme of learning relationships. Chapter Three centers on the way helping professionals can promote the development of effective learning relationships with people they encounter in the course of their practice. The discussion is particularly concerned with ways to develop and exercise influence within learning relationships.

Chapter Four discusses facilitation in group learning situations. The topics include the stages groups pass through in the course of their development and the variety of roles group members can assume. The discussion concludes with an exploration of the effective facilitation of experiential learning and with a variety of community education strategies that are together known as popular education.

The next four chapters deal with various elements included in the cycle of planning for effective teaching and learning. Chapter Five focuses on the importance of performing a learning needs and resources assessment prior to teaching. This includes determining that teaching is indeed what is required in a given situation, together with a review of the needs perceived by those who will be engaged in the teaching or learning process. The next stage in the planning cycle, to develop an overall design for the teaching intervention, is discussed in Chapter Six. People in the helping professions are encouraged to develop a systematic teaching plan that will attract and sustain learners' motivation. However, there is also a recognition, throughout the book, that teaching may occur in much more spontaneous ways and that learning may result from an emerging process rather than a deductive anticipatory design.

Chapter Seven describes a selected range of learning resources that can be used to complement an overall teaching plan. Practitioners are encouraged to modify existing resources, or to create their own materials when necessary. Chapter Eight includes a discussion of issues related to the evaluation of teaching and learning.

Formative evaluation and summative evaluation are seen as important ways to keep learning on track and to generate data that may be used for teaching improvement. The discussion then shifts to an examination of ways to ensure what is learned will result in lasting and contagious change. These two topics are discussed as "transfer of learning" and "the diffusion of innovations."

Chapter Nine contains a review of the major themes of the book, ways to promote continuing improvements in teaching, and a discussion of some of the trends that may shape teaching in the human services. The book concludes by taking the reader back to a reconsideration of the teaching challenges described at the start of the opening chapter.

A Note on Terminology

An effort has been made to reduce the amount of unfamiliar terminology, or jargon, in this book, but inevitably some such language does appear. A deliberate effort has been made to select only those terms that seem to have some specific descriptive power, and I hope this will become apparent to the reader. Many of these terms represent a reframing of concepts that are already in use in the human services. They are renamed to place them within the context of adult education.

Acknowledgments

First, let me say that I am most grateful to the University of Victoria for granting me the period of study leave during which this book was completed.

This book represents learning I have accumulated from many different sources. Some of these ideas came from my own professional education, but others—the most influential—have come from those who participated in the courses I have taught and the workshops I have designed and facilitated. These learners took time and risks in sharing their feedback on my efforts, and I have always been impressed with their commitment in helping me understand and improve my teaching. This is equally true of the members of a wide variety of self-help groups, who I have counted as friends and colleagues over the years. They have taught me about the power of peer learning and experiential knowledge, and from them I have learned about the potency of partnership in the helping enterprise. It is these two groups of people, the learners and the self-helpers, that are primarily responsible for teaching me the skills that eventually resulted in a national teaching award.

Many people have offered ideas and encouragement, including Hector Balthazar, John Farquharson, Marjorie Martin, and Barbara Judson, who brings enthusiasm, energy, and partnership to our collaboration in running the teaching development center at the University of Victoria.

Finally, my thanks to two other very special people: to Kristen, who thinks I am not too old to learn, and to my in-every-way-delightful partner, Maria, who learns with me every day and is my most influential teacher.

Fide et Fortitudine
(Motto of the Clan Farquharson)

Victoria, BC, Canada   Andy Farquharson
August 1995

The Author

· ·

A ndy Farquharson is a professor in the School of Social Work
and director of the Learning and Teaching Centre at the University of Victoria, Vancouver Island, British Columbia. He received
his B.A. degree in psychology (1962) from Bishop's University and
his M.S.W. degree (1965) from McGill University. He was subsequently granted an M.Ed. (1972) and an Ed.D. (1975) from the
University of Toronto.

Andy has worked as the director of family counseling services in
Vancouver and Toronto and has been a professor and continuing
education administrator in Newfoundland, Ontario, and British
Columbia. He has consulted widely, particularly on issues related to
adult learning and self-help groups. Andy has designed and facilitated numerous professional development workshops, and in 1986
he was selected to join the first of ten groups of 3M fellows who
were recognized as outstanding university teachers in Canada. In
addition to publishing in books and professional journals, Andy has
produced several professional development learning kits that blend
print and audiovisual media.

Teaching in Practice

Teaching and Learning as Facets of Professional Practice

The scene is a hospital. A nurse is helping a young woman recently diagnosed with diabetes learn the intricacies of correctly filling a syringe in order to inject herself with insulin.

The scene is a community hall in a low-income neighborhood within a large city. A community worker is helping a group of people who live in public housing sort out ways they might take some of their grievances to the appropriate authorities.

The scene is the office of a family physician. She is helping two generations of a family understand what the alternative care options may be for their aging parent and grandparent, who has suffered a disabling stroke and is no longer able to care for himself in his own home.

The scene is a drop-in shelter for street youth. A young social worker is chatting informally with a group of teens. In subtle ways he is posing questions that encourage them to exchange ideas about how they might defuse situations that carry the potential for confrontation.

All of these situations have two common elements: the helpers are representatives of one of the human service professions, and the actions of these professionals are intended to promote learning. Thus these professionals are either explicitly or implicitly engaged in the act of teaching or the facilitation of learning. They are either transferring knowledge and skills to others directly, or enabling learners to transform current knowledge to fit their own unique circumstances, or helping people learn by generating their own new understandings or meanings.

These situations illustrate the focus of this book: an examination of the opportunities to teach that arise in human service practice, and an exploration of the ways in which helping professionals can use teaching to influence change.

The umbrella term "human service professional" is used to describe a range of professionals whose primary role is to extend support, healing, and information to their fellow citizens. These helping professionals include family physicians, probation officers, clinical and public health nurses, employee assistance counselors, public health educators, community psychologists and psychiatrists, teachers and pastors, and community development workers and social workers. More broadly, the term "human service professional" might be expanded to include practitioners who already identify themselves as engaged in educational activities. This would add those involved in various forms of adult basic education (such as English as a second language programs and literacy programs) and those strategically located in the service network, including pharmacists, occupational therapists, special education teachers, and others. These kinds of helping professionals, too, are often involved in working with adult learners.

As the above scenarios illustrate, a daily reality for these professionals is that they are increasingly called upon not only to help but to teach the people who come to them for service. They are also involved in promoting learning for their colleagues and the public at large. In various situations this teaching may consist of one-to-one instruction, the facilitation of group learning, presentations to large groups, or broad-scale public education.

In addition, the rapidly expanding knowledge base in each of the human service professions, coupled with the changing demands of practice, require that professionals actively pursue their own continuing learning. The growing professional must advance his or her knowledge and skills, both as a teacher and a learner; thus many of the ideas that follow may be applied to a personal program of continuing professional development.

Fortunately, much of the knowledge, attitudes, and skills human service professionals bring to their practice is very similar to what is required for effective teaching and facilitation of learning. Thus many of the concepts associated with productive teaching already have parallels in the ideas that inform other aspects of practice in the human service professions. These concepts include the development of clear and collaborative working relationships among partners in a helping or learning enterprise; effective interpersonal communication skills, including active listening and sensitive feedback; and the goal of promoting increasing levels of self-determination and self-direction on the part of the patient, client, or learner. For this reason, practitioners who need to engage in teaching may need merely to reframe some of their current activities and rename some of their existing strategies to make their teaching more visible and intentional. This heightened consciousness should in turn promote more deliberate and continuing attention to teaching improvement. The recognition of teaching as an important and often seamless part of their professional practice may encourage practitioners to explore the wealth of practical information about effective learning and instruction.

Teaching in a variety of service situations can also be a concrete, discrete intervention that produces tangible and measurable results of its own. It therefore holds the promise of being both a creative and a rewarding activity for the human service practitioner. In this chapter the focus is on the subtle and not-so-subtle ways teaching and learning can affect the daily activities of human service professionals. The discussion addresses the various types of learners who may be targets of teaching interventions, and explores some of the social changes that have contributed to the increased need for effective teaching in daily human service practice.

Teaching and Learning in Human Service Practices

An initial challenge is to become aware of the myriad ways professionals are already engaged in teaching in their day-to-day practice. These may not be clearly evident, because of the relatively narrow and formal ways in which many people think about teaching and learning. All too frequently these narrow conceptions obscure the more informal and ephemeral ways in which teaching and learning occur. For example, many people associate teaching only with activities that take place in a formal setting, in which one person is specifically designated as the teacher and others as the students. In reality much teaching in the human services setting is informal, implicit, transitory, and at times largely learner-directed. That is, learning is primarily directed and carried out by the learner, with or without a person formally designated as "the teacher." A Canadian researcher, Allen Tough (1979, 1982), has done much to advance a broader conception of learning, to include activities that take place without the presence of formally assigned teachers and beyond the confines of the classroom. In essence, Tough draws attention to the kind of informal learning everybody engages in as they learn to live in relationships, maintain their health, and manage many of the other challenges of daily living. For example, Tough sees learning how to buy a first house, learning how to live with a physical disability, or learning how to manage personal finances as examples of predominantly informal and self-directed learning projects.

One way to appreciate the differences—or, more accurately, the continuum—between formal and informal adult learning is to consider the metaphor of an iceberg (Figure 1.1). The visible tip of an iceberg might be likened to the kind of formal learning we associate with structured education, training, and professional development programs. In such programs the teacher is clearly defined; he or she has an explicit, structured contract with the learners, who occupy their designated role of student, patient, or client. This is the kind of learning that society most readily recognizes and values.

However, as previously noted, a large part of the daily learning people accomplish takes place informally and without regard to educational institutions or the people society formally designates as teachers. This learning is reflected in the larger, less visible portion of the iceberg that lies below the surface.

The limitation of the iceberg metaphor is that it suggests a tidy distinction between formal and informal learning. In reality there is a more interwoven process produced by the dynamic interplay between formal and informal learning. This point can be illustrated by the following example. A single mother living in a tightly knit low-income neighborhood developed a skin lesion of unknown origin. She sought the advice of family and friends in an attempt to learn about the cause and treatment of this condition, to determine what her level of concern should be, and to decide whether she should seek professional assistance. On the advice of these influential people the woman did proceed to seek professional advice. The medical practitioner's assessment and recommendations were then carried back to the informal network, where they were discussed and modified by the woman's peers.

Figure 1.1. The Iceberg of Learning.

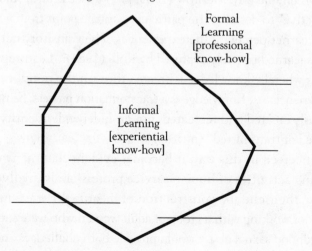

Such is the continuous ebb and flow of formal and informal learning. This is a continuing process, because knowledge does not remain static and different sources of understanding can reinforce, contradict, or modify one another.

In this book learning is conceived of as a process of meaning making; learners are thus meaning makers (Postman and Weingartner, 1969; Cranton, 1994). The metaphor of meaning making is based on the notion that learners actively create the reality they perceive; therefore their reality is shaped by their previous experiences, their assumptions, and their needs. Postman and Weingartner (1969) describe how the metaphor operates in the learning process: "The meaning-making metaphor puts the [learner] at the center of the learning process. [The aim of teaching is] to help [learners] improve their unique meaning-making capabilities. And this is the basis for learning how to learn, how to deal with the otherwise 'meaningless,' how to cope with change that requires new meanings to be made" (p. 97).

Such meaning making can take place in formal settings, with people designated as teachers, or it may occur in informal ways, or it may involve a blend of both formal and informal learning.

It follows that each individual tends to make meaning in his or her own unique way. Mezirow (1985, p. 5) uses the term "meaning perspective" to describe the particular vantage point from which a given learner perceives life experiences. The transitory nature of what is learned is nicely captured by Kolb (1984): "Learning is the process whereby knowledge is created through the transformation of experience. . . . Knowledge is a transformation process, being continuously created and recreated, not an independent entity to be acquired or transmitted" (p. 38).

Conceived in this way, it becomes evident that many of the teaching activities of human service professionals involve supporting their clients' construction of meaning. For example, a counselor working with a group of adult women who were survivors of childhood sexual abuse would provide both challenges and support as these women struggle to assign meaning to these painful experiences.

Teaching, for the purposes of this book, may be considered any activity undertaken with the specific intention of promoting learning. That is, in this book the focus will be primarily on the type of teaching that occurs at the tip of the iceberg, in which the human service professional consciously, purposefully assumes the role of teacher. There are, of course, many less formal situations in which practitioners encourage learning in the course of their other duties.

Two further examples illustrate these alternative modes of teaching practice:

Formal teaching. A respiratory therapist makes a presentation to parents of asthmatic children in order to help them understand some of the new technologies and techniques in her discipline.

Informal teaching. A community worker helps a group of low-income residents form a neighborhood association. In the course of these activities he takes advantage of opportunities to help these people learn some of the skills of effective lobbying.

This exploratory discussion will not address situations in which informal teaching occurs, even when there is no conscious and deliberate attempt to do so. For example, unintended teaching might occur when a human service professional unconsciously models a behavior that other people subsequently learn and adopt. Given the power inherent in the positions occupied by human service professionals, this kind of unconscious and unwanted teaching can take place quite readily. For example, a story is told of structuring a ward in a mental hospital to conduct what is known as milieu therapy. As part of this simulation, patients were asked to take on the roles of physicians and other health care providers. One patient assigned to play the role of a psychiatrist promptly consulted his watch and announced that he had to leave for another meeting.

Obviously some unintentional but important teaching had taken place in earlier encounters between patients and the professionals working in this setting.

Like "teaching," the word "education" is used in this book in a restricted way, to refer to systems and structures that have been developed specifically to promote teaching and thereby support learning. Used in this way, "education" becomes a descriptive term for the formal apparatus of institutions, classrooms, and teachers that are created to support learning. This definition will not be satisfactory to some, but it should be understood in this discussion as the more restricted way in which education is conceived.

It is not easy to select a word or phrase that captures the activities of human service professionals as they engage in teaching interventions. In the literature there are references to the "community change educator" (Franklin, 1976), the "self-care educator" (Levin, 1978), the "consumer educator" (Gartner, Greer, and Reissman, 1979), and the "client educator" (Mann, 1985). There is probably no concise way to reflect the rich variety of teaching activities that are undertaken by a wide range of human service professionals. For this reason, helping professionals who teach in the course of their practice are simply designated as "practitioners" rather than the more cumbersome label of "practitioner/teacher," although it may be a little more accurate.

A final task in clarifying the terminology used in this book is to define what is meant by the term "learner" and why this has been chosen as the preferred designation for those people who are the targets of teaching. Many human service professionals refer to those who use their services as "patients," "clients," or "students." The difficulty with each of these terms is that they are too limiting. Thomas (1967) has suggested that a problem with the construct of "student" is that this role requires a cluster of activities that may not fit easily within an individual's particular style of learning. Further, the connotation of the student as *consumer* obscures the role of the learner as *producer* of his or her own learning. This issue will be explored in greater detail in Chapter Three, but at this point it should be noted that the term "learner" is used here to embrace not only students, but also patients, clients, constituents, and human service colleagues. Thus the focus in this book will be on the activity of learning rather than the particular role construct of client, patient, or student. A familiar slogan observes that "students are a lot like people." This reminder might well be extended to include patients, clients, and constituents as a way to ensure that their humanity is not lost within various role constructs.

Learners in Human Service Practice

Teaching and learning are integral aspects of the helping process, and it is important to identify the diverse individuals, groups, and communities that may become involved in teaching interventions.

Individuals

The literature on patient education, a field pioneered primarily by the nursing profession (Haggard, 1989; Rankin and Stallings, 1990; Redman, 1993; Babcock and Miller, 1994), yields some practical examples of the ways in which helping professionals engage in teaching with individuals. These include such activities as teaching home management skills to people on renal dialysis, teaching people how to control hypertension, and teaching diabetics how to inject insulin.

In a quite different field of practice, a probation officer might need to engage in explicit teaching either to help an offender thoroughly understand the terms and conditions of a probation order or to enable a judge to learn more about the contextual factors that should be considered in arriving at an appropriate sentence. A third example can be found in the situation of a medical social worker who needed to help a couple in their middle years learn about a variety of community care alternatives for the husband's mother, who was suffering from Alzheimer's disease. As an adjunct to her direct teaching with this couple, the social worker developed an instructional pamphlet that could be used for further reference. This example also illustrates the way in which individual teaching might be accomplished with indirect instruction that does not involve face-to-face contact between teacher and learner.

Similarly, it should be noted that many of the teaching strategies presented in this book can be applied to the development of effective self-instructional print resources and other ancillary teaching and learning tools. Some considerations for the development of these kinds of materials are dealt with in Chapter Eight.

Small Groups

In many instances teaching and learning in human service settings takes place with small groups of learners; informal learning may be exchanged between people with shared concerns, among family members, between members of the general public, or within groups of professional colleagues.

Less formal group teaching may occur in work with families and others who are confronting a life crisis such as a death in the family. More formal, structured group teaching may be used to help people learn a wide assortment of life skills, from budgeting to parenting, mediating, and lobbying. Formal group teaching (staff training and development) may be the strategy of choice in many situations: for example, when helping a professional staff learn how to administer a new policy or use a new piece of medical or communications technology.

Communities

The third target group of learners are those clustered into existing communities; usually these contain larger numbers of learners than the groups discussed above. These communities may be defined in geographic terms, as comprising people who live close to one another in a given neighborhood, town, or region. Alternatively, the boundaries of a community may be understood in functional terms, to include people who share a similar concern or status such as homelessness or sexual orientation. This distinction is frequently blurred—in reality, many communities that are the targets of teaching can be defined both geographically and functionally. For example, a family physician might engage in teaching with the parents of high-risk infants (a functional community) who are all drawn from the same neighborhood (a geographic community).

Many activities that are commonly part of community development may be viewed as teaching and learning interventions at the community level. From this perspective the role of community worker is recast as that of teacher. Such roles may involve direct teaching to help increase the knowledge and skills of a particular group of citizens (for example, teaching organizing and lobbying skills), or they may require more indirect teaching through the facilitation of learning (for example, linking people with shared learning needs and liberating resources to support community learning). Many of the exciting new initiatives in this type of teaching may be found in the growing literature in the field known as popular education (Freire, 1973; Arnold and Burke, 1983). A popular education approach to the facilitation of learning by community groups is explored in some detail in the latter part of Chapter Four.

Professional Groups

Professional colleagues from the same or allied helping professions are also targets for teaching by human service practitioners. Most frequently this involves group teaching (so professional colleagues are really just a more specific target group). Practicing professionals may be invited to teach in university and college preservice programs, or—more frequently—they may be asked to act as a resource for in-service programs that train practitioners in new skills or offer ongoing professional development. Learning by fellow professionals may also be facilitated more subtly, in the course of collaborative work by interdisciplinary teams. In this context there is typically a continuing need to help other team members learn from the expertise each member brings to the process of cooperative problem solving. There is also an ongoing need for people in different professions to keep others informed about their roles and their individual contributions to the collaborative effort. This book should encourage professionals in the human services to take advantage of any and all opportunities to teach their peers and to facilitate collegial learning. Teaching can be as tangible and purposeful as any other aspect of professional practice. Effective teaching with professional peers can be an important way to apply many of the ideas contained in this book.

Individual Professionals

A final target for teaching are practitioners themselves as they engage in ongoing professional development. In order for professionals to remain abreast of trends in a particular discipline, they must be proactive in managing their own continuing professional development. This is particularly important given the limited life span of knowledge within many human service disciplines—old knowledge, skills, and attitudes are continually displaced by the wealth of new information on ways to improve professional practice.

Examples of both formal and informal teaching interventions with this range of learners—individuals, families, groups, communities, colleagues, and professionals themselves—are outlined in Table 1.1.

It is evident from these examples that frequently when practitioners engage in informal teaching interventions, the teaching relationship is based on an implicit understanding rather than an explicit agreement or contract between the parties. The need for such an arrangement occurs when the practitioner believes a target learner would be reluctant to assume the role of student or learner. Or the practitioner might conclude that the targeted learner or learners will resist the content of what is to be learned if it is taught in an explicit fashion. Examples of this kind of implicit teaching may be found in the relationship between parents and

Table 1.1. Teaching in the Human Services.

Formal Teaching	*Informal Teaching*
INDIVIDUALS	
Mary, a social worker, teaches her client some management skills [budgeting, tracking expenditures, and so on].	Mary informally teaches a client about responsibility by thoughtfully planning how to respond to his late arrival at interviews in a way that will promote learning.
FAMILIES	
Jane, a family counselor, uses her initial sessions with the W family to teach them about their rights and responsibilities in the counseling relationship.	On a home visit to the W's, Jane observes that the daughter leaves the room whenever her parents argue. She uses this observation to help the parents learn a little more about the consequences of their communication patterns.
GROUPS	
Bill leads a group for men who batter. He helps them understand two possible reasons for their abusive behavior.	Bill has established contact with a group of street kids. One of his goals is to try to positively influence their eating habits, and he takes advantage of information opportunities to teach them the basics of good nutrition.
COMMUNITY	
Chris works with a local AIDS support group to develop an educational pamphlet on the disease.	Although not gay himself, Chris has a goal of positively altering community attitudes toward lesbians and gay men. He uses his social contacts to push this agenda, while respecting the limits of his "outsider" perspective.
PROFESSIONALS	
Carol, a community nurse, develops a one-day workshop to teach her colleagues about the nature and effectiveness of self-help groups.	Carol uses the weekly meetings of her interdisciplinary medical team to informally help her colleagues understand her role on the team and in the community.
PERSONAL CONTINUING EDUCATION	
Stan, a college nursing instructor, has a long-standing interest in creative problem-solving. He obtains funding to attend an institute on this subject.	Stan wants to try to improve his teaching. He decides to keep a journal recording various facts and his assumptions and feelings following each teaching episode.

their children. In these situations teaching may need to be very subtle, because the child's awareness of the parent as a teacher can be repugnant—particularly to adolescents!

There are important ethical issues raised by implicit teaching and the right of people to be consciously aware of all that is taking place within the context of their relationship with a helping professional. These ethical concerns will be explored in Chapter Nine, but at this point it will suffice to note that professionals in the human services need to be constantly alert to the potential for domination and for violation of people's right to self-determination. This is particularly important when a practitioner engages in implicit teaching with a client.

Teachable Moments: Finding Teaching Opportunities

Human service professionals recognize that there are certain moments when people are more open to change. Havighurst (1970) uses the term "teachable moments" to describe these times, when individuals, groups, and communities find that their existing mode of functioning has been disrupted in some fashion. On these occasions people are open to developing new meanings and behaviors as they work to restore balance in their lives. These periods of disequilibrium are sometimes predictable; for example, certain challenges are associated with the various stages of human development (puberty, adolescence, adulthood, middle age, and old age). On the other hand, times of imbalance may also result from unexpected or capricious crises such as job loss, health problems, geographical relocation, and relationship difficulties. In any event, teaching will be much more potent if it is delivered during these teachable moments and if it is related to the learning needs of the persons involved.

One of the most attractive aspects of teaching in practice, as opposed to teaching in formal educational programs, is that the practitioner is much more likely to be present when these teachable moments occur. Developing acuity and skill in spotting and building on these opportunities is a satisfying lifelong challenge. Once developed, these skills can be applied to work with individuals, groups, communities, and organizations. The failure to detect and respond in a timely way to these crucial teaching opportunities can leave the practitioner attempting to teach people what they no longer wish to know.

The key to building on teachable moments is to identify *what* the learner needs to know and *when* he or she is likely to be receptive to this material. To illustrate the challenges in taking advantage of teachable moments, there is an apocryphal story that goes as follows: a young, single mother of a five-year-old was experiencing an increasing need to give her young son some basic information about what are euphemistically known as the facts of life. However, she was sensitive enough to recognize that she should perhaps wait for a teachable moment to impart this information. Finally the day arrived when her son queried, "Where did I come from, Mum?" The mother pounced on this opportunity and launched into a lengthy, well-rehearsed explanation of human reproduction. Her son's eyes began to glaze over. When she paused momentarily he was able to say, "That's interesting, 'cause Billy comes from Montreal!"

There are a couple of lessons to be learned from this cautionary tale. First, practitioners need to be sure that their perception of a teachable moment is accurate and that the learner is really ready to learn what the practitioner wants to teach. For example, a client might express readiness to change an undesirable behavior, without demonstrating any ability to do so. Second, the professional needs to guard against overloading the teachable moment. There is a danger of telling the learner more than he or she ever wanted to know about a particular topic, if practitioners have enthusiastically overprepared for this moment. An example of this might be parents who seek advice about a child's behavior and wind up in family therapy, when they only wanted some simple, practical suggestions. One way to avoid these kinds of situations is to apply the principle of parsimony: teach as little as possible in order to promote learning.

The following example illustrates how a practitioner might have to be patient in waiting for an appropriate teachable moment:

> A family counselor had seen a woman three times who was experiencing vicious verbal assaults from her husband. On each occasion the woman expressed a desire to leave him, but she seemed unable to follow through. At the next interview the counselor asked if her young daughter was also experiencing this angry criticism, and the mother acknowledged that she was. The counselor helped her explore what this might mean for the child in the long term, and this triggered a teachable moment during which the mother mapped out firmer plans to leave.

Developmental Learning Opportunities

Some wag made the observation that "Life is a learning experience," and this is the thrust of this learning principle. The suggestion is that people are often interested in learning that is directly related to the developmental tasks they currently confront. Knox (1977) wrote a most comprehensive, useful resource on this topic, in which he notes: "The term *development* refers to the orderly and sequential changes in characteristics and attitudes that adults experience over time. . . . An understanding of these . . . relations [and roles] in the lives of adults can increase the ability of practitioners to predict trends and assist adults in their efforts to learn and change" (p. 9).

Recognition of some of the common life tasks and role transitions people experience makes it possible for the practitioner to predict and thus plan for certain kinds of teachable moments. The kinds of teaching and learning opportunities that can be mobilized around developmental tasks range from formalized programs of family life education to informal learning within self-help groups. Some examples of more formal programs include prenatal classes, infant stimulation programs, parent education programs, marriage enrichment courses, and preretirement planning workshops. More autonomous self-help groups include parents-of-twins, solo parents, "tough love," and widow-to-widow programs. These kinds of educative and supportive programs can serve a range of issues and appeal to a variety of learning styles.

Practitioners are encouraged to scan for other opportunities to structure teaching and learning activities around teachable moments triggered by the challenges associated with the various stages of human development.

Critical Learning Opportunities

Other teachable moments occur with unexpected crises such as the onset of an acute illness or the loss of employment. These types of situations may stimulate two alternative types of learning: learning to find meaning for what has occurred and to live with the situation, or learning to find ways to alleviate the circumstances. There are important learning tasks involved in responding either way to these challenges. In recognition of the coping tasks associated with these kinds of critical events, many human service programs are established in such a way that they can be easily accessed at the times and places such events are likely to occur. Examples include relocation counseling agencies, divorce and separation counselors, employment and reemployment services, and hospital-based social service and emergency departments. In the future practitioners are likely to find other creative ways to develop services around this concept of the teachable moment, and this will increase the probability that teaching is accessible where and when people are most motivated to learn. Teaching opportunities that occur in conjunction with unpredictable life crises are reflected in the following examples:

The senior staff of a school district organized a quick response team, which could be rapidly deployed when critical events affected members of the school community. Typical situations this team has addressed include helping high school students learn how to cope with the trauma of the suicide of a classmate on school grounds, helping a group of teachers learn how to help parents deal with their concerns about a life-threatening viral infection that had claimed the life of several students, and setting up a support group for teenagers who were caught in the middle of a marital breakup.

Employee assistance counselors employed on a military base designed an educational program for families faced with relocation across the country following a scheduled base closing. They also helped establish a mutual aid group for spouses of military person-nel serving in war zones overseas.

In these kinds of situations, while the critical events may be relatively difficult to predict, there is some lead time for the practitioner to plan a teaching intervention. However, there are many other circumstances when teaching opportunities are indeed "moments," in the sense that they are ephemeral and fleeting (for example, when a frail elderly person asks what the options may be if he or she is no longer able to live independently, or when a chance question in an interview with the local media offers the professional an opportunity to provide some effective public education). These subtle opportunities offer the practitioner a potent way to influence learning—if they can be detected and tapped in a timely fashion. This point is crucial, because unless the professional is consistently reflective and responsive in the course of his or her daily practice, these momentary teaching opportunities can be missed. One of the hallmarks of connoisseur practitioners is their ability to detect and respond quickly to these opportunities. In metaphorical terms, it is all too easy to spot only the retreating rear lights of a teaching opportunity after the learning vehicle has already passed by the practitioner. The following examples illustrate some of these more fleeting teachable moments:

A family physician had been concerned for some time about the sedentary lifestyle and weight gain of a patient in his early thirties. Initial attempts to raise these concerns were rebuffed. Later, when a medical problem occurred related to the excess weight, the patient was more receptive to a teaching intervention.

An occupational therapist was concerned about the racial stereotypes expressed by her colleagues. She waited patiently until some comments were made about "immigrants." Then she pointed out that she herself was not born in North America, and she proceeded to share some of the negative experiences and consequences she had encountered due to the prevalence of such stereotypes in North American culture.

The administrative staff of a community college rejected attempts by college counselors to introduce teaching initiatives addressing issues related to sexual harassment. A program was finally introduced following serious harassment charges brought by three female students against a male instructor.

A special education teacher working with primary-school children with multiple disabilities was concerned that other team members (a psychologist, a speech therapist, a social worker) were tending to treat a seven-year-old boy as though he were a cuddly preschooler. The child was undersized for his age, and undeniably cute, but this kind of attention was tending to reinforce some very immature behavior. Eventually, at a team meeting, the social worker mentioned that the boy's parents had complained about his immaturity. The teacher then used this opportunity to do some informal teaching about the need for all team members to be consistent in responding to this child.

A community worker was concerned about poor fish-handling practices in a northern fishing community. Rough treatment of the fish and inadequate icing were contributing to rapid deterioration of the product. The community worker, a relative newcomer, had been able to establish only limited credibility, and he could not get community leaders to hear his concerns. Some time later, following a long spell of hot weather, an itinerant fish buyer indicated he was only prepared to buy 40 percent of the catch. The community worker encouraged him to be specific about his concerns about the quality of the product, which helped create a climate for teaching some new fish-handling procedures.

An appreciation of the value of gearing teaching to teachable moments may be one of the most effective ways to increase the effectiveness of teaching interventions in the human services. One striking example of a large-scale initiative based on this principle was a program for peasant healers in China, known as the Barefoot Doctors program (De Geyndt, Zhao, and Liu, 1992). This interesting project presented a challenge to practitioners—to rethink some of their cherished notions about professional education.

The Barefoot Doctors program was undertaken following the revolution in China, when the authorities decided they wished to improve the standard of medical care at the local level. They wisely recognized that while there might be no formally trained doctors in a particular community, there were likely to be individuals who were locally accepted as healers. The Barefoot Doctors project recruited a number of these local healers for accelerated training in techniques of Western and traditional Chinese medicine as well as methods for harvesting and preserving medicinal herbs. These individuals were rewarded with a pedal-driven bicycle-cum-stretcher and returned to their local villages. They continued to carry out their traditional occupational roles, using their enhanced medical skills whenever these might be required.

Inevitably the barefoot doctors encountered diseases and injuries that were beyond their current competency; on these occasions they would load the patient onto the stretcher and peddle off to the nearest medical facility. The patient would be admitted for care and the barefoot doctor would remain for continuing education related to the patient's condition. For example, if the patient required an appendectomy, the barefoot doctor would be taught about diagnosing this condition and about postoperative care of the patient. In this manner these peasant doctors obtained an extraordinary level of skill through a process of recurrent education. The elegance of this model of continuing professional development is that the learner always receives a piece of new learning at the precise moment when there is motivation for this learning. This is in marked contrast to the Western model of professional education, in which great quantities of teaching are provided up front prior to practice. By the time these skills are actually required, much of this learning may have been lost. There seem to be plenty of implications in this experience-driven, direct teaching method for the human services and for the design of teaching programs.

In summary, the concept of the teachable moment underscores the fact that teaching is more effective when learners are naturally motivated to learn what is being taught. This kind of motivation is often associated with predictable life transitions, with unexpected life crises, or with more ephemeral teaching opportunities. In order to respond effectively to these opportunities, the practitioner needs to be patient, perceptive, and creative.

Expanding Opportunities for Teaching in Practice

There appear to be several factors that have contributed to the increasing interest in teaching and the promotion of learning in the human service professions. These include changing conceptions of health and well-being (Epp, 1986, 1988); altered expectations of service users (Powell, 1987); the rapid expansion in many fields of knowledge; and a new appreciation of experiential knowledge as a complement to scientific and professional know-how (Schön, 1983; Belenky, Clinchy, Goldberger, and Tarule, 1986). There is a dynamic interrelationship between these factors, and together they have contributed to a profound shift in the conceptualization of the role of human service professionals. This is not a trivial adjustment—it represents a brand new paradigm for constructing the multiple activities of helping professionals. This new perspective reveals a multitude of teaching opportunities, and to the extent that professionals recognize and accept their role as teachers, they can be a key resource in the promotion of individual, group, and community learning.

One aspect of this new paradigm for the human services is that it incorporates a much broader understanding of the concept of health. This new understanding recognizes that health embraces much more than the simple absence of disease. Likewise, this view has broadened practitioners' understanding of the impact of stress on their clients' physical well-being; this in turn has heightened their appreciation of the importance of social supports to buffer the effects of such stress (Gottlieb, 1985). These understandings are coupled with a greater acknowledgment of the role of public policy in promoting health. Indeed, the term "*healthy* public policy" is now used to reflect this perspective.

At the same time, there has been an increasing demand from service users to participate more fully in the design and delivery of human services. Several studies conducted over a span of years have documented consumer dissatisfaction with the delivery of human services (Mayer and Timms, 1969; Maluccio, 1979). These criticisms often stem from the class, culture, and gender barriers that interfere with communication between service providers and consumers. To some extent this has been the result of a model of service that was essentially nonreciprocal: one party giving or prescribing and the other receiving. This is reflected in the words of Ivan Illich (1987), who observes that "professionals tell you what you need and claim the power to prescribe" (p. 17). This power of prescription carries with it the possibility of overemphasizing the need for professional intervention. The inherent danger in this situation is also noted by Sarason (1972), who observes that professionals rarely define a problem in terms that do not require their own (professional) presence in order to achieve a solution.

In a related development, human service professionals have also become increasingly aware and accepting of the ways in which lay people who share physical, social, or psychological concerns can benefit from the kind of self-directed learning that takes place within self-help groups (Powell, 1987; Cardinal and Farquharson, 1991). Much of what is learned in such groups is based on experiential knowledge derived from the direct life experience of the members. Similarly, there is emerging acceptance among all types of professionals of the concept of experiential ways of knowing—ways of knowing that do not rely exclusively on a process of technical rationality (Schön, 1983). The understanding derived from inquiry based on technical rationality and the scientific method may be referred to as professional knowledge, while experiential knowledge refers to the understanding extracted from the direct, nonscientific, and unquantified experience of the learner. One way to conceptualize these two domains of knowing is to modify the metaphor of the iceberg (see Figure 1.1). This visible, revered tip of the iceberg, representing knowledge based on technical rationality, should not be allowed to downplay the importance of the experiential know-how that lies below the surface. In reality, experiential knowledge interacts with technical/rational knowledge to inform much of the daily behavior of both professionals and the general public. There tends to be an interweaving of these different ways of knowing.

Schön (1983) advances the argument that the high-functioning professional draws on both technical rationality and experiential knowledge to inform his or her practice. His view is that there can be a positive synergy between these two ways of knowing. The challenge he poses is for professionals to learn from the experiential wisdom of those they work with, and to grow in understanding as they engage in reflective practice. This issue is given more attention in Chapter Two.

Foundations of Teaching in Human Service Practice

The preceding discussion addressed some of the social trends that have contributed to the developing interest in teaching as a practice intervention. At the same time, it should be acknowledged that teaching is not a new activity in the helping professions—all efforts to promote changes in behavior are ultimately exercises in teaching or the facilitation of learning.

There are at least four fields of practice that lay the groundwork for the current interest in teaching strategies and contribute to the knowledge base for pursuing teaching in human service practice: patient education, health promotion, community education, and professional education.

Patient Education

Patient or client education has for a long time been a concern of the medical professions in general and of nursing in particular (Haggard, 1989; Rankin and Stallings, 1990; Redman, 1993; Babcock and Miller, 1994). It has been defined by Squyres (1980) as "planned combinations of learning activities designed to assist people who are having or who have had experience with illness or disease in making changes in their behavior [that are] conducive to health" (p. 1).

Much of the early work in this field was concerned with ways to ensure that patients would comply with directives given by helping professionals. In time, however, studies of patient noncompliance contributed to an appreciation of how individual people construct their understanding of wellness, and how this process might be used to help them achieve and maintain the level of wellness their doctors prescribed. A person's "health belief model" (Becker, 1974), or wellness paradigm, came to be recognized as a key variable in determining patient compliance or noncompliance with a professionally recommended health regime. There is a great deal of useful information on this subject in the general patient-education literature. In particular, Becker's health belief model serves as a reminder of the need to be alert to demographic and psychosocial variables that can enhance or impede learning in specific circumstances.

Health Promotion

The field of health promotion developed in part from earlier work in patient education and family life education, but it has expanded to include a concern with healthy public policy and disease prevention. The elusive nature of the concept of health promotion is reflected in the following statement from Health and Welfare Canada (1989): "[Health Promotion] is something quite original, which is not health care, or health education, or health administration, or public health, although all these form part of its lineage. Health Promotion is more than the sum of its parts" (p. 1).

A key milestone in the health promotion movement was the publication of *Achieving Health for All: A Framework for Health Promotion* (Epp, 1986) by the Canadian government. This document in essence shifted the focus from individual lifestyles to the influence of the environment on health. Its plan for action focused on self-care, mutual aid, and the creation of healthy environments. The first two of these domains rely heavily on teaching and learning processes.

Community Education and Development

Community education and development is a huge field of practice, ranging from modest outreach efforts at community colleges and schools to radical learning initiatives such as those proposed by Paulo Freire (1973) and, more recently, by popular education practitioners (Arnold and Burke, 1983). The practitioner whose primary target for change is the community may find it helpful to reframe much of his or her work to involve teaching or the facilitation of learning.

Professional Education

A final field of practice that is a source of ideas about teaching and learning is the area of professional education. This domain of education includes both the initial training of human service professionals and the continuing education of those who are already in practice. The literature on higher professional education (Knowles and Associates, 1985; Baskett and Marsick, 1992) is already large and is growing rapidly. Likewise, a great deal has been written about the creation of programs for continuing professional development (Houle, 1980; Willis, Dubin, and Associates, 1990).

This snapshot of these four fields of teaching practice should not exclude the many other ways in which the human service professional may help his or her clients or the community through teaching. In Chapter Two the focus shifts to a consideration of how teaching in practice may be improved by drawing on ideas from an allied human service profession, the field of adult education.

2

Viewing Clients and Patients as Learners

As indicated in Chapter One, this book draws attention to the multiple ways in which helping professionals are called upon to teach, and it provides an introduction to the wealth of knowledge about effective teaching in the human services setting. This chapter focuses on an expanded understanding of different conceptions of the learning process, discussing a number of principles to guide the facilitation of adult learning.

Teaching Philosophies

In beginning this exploration of the learning process, helping professionals are encouraged to reflect about the perspective or philosophy they bring to the teaching aspects of their professional practice. What values and assumptions guide your professional decisions regarding when, what, and how to teach? The importance of clarifying your personal perspective is noted by Stephen Brookfield (1990): "Develop a theory of practice, a critical rationale for why you are doing what you are doing. . . . Without a personal organizing vision we are rudderless vessels tossed around on the waves and currents of what political whims and fashions are prevalent at the time. Our practice may win us career advancement, but it will be lacking in the innate meaning that transforms teaching from a function into a passion" (p. 195).

The following discussion of two distinct approaches to understanding and guiding the learning process should illuminate some embedded philosophies about learning that practitioners bring to their teaching. The two approaches are known as positivism (or logical positivism) and constructivism. While they are introduced here as discrete philosophies, it is possible to blend strategies from each approach in developing helpful teaching interventions.

Positivism

Positivism refers to a logical, scientific approach to inquiry, in which hypotheses are tested and conclusions are reached that are irrefutable and can be independently verified. The type of professional knowledge that characterizes the tip of the metaphoric iceberg (see Figure 1.1) is most frequently characterized by positivist inquiry.

The basic assumptions that underlie a positivist approach to teaching are that learning needs can be closely determined, learning objectives can be sharply framed, and teaching is always a rational and sequential process. Positivism embraces what Joyce and Weil (1986) call a "family" of related theories, including behavior modification and mastery learning.

In positivist teaching the locus of control is primarily the teacher. Teaching is tightly structured, and learning outcomes are stated in behavioral terms. This type of approach is often characteristic of training programs in business and industry, and it may also be found in the human services in the training of paraprofessionals. As a practice strategy, a more positivist approach may be used by those with a background in behavioral psychology and in situations in which learning outcomes can be closely specified. Some of the key figures who favor this type of approach to teaching include Robert Mager (1984), who has written extensively about the form and function of learning objectives, and Robert Gagné (Gagné and Driscoll, 1988), who has influenced the design of numerous training programs.

Constructivism

In Chapter One, learning was described as a process of meaning making, involving the active construction of meaning by the learner. This perspective on the learning process is known as constructivism (Candy, 1989); it offers a practical way for human service professionals to understand situations that appear to require some kind of teaching intervention. Constructivism proposes that each individual creates or constructs the reality he or she experiences. Mezirow (1985) takes a similar approach; he speaks of mediating constructions, or meaning perspectives. He describes them this way: "Meaning perspective refers to the structure of cultural and psychological assumptions within which our past experience assimilates and transforms new experience. . . . They guide the way in which we experience, feel, judge and act upon our situation. . . . By defining our expectations, it also selectively orders what we learn and how we learn" (pp. 21–22).

Whitman (1993), in a review of the literature on constructivism, points out that people engage in individual, *cognitive* constructions when they draw on experiential and technical data to assign meaning to new experiences. They construct "meaning maps" as a way to account for these events. (This is illustrated, for example, in the way a counselor "constructs" or accounts for what appears to be taking place within a family that is experiencing interpersonal difficulties.) In turn, these individual constructions are modified through a series of *social* constructions when they are shared with other people. Input from a variety of people continuously shapes and modifies the explanatory constructs of the individual. (A practitioner's initial construction might be modified during a case consultation with colleagues, for example.) The value of constructivism for practitioners is that it serves as a reminder that each learner constructs the world differently. Thus, as Whitman (1993) says, "the teacher's role is to help learners use personal experience to understand the world in their [the learners'] own way" (p. 2). The constructivist model under-

scores the role of the teacher in developing a partnership relationship that fosters the development of active learning and an increased
independence on the part of the learner. The concept of social constructivism points to the need for collaboration—to help people
learn from the varied perspectives of their peers and of the practitioner. Finally, constructivism offers a way to take into account the
mediating effects of gender, class, and culture, as these impact sig-
nificantly on the process of constructing meaning.

The following example illustrates one way in which a constructivist perspective might shed light on an unsuccessful teaching
intervention:

> A physician, employed by an international aid project, was teaching
> basic hygiene to a group of peasant women in a developing country.
> She set up a table with two bowls, one filled with mud and the other
> with soapy water. She immersed her hands in the mud and then held
> them up, asking if they were clean or dirty. "Dirty!" the women cho-
> rused. She then washed her hands in the suds and again asked for
> an evaluation. "Clean!" came the response. Then, as a final check,
> she once more put her hands in the mud and asked for comment.
> Much to her chagrin, the judgment of the participants was that her
> hands were now "Clean!"
>
> "Why?" she asked. The learners responded that her hands were
> clean because only moments before she had washed them.

A constructivist analysis of this situation would suggest that one of
the factors at play here is a different construction of the concept of
"clean." This example also illustrates a variation between different
groups in the extent to which "cleanliness" is seen as a useful or
desirable guiding construct. Is cleanliness next to godliness, or is it
merely an artifact of foreign folklore?

In summary, the theory of constructivism points to the individual nature of learning, to the mediating effects of the perspectives
of others, to the value of experiential knowledge, and to the impor-

tance of active learning. In human services practice there will be situations that require either a positivist or a constructivist approach; but for the most part elements of both perspectives can be used at different stages of a teaching intervention. Most frequently the spontaneous and emergent nature of much of the teaching that occurs in human services practice dictates the need for a more constructivist approach.

Stages of Learning

Another approach that may help practitioners think about effective teaching is to understand that learners pass through identifiable stages as they learn, becoming increasingly strategic in their thinking. Commonly referred to as levels of cognitive development, these stages can serve as a guide to the way that teaching is calibrated to ensure that it both reaches and stretches the learner.

William Perry (1970, 1981) is the person who has been most frequently identified with this area of study. In his work on ways of knowing, Perry suggests that students advance through a series of evolving meaning perspectives, or positions, in the course of their intellectual development. He sets out an elaborate scheme of different levels of intellectual development, which can be reduced into three basic categories: dualism, multiplicity, and contextual relativism.

Perry says that at the first level, dualism, learners tend to frame their experience in terms of polar positions: good/bad, right/wrong, us/them. At this level, learners tend to rely on the opinions of authorities to give them "the truth." Over the course of time, however, many learners abandon this dualistic position, as they come to understand that there are multiple perspectives on the nature of truth and goodness. What is most puzzling for learners at this stage of their cognitive development is that these various perspectives often seem to contradict one another. This recognition of the existence of competing authorities necessarily undermines the learner's faith in any single viewpoint, and it may lead the learner to believe that all answers are equally true. But Perry believes that as the learner continues to evolve intellectually, he or she will eventually come to a position of contextual relativism. That is, learners will arrive at the understanding that truth is relative, shaped by a given context and by the particular perspective of the knower or meaning maker.

Stimulated and challenged by Perry's conclusions, Belenky, Clinchy, Goldberger, and Tarule (1986) wrote their own groundbreaking response, derived from their direct experiences with women as knowers. These authors found that Perry's ideas failed to resonate with their own learning experiences as women. They concluded that this was due to the fact that Perry's original study mostly drew on the experiences of a group of privileged male undergraduates at Harvard. In their book, *Women's Ways of Knowing*, they articulate an alternative model of cognitive development, based on the intellectual journey experienced by women.

There are some parallels between the work of Perry and the conclusions reached in *Women's Ways of Knowing*. Belenky and her colleagues outlined four main stages in their own process of cognitive development: received knowing, subjective knowing, procedural knowing, and connected knowing. Each of these stages in turn embraces several related subcategories. In simple terms, their model suggests that women learners proceed from a state of silence, in which they receive knowledge through the voices of others, toward a state of subjective knowing, in which they begin to listen to their own inner voice and to validate a separate sense of self. In the last two stages, women are seen as having developed their capacity for procedural knowing (after developing skills in systematic analysis and thinking procedures) and then, in turn, their capacity for connected knowing, which enables them to establish contact with the knowledge of others. Finally, these various voices become integrated into what Belenky and her colleagues describe as "constructed knowledge." They describe this as the recognition that "all knowledge is constructed and the knower is an intimate part of the known" (p. 137). In effect, their discussion takes us full circle, back to the earlier exploration of constructivism.

The implication of these theories of cognitive development on teaching in the helping professions is that they underscore the need to individualize teaching methods. That is, it is important to pay close attention to the cognitive position of individual learners in selecting the material to be taught and deciding on the manner in which it should be presented. The aim is to introduce ideas that are understandable and that, given the current cognitive position of the learner, also promote continuing intellectual development.

Schmidt and Davidson (1983), Daloz (1986), and others have suggested specific ways teachers can tailor their instruction to different cognitive stages, mostly by teaching to the leading edge of the learner's current cognitive level. The aim is to ensure comprehension while fostering further intellectual development. It is apparent that frustration can arise when there is a significant mismatch between the demands of the practitioner and the intellectual position of the learner. This may partly account for the clash in expectations that can occur between professionals and their clients (Mayer and Timms, 1969; Maluccio, 1979), although other factors, including class and culture, may also be at play in such situations.

The following examples illustrate how an understanding of the cognitive positions of learners might be used to shape a practitioner's teaching interventions:

A social worker in an intermediate care facility found that several of her elderly clients seemed to favor a dualist mode of thinking. Accordingly, when helping them to learn about group relationships she tended to offer quite concrete suggestions and to teach them specific behaviors that might help them resolve their interpersonal conflicts.

A counseling psychologist was working with a group of parents of preschoolers to help them expand their parenting skills. Each parent seemed to adhere fairly rigidly to the doctrines of the particular parenting expert he or she favored. This resulted in some rigidity and relatively little independent thought. Gradually, by posing numerous hypothetical parenting challenges, the psychologist was able to help these parents learn that they needed to create some of their own solutions, apart from what the experts offered. These would need to be suited to their own circumstances, the personalities of their children, and their own perspectives on parenting.

Residents of a low-income housing project tried to establish a day care facility based on a model used in another city. They experienced difficulty in moving their plans forward. A public health nurse, through her support and gentle teaching, was able to help them learn ways to develop an original day care model based on their own particular perceptions of care and the resources available within their own community.

Styles of Learning

Another important way in which learners differ from one another is in their individual ways of conducting learning. Learning style has been defined as "the individual's characteristic ways of processing information, [of] feeling and behaving in certain situations" (Smith, 1982, p. 24). There is considerable interest in the concept of learning styles, and there are a number of different conceptions of how individuals differ in this regard (Myers and Myers, 1980; Gregorc, 1982; Kolb, 1985; Butler, 1986; Ingham and Dunn, 1993). These conceptions of learning styles range from the now somewhat questionable distinction between right- and left-brain learning all the way to highly structured models like the Myers-Briggs Personality Type Indicator. Many of these newer learning style inventories promise a high degree of precision in measuring individual styles.

The work of David Kolb (1984) stands out among these learning-style theorists because his approach is relatively straightforward. His model also has added value in that it provides a way to understand the process of experiential learning. Kolb suggests that learning style is shaped by two variables: concrete-to-abstract and active-to-reflective. He sees these two continua intersecting as illustrated in Figure 2.1.

These four dimensions of learning are defined by Kolb in the following way:

Learning from concrete experience. This dimension relies heavily on experience-based input.

Learning from reflective observation. This phase involves gathering all available data generated by an experience.

Figure 2.1. Kolb's Dimensions of Learning.

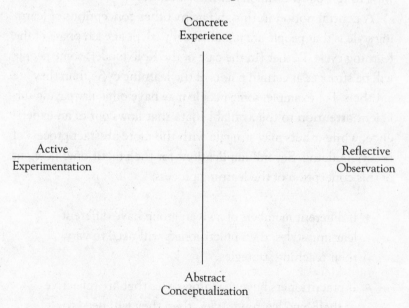

Learning from abstract conceptualization. In this phase, learning is advanced by the generation of analytical and conceptual hypotheses or theories in an attempt to explain the data generated by the learning experience.

Learning from active experimentation. This is the "doing" phase of learning, when the utility of the theories that have been generated are tested in action. This in turn generates more data.

Kolb suggests that when people are learning they constantly cycle and recycle through these stages, in a predominantly clockwise fashion. That is, learners have an experience, reflect on the cognitive and affective data generated by the event, use these data to construct theories to account for the experience, and finally find ways to test out the validity of these theories.

A central notion in this and many other conceptions of learning style is that people are not all equally adept at each phase of the learning cycle. Rather (in the case of the Kolb model) some people will be stronger at certain points of the learning cycle than they are at others. For example, some people may have difficulty paying sufficient attention to the available data that flows out of an experience, while others may struggle with the more abstract process of theory-building. Several implications for the practitioner flow out of this conception of the learning process:

- If different members of a given group have different learning styles, then practitioners will need to vary their teaching strategies.

- If practitioners have teaching styles that are reflective of their own learning styles, then they will need to recognize that their teaching may well pose difficulties for learners who have styles that differ markedly from their own.

- Groups of learners whose different learning styles represent different strengths can provide important learning resources for one another. For example, those with a particular strength in reflective observation may complement those who are more adept at abstract conceptualization. This kind of complementary blending of learning styles is one of the factors that can contribute to the potency of group learning and teamwork.

- Different learning tasks may demand particular learning styles. For example, reflective observation may be important for parents trying to identify their child's strengths and weaknesses, while active experimentation may be more useful in testing alternative ways of responding to the child's behavior.

The implications of these different learning styles are illustrated by the following examples from human service practice:

Blend of teaching strategies. In planning a workshop on money management, a vocational counselor developed a plan that included a priority-setting exercise, a system for keeping track of expenditures, some theories on debt reduction, and a sample grocery shopping expedition.

Mismatch of teaching and learning style. A social work student who had completed the Kolb Learning Style Inventory approached her instructor because of her learning difficulties. She had scored low on abstract conceptualization, which was a key attribute of the instructor's teaching style. Mutual recognition of this mismatch enabled teacher and learner to arrive at a more effective accommodation of their respective teaching and learning styles.

Heterogeneity of learning style. A special education teacher and her three teaching assistants were conscious of some difference in their approach to learning and problem solving. However, when they compared their Learning Style Inventory scores they found that, as a team, they had complementary strengths that covered all four quadrants of the Kolb model.

Demands of the learning task. A group of child protection workers with learning styles that tended to rely heavily on concrete experience and active experimentation experienced difficulties in learning a new statistical program. This piece of software required close attention to data and comprehension of some fairly sophisticated theoretical constructs. The staff trainer who was helping them to learn this material recognized that she would need to provide support and strategies for data collection and theory building.

There is a good deal of ongoing research in the area of learning and teaching styles. Practitioners can expect that new findings will help them to be more precise in taking account of individual differences as they plan future teaching interventions. At present, however, there is only an imperfect and often contradictory understanding of learning styles. Cranton's advice (1994) is that teachers can simply accept that people learn differently and try to respond flexibly to their diversity.

Knowles's Principles for Effective Teaching

Adult Education is a relatively new but rapidly growing discipline. One of the pioneer theorists in the field, Malcolm Knowles, continues to be frequently cited, perhaps because he writes with such unfailing humanity and practicality. Knowles (1985) suggests that there are three principles that teachers should consider when working with adult learners. These principles are part of a constructivist model of the learning process. They stress the need for practitioners to take into account the following factors: the self-concept of the learners, their accumulated life experiences, and the purpose or application they have in mind for the material they are learning. (Another consideration is the learner's motivation, which may be stimulated by so-called teachable moments. This was addressed in Chapter One.)

These three factors structure the following review of guidelines for facilitating adult learning. It is important to recognize, however, that a number of other authors have added to, and sometimes challenged, Knowles's ideas. These commentators include Brundage and MacKeracher (1980), Smith (1982), Knox (1990), Brookfield (1986, 1990), and Cranton (1989).

The Learner's Self-Concept

In working with mature learners, practitioners need to understand that there are two ways in which learners' self-concept becomes an important consideration. First, adult learners want an opportunity to exercise some direction over the processes and/or outcomes of their learning. This parallels their wish to become increasingly self-directing over other aspects of their lives. Second, the way adults view and value themselves—that is, their self-concept (Satir, 1972; Corey, 1991)—has an important influence on the way they engage in learning activities.

There are two discrete but interrelated components that together compose a person's self-concept. The first element is an individual's self-image, the construct each individual forms about himself or herself: tall or short, attractive or unattractive, majority or minority. A person's sense of self and his or her abilities may not necessarily conform to his or her current attributes or to the way in which that person is perceived by others.

The second element of self-concept is self-esteem. Self-esteem is the value people place on the image they have constructed of themselves. An easy way to recall this relationship between self-image and self-esteem, as constituent elements of self-concept, is by means of a simple formula: SC = SI + SE (Self-Concept = Self-Image + Self-Esteem). The advantage of recognizing the two constituent ingredients that compose a person's conception of self is that practitioners may encounter people who experience learning difficulties related to some aspect of their self-concept. This may result from a poor self-image, low self-esteem, or both. In order to take into account issues related to the learner's self-concept, two teaching guidelines can be followed:

Respect and Partnership

It has been noted that as people mature they have an increasing need to gain and sustain a measure of control over themselves and their social environment. In their learning environments, people wish to be treated with respect, to be valued as having some existing level of competence, and to be recognized as wanting to have some degree of input into what happens to them. To the extent that people experience these conditions of respect and partnership, they are more likely to be collaborators in the learning process. In contrast, if learners experience the learning process as overly demanding or excessively directed by others, their motivation to learn will be correspondingly reduced.

Some examples of the consequences of failing to honor these principles of respect and partnership are reflected in the following teaching situations:

Miss Jones, a home economist raised in a large urban center, told residents in the remote, rural community where she was employed that their nutrition practices were inadequate. She decided that she would teach them alternative methods. Not surprisingly, the classes were sparsely attended. (There was even some graffiti about Miss Jones in the washroom of a local tavern: "Miss Jones eats . . . french fries!")

A social worker assigned a new client who had just become a mother at the age of fifteen launched into a rather didactic teaching intervention on parenting skills. The teenager became increasingly withdrawn during this experience, and then she failed to return for a scheduled second interview. Later the social worker learned that the teen had successfully raised her three younger siblings following her mother's death some six years earlier.

Learner Self-Image and Self-Esteem

Practitioners recognize that how learners perceive themselves influences the expectations they bring to learning situations. The presence of the teacher or other learners may trigger uncomfortable memories of earlier, unsuccessful or denigrating learning situations. These feelings may be reactivated in the current learning situation.

In working with learners who have low self-esteem, practitioners find that even modest critical feedback will tend to promote a strong and often fearful reaction. The learner may respond with a fight, with flight, or with the mobilization of a variety of defense mechanisms, including denial, projection, and rationalization. Due to their internalized self-image, learners may fear that they are incapable of achieving a particular learning goal. In such situations the teacher may run across a variety of negative learner self-attributions (Bandura, 1977a) that reflect a learner's belief that he or she lacks the capacity to learn. In addition, learners may be blocked by a failure to recognize or accept that they need to engage in a particular learning activity. Now to address each of these learning blocks in a little more depth.

Fear of formal learning situations. Many of the people professionals encounter as patients or clients have not experienced a great deal of success in the role of "student." For example, many adults who return to formal education after a long absence bring with them a reservoir of negative memories and feelings derived from earlier school experiences. These may include the pain of failure, the shame of ridicule, and the tyranny of boredom. In contrast, the majority of human service professionals have, by definition, not only survived, but prospered in their schooling experiences. It is therefore easy for these professional helpers to lose touch with the fear learners may associate with something as apparently innocuous as a parenting course. People like this will approach such experiences with a fear of being judged or being made to feel foolish in front of others if their self-perceived inadequacies become revealed. The practitioner needs to be aware of this potential and take all necessary steps to reduce such anxiety. The aim is to bring these thoughts and feelings to a level where learners are ready to engage in some of the inherent risk-taking that is associated with learning. For example:

> The staff of a recreation center found that 30 percent of those who inquired about a beginners' fitness class failed to show up for the program. In a follow-up study of these nonattendees it was found that many of them were acutely self-conscious because of perceived excess weight, the fear of being embarrassed, and doubts about their ability to do the required exercises. For several of them these fears were compounded by uncertainty about the type of shoes and clothing they should wear to the first class. The staff responded with a user-friendly brochure mailed out to all those who had made telephone inquiries. This material included tips on clothing, some photos of earlier classes, and the names and phone numbers of mentors who had already taken the course. This had a positive effect on enrollment in subsequent classes.

Fear of feedback. Feedback is an essential ingredient for learning and change because it gives learners and teachers information about the consequences of their behavior. Knox (1990) says that "feedback includes all ways by which learners obtain information about how their learning activities are progressing. It includes self-assessments as well as reactions by [others]" (p. 159).

This evaluative data enables the practitioner and the learner to track progress and to redirect their future teaching and learning activities. However, learners who have an inaccurate self-image or shaky self-esteem can be blocked from gathering and responding to the feedback that may be available. In these circumstances such people may receive genuinely positive feedback, but if it in some way varies from how they perceive themselves, they will discount these positive messages. Again, a variety of defense mechanisms can come into play to make this possible (Frew, 1986). And even small quantities of negative or critical feedback that do succeed in making it through these defense mechanisms can be experienced as disproportionately devastating by a person with a poor self-concept.

Finally, practitioners should recognize that not only individuals can have a poor self-concept. Groups, organizations, and communities can likewise suffer from a poor self-image or low self-esteem, and this becomes a factor for practitioners who work with groups or in organizational and community development. For example:

> Many of the residents of an isolated, single-industry boomtown in the Canadian north tended to dislike a number of aspects of life in that community. However, they were very angry when counseling staff at the local college initiated an educational film project that intended to document the situation of women living in that community. The residents, particularly the men, perceived this as a further criticism of their town; the film was experienced as an attack on their already fragile collective self-concept.

Faulty perceptions of entitlements and capacities. Learners can also be blocked by their not recognizing abilities they have or by their not valuing those abilities. Chapter One touched on some of the differences between the role of student and that of learner. Many people have not previously prospered in the student role, and they may also fail to appreciate some of the important learning accomplishments of their past. For these reasons the practitioner may frequently have to help such learners overcome negative self-attributions. These may include both a perceived lack of capacity and a perceived lack of entitlement. Some examples:

A nurse was confronted with the task of teaching a lighthouse keeper how to change his wife's surgical dressings when they returned to their isolated home. The husband seemed to be particularly fearful about this learning task, and after careful exploration the nurse determined that the man saw himself as a very clumsy individual. He was convinced that he would make a mistake that could prove life-threatening to his wife. Having diagnosed this learning block, the nurse helped him review what he had already learned in several first aid courses, as well as reminding him of the important assistance he had once provided a victim of hypothermia. This served to bolster the man's confidence in approaching the task of learning how to care for his wife.

A public health educator helped a group of tenants in a low-income housing development learn how to lobby for better neighborhood health services. However, when his teaching sessions were completed, no action was forthcoming from the tenants. In consultation with those who had attended his sessions, the practitioner reached the conclusion that the participants shared a collective self-concept of being unworthy of taking action on their own behalf. They had internalized the notion that they did not deserve a more equal share of resources. The nature of the educator's teaching intervention had to change in order to address this issue.

A different type of resistance to learning may be evident in situations in which learners believe that the learning task at hand is not their responsibility. Their self-concept does not include the notion that they should incorporate the particular knowledge, attitudes, or skills that are being taught. For example, a practitioner proposing a continuing education workshop for nurses might meet this response: "Real community health nurses don't have to know how to do foot care."

Other groups of learners may feel no need to learn what the practitioner wishes to teach, because they do not see the learning task as fitting with their self-concept. For example, some people may see no need to expand their repertoire of parenting skills, and others may reject the need to learn to use more inclusive language. It is therefore important for the practitioner to develop an appreciation for the unique perspective of the learners in each situation. For example:

> An employment counselor ran into difficulty recruiting a group of unemployed former shipyard workers for a retraining program. The course required participants to achieve a basic level of typing skills. However, the workers saw this as demeaning, and they could not accept that it was an essential aspect of achieving computer literacy.

> A primary school had a number of students with a range of moderately severe physical disabilities. These children required a good deal of physical support, including assistance with toileting. This duty was normally performed by teaching assistants, but when they were unavailable the classroom teachers needed to carry out these activities. The teachers were very resistant to learning the toileting procedures, because they did not see this as part of their professional role.

In summary, practitioners need to assess the self-concept of patients and clients when planning to teach them or to facilitate their learning. Learning can be impaired when learners lack the expectation of success or when what is to be learned does not fit with how they see themselves.

The Learner's Life Experience

Knowles (1985) points out that as people mature, their accumulated life experiences increasingly define the way they see themselves and the world. This perception fits with a constructivist understanding of the learning process, in which knowledge is inextricably intertwined with personal experience: "Each experience with an idea—and the environment of which that idea is a part—becomes part of the meaning of that idea" (Duffy and Jonassen, 1991, p. 8).

There are three reasons why practitioners need to understand and tap into the wealth of accumulated experience learners bring to each new learning opportunity. First, it is important to assess the nature and extent of this prior learning in order to gauge how to design the new learning to fit with, and build on, the learners' existing level of understanding. Second, to the extent that the practitioner is aware of the past experiences of individual learners, he or she can use metaphors, analogies, and examples that will be meaningful to particular individuals. This is a useful way to illuminate new ideas or skills, by linking them to knowledge, attitudes, and skills the learner already possesses. Finally, if these accumulated experiences can be drawn out and shared, learners can become a rich learning resource for one another.

The Level and Context for Learning

In planning a teaching intervention, practitioners need to assess the existing knowledge and skills of potential learners. This assessment should, where possible, address the entry-level abilities and motivations learners bring with them. It is preferable to identify the appropriate level at which to begin teaching prior to the start of the teaching episode, but situations arise where this is not possible. In these circumstances a quick assessment of learning needs, abilities, and motivations may be inserted at the start of teaching. This type of on-the-spot reading of the group is sometimes described as "emergent assessment." Issues related to the assessment of learning needs and capacities are explored in greater depth in Chapter Five.

The following examples illustrate how different kinds of assessments might be carried out:

Formal prior assessment. An experienced community educator was asked to design community development training for a group of community health nurses. The sponsoring agency assumed there was a

very low level of competence among the learners, but the trainer conducted a number of focus group interviews to check the entry-level
knowledge and skills of potential participants. He found that they had
a good deal of related experience to draw on, and he determined that
the learning goals could be more sophisticated than those proposed
by his employer.

Informal prior assessment. A social worker at an immigrant aid
agency decided to reach out to a group of newly arrived refugee
women who tended to congregate at a neighborhood Laundromat.
She felt that they might need to learn additional life skills in order to
participate fully in the new culture. The worker first engaged the
women in a series of lengthy, informal discussions to try to establish
their existing repertoire of coping skills.

Emergent assessment. A speech therapist was asked to present theories of stuttering to parents of children with a variety of speech difficulties. Faced with this diverse group of learners, he began by asking
them to indicate what they already knew about stuttering and what
they were hoping to learn from the session.

It is also helpful for the practitioner to assess psychological factors derived from past experiences that may influence the teaching
intervention. For example, people may have developed a resistance
to certain topics, or they may have had experiences that make them
uncomfortable with the proposed context in which the learning will
take place. For example, some health-related support groups may
prefer to meet somewhere other than a hospital or medical setting
because some members may be inhibited by medical settings. Some
other examples:

Content resistance. A practitioner employed by an AIDS information
and support agency was asked to develop an educational program
for personnel at a military base. It was anticipated that there might

be some resistance to the program, which could trigger latent homo-
phobia at the base. Accordingly, the base commander opened the
first session by citing statistics on the estimated number of gay and
lesbian members of the military. This presentation was followed by
an army doctor's citing data on the heterosexual transmission of HIV.

Context resistance. A psychologist was invited to facilitate the meetings of a support group for parents of children with terminal illnesses.
The parents were adamant that they did not wish to meet in the hospital, as they had already spent too much time there and it had very
painful associations for them.

In summary, it is important to assess the accumulated experience
of the people who are to participate in a learning event. This information may be used to plan at what level to pitch the presentation
and to identify psychological or contextual factors that might
impact the learning climate.

Grafting: Understanding the New in Terms of the Old

This principle rests on the perception that learning is an active
and constructive process. It recognizes that both teachers and learners bring with them a rich storehouse of meanings derived from
their accumulated life experiences. Thus new meanings will tend
to be understood to the extent that they conform to meanings
learners have already accumulated. For example, if people are thrust
into some totally unfamiliar and alien situation, they begin to assign
meaning to this new situation by comparing it with past experiences
that seem to have some similarity. That is, people tend to seek out
metaphors and analogies from past experience that might account
for their present circumstance. An anonymous author expressed this
process elegantly with this observation: "A metaphor is a person's
pogo stick for crossing the terrain of the unknown." People venture
forward in their understanding by comparing new experiences with
meanings developed in the past.

Enriched Communication

Another reason for practitioners to understand some of the prior experiences learners bring with them is to enrich their communication with them. The lives of teachers and learners often overlap in only limited ways; thus much of their respective life experiences remain hidden from each other. This restricts the extent to which both parties can explain their thoughts, ideas, and feelings. Metaphors and analogies that relate to the life experiences of learners can be used to illuminate important new ideas. This is evident in the following situations:

A marriage counselor was working with a couple. The husband was employed as a commercial fisherman. The counselor wanted to help this man look at some of his unproductive patterns of communication. She accomplished this by using nautical analogies to support the points she wanted to make. These included the way tides reflect the pull of the moon and the function of radar as a feedback system.

A physician raised and trained in a large urban center was assigned to work in a predominantly Inuit community in the Canadian Arctic. On his arrival he made a concerted effort to learn about the hunting and gathering economy of that community. This gave him a meaningful range of analogies he could use to illustrate some basic principles of public health.

To the extent practitioners learn about learners' prior experiences, they can tap into this storehouse of existing analogies to make learning more meaningful. Such explorations of their personal experience is therefore driven by much more than idle curiosity.

Sharing Learning

Perhaps the most important reason for encouraging learners to share their accumulated experience is that in this way learners can be a resource for one another. In two-way communication of experience there are obviously benefits to both parties. Less obviously, there are also benefits to those people who may become involved in teaching or in sharing their own prior experiences. In most situations where peer learning is encouraged, a continuous, reciprocal exchange of experiences ensures that all parties enjoy the benefits of being both teachers and learners.

The reciprocal sharing of teaching and learning are evident in these situations:

> In a family life education group for single fathers, the participants were divided into small groups to share their recollections of the most positive examples of parenting that they had witnessed during their own childhood. This exercise was later evaluated as the most useful session in the program.

> In a community education project geared to reduce the number of native children who become school dropouts, elders and other members of a First Nations community were encouraged to share experiences and stories that they had found to be effective in similar situations.

> A nurse in a diabetes clinic invited members of a group of parents of diabetic children to share with other participants some of the dietary tips they had learned over the years.

These kinds of peer learning situations often have added impact because of the sociocultural similarities between the learners and the teachers. Such similarities, which may be based on factors of class, ethnicity, gender, and social role, can facilitate communication. Frequently it is the shared "insider" status of those involved in peer learning that lends increased credibility to the experiences they share. Similarly, there is frequently a reduction in the power differentials present in many professional helping relationships.

The benefits to those who share or "teach" in group learning sessions may be less evident, but they are nonetheless important. The dynamic in these kinds of situations is described by Reissman (1965) as "Helper 'Therapy,'" indicating that it is frequently the person who is extending help (in this case the human service practitioner) who receives the greatest benefit. This results from a blend of three factors. First, the helper (peer-teacher) has the opportunity to reciprocate or repay some of the benefits he or she has derived from the sharings of other group members. Second, the act of teaching or sharing involves the helper in recalling and clarifying the valued experiences he or she wishes to share with others. Finally, there is a dynamic of self-persuasion, as those doing the teaching are themselves persuaded as they listen to their own persuasion of others.

Practitioners also gain by learning from the experiences of their clients (Maluccio, 1979). The following examples illustrate how both peer learners and human service professionals can benefit from the exchange of accumulated prior learning:

> A woman who was a participant in a job readiness workshop suffered from a marked lack of self-confidence. However, when the discussion focused on budgeting, she was able to contribute a number of ideas from her experience keeping the books for her brother's gas station. She received much positive feedback from the other learners, which bolstered her self-esteem. In turn, this enabled her to participate more fully in the program.

In an earlier discussion of the distinction between professional and experiential ways of knowing, it was noted that professionals can learn much through active reflection about their practice. In particular, practitioners can learn from the experiential and cultural wisdom of their patients and clients. For example:

> A public health nurse found that she was working with an increasing number of recent immigrants from Southeast Asia. These people had

brought with them a number of traditional health practices from their countries of origin. The nurse made an effort to learn about these practices and to incorporate some of them into her own practice.

In more formal and extended training programs it is possible to create structured opportunities for learners to engage in peer teaching. These presentations may be planned as face-to-face encounters in seminars or workshops, or participants might be asked to prepare learning materials that can be of benefit to others (Farquharson, 1985). In both face-to-face peer teaching and mediated peer learning there are benefits to teachers and to learners. These approaches build on the demonstrated advantages of peer teaching (Whitman, 1988).

To summarize, there are four reasons why a practitioner would wish to draw out the previous life and learning experiences of a client or patient: to establish the appropriate level at which to pitch the teaching intervention, to link prior learning with present learning, to enrich communication by tapping into existing knowledge that can be used to illuminate new ideas, and to enable learners to learn from one another.

The Learner's Purpose for Learning

It is important for the practitioner to develop an understanding of the range of motivations that may exist within a given group of learners. Professionals can all too easily assume that the members of a group of learners all share a common motivation for learning a particular topic, and that this motivation fits seamlessly with what the practitioner is motivated to teach. All too frequently one hears human service professionals complaining that a particular learner or group of learners lacks the motivation to learn about a particular topic. What this statement may more accurately reflect is a lack of a fit between the teacher's motivation and that of the learners.

In reality there is usually a good deal of variation in different learners' motivations, and there is further variation between these motivations and those of the teacher. Not only may motivations vary from one participant to another, but the collective motivation of a group of learners may not match those of the teacher. These kinds of mismatches can occur when teachers and learners have different conceptions of how they wish to apply what is learned. The following examples illustrate a range of alternative applications that learners may have in mind:

> A large social agency offered an in-house staff development workshop on mediation skills. The workshop leader assumed that the participants would all wish to apply these skills to their work with clients, and thus all of the leader's illustrations were work-related. In fact, more than half of those participating had quite different applications in mind: resolving family conflicts, using more effective bargaining techniques, resolving neighborhood disputes.

> A community education and recreation center decided to offer a course on "How to Chair a Meeting." At the start of the first session the instructor, a community development worker, distributed cards and asked the twenty-two participants to record what they hoped to do with what they learned in the sessions. The fifteen different reasons they gave for being there included (1) to be able to run neighborhood meetings, (2) to learn what a politically involved spouse was talking about, (3) to be able to straighten out a parent/teacher group, (4) to prepare for law school, and (5) because another, preferred course was filled.

Learners may not necessarily share the practitioner's view, based on his or her readings of basic educational theories, that new, learned behaviors should be used flexibly. Rather, adults may tend to have a clear idea of how they wish to apply what they learn, and they usually prefer to make this application in the near future. As a result these types of learners may simply want to learn a checklist of new behaviors, and they may feel less of a need than the teacher does to understand the theoretical principles on which these actions may be based.

In a parenting course the professional leader felt it was important to deal with some of the more theoretical aspects of family functioning. Eventually one of the working-class parents in the group burst out with, "Why don't you cut all the B.S. and tell us what to do when he's caught shoplifting?"

An association of human service professionals offered a two-day professional development institute on "Helping Through Teaching." A needs assessment prior to the event revealed that most of those who signed up indicated that they wanted practical guidelines for teaching in practice, and very little of "that theoretical stuff."

Thus learners can be frustrated if a teaching intervention does not directly address the application they have in mind. For example:

A young man involved in an outreach program for street youth approached one of the program's counselors for information about enrollment in a course for cooks. The counselor launched into a lengthy explanation of various courses that could lead to a career as a restaurant chef. A few questions would have clarified that the youth wanted to learn about apprenticeships for serving as a cook's helper at a logging camp.

Another consideration in focusing on the orientation of the learner is to try to understand the extent to which the learner is a voluntary participant in the process. Frequently helping professionals find themselves working with people who have been required to participate in a particular program. An example of such a coercive situation might be a reeducation course for convicted drunk drivers who must attend as a condition of their sentence. In all likelihood there will be a number of reluctant or downright recalcitrant learners in such a group. In other situations participation may appear to be voluntary, but people may have experienced more subtle pressure to attend. For instance, some professionals must accumulate a set number of hours of continuing education as a requirement for the annual renewal of their professional licenses.

In other circumstances people may attend voluntarily, but with less than the desired amount of motivation. For example, a couple might agree to attend a marriage preparation class if it is required by the pastor they wish to perform their wedding ceremony. This by no means ensures that they possess the intrinsic motivation that may be necessary to learn from this experience. In situations where the practitioner is working with nonvoluntary or reluctant learners, he or she may have to use some degree of coercion while trying to establish a more benign form of authority. (Chapter Three covers alternative forms of influence, and how practitioners can make use of statutory authority while also building credibility with their learners.)

However, there are a limited number of situations in which practitioners must attempt to teach involuntary learners; the majority of teaching situations in the human services involve learners who are exercising some degree of choice in their participation. Indeed, unless a spark of personal involvement can be ignited and fanned, it is unlikely that much learning will occur. To rephrase an old maxim, "You can take a learner (horse) to a learning opportunity (water), but you can't make him or her learn (drink)."

The willing participation of learners in much of the teaching that takes place in human service practices is a factor that contributes to the effectiveness and satisfaction of this approach. Voluntary participation also means that learners are free to withdraw from the teaching situation whenever they wish (much like the behavior of professionals shopping around for worthwhile sessions at a professional conference). This phenomenon of learners "voting with their feet" should encourage practitioners to involve learners as much as possible in shaping the learning process to meet their personal needs. It should also underscore the need to be very specific when advertising the focus of a formal learning event, so that potential learners can accurately assess what is being offered. For example, a workshop on caregiving was advertised in a community newspaper, with the intention of providing information for lay people caring for a dependent relative or friend. Unfortunately, several nurses from a neighboring town signed up for the session with the expectation that the workshop would focus on the needs of professional caregivers.

In summary, mature learners often participate voluntarily in learning and bring with them individual expectations of what they will learn and how they will use it. It is helpful for the practitioner to take account of these motivational considerations when planning teaching interventions.

3

Developing Learning Relationships with Clients, Patients, and Colleagues

The quality of the relationship that develops between teachers and learners is an important ingredient in the success of any teaching or learning endeavor. Not only are such relationships important for the immediate learning situation, but they also build confidence for future learning experiences. As noted by Gerard Egan (1990), each learning relationship tends to have a unique character: "Effective helpers use a mix of skills and techniques tailored to the kind of relationship that is best for each client" (p. 59).

Daloz (1986) adds another dimension in noting that "teaching is most of all a special kind of relationship. . . . Of course the teacher has to know something, but what we know is of value only as we are able to form it in such a way that our [learners] can make use of it for their own evolving ways of knowing" (p. 14). In human service practice, the goal is to build learning relationships that combine optimum levels of challenge and support for the learner and that are characterized by three interrelated processes: empowerment, critical reflection, and self-direction.

Empowerment

The difficulty in arriving at a concise definition of empowerment is that the word is used to describe both a state of being and the process of arriving at that state of being. The term "empowerment" may be used to describe changes in individuals, changes in larger, controlling structures, or changes in the systems that mediate the relationship between individuals and these larger social systems (Rappaport, 1984). For example, for a person with a physical disability, empowerment might represent a personal transformation resulting from his or her realizing previously untapped potential. Empowerment might also be evident in changes in a government service for people with disabilities as it begins to hire these people to work within the organization. Finally, empowerment might describe the experience of a lobby group for physically disabled people whose members come to realize their ability to influence the policy-making process. Definitions of empowerment abound, but for this examination of teaching in practice the description developed by Cochran (1985) has practical utility: "An interactive process involving mutual respect and critical reflection through which both people and controlling institutions are changed in ways which provide those people with greater influence over individuals and institutions which are in some way impeding their efforts to achieve equal status in society, for themselves and those they care about" (p. 5).

Another useful definition is framed by Shor (1992), who focuses more directly on the nature of empowering education: "Empowering education . . . is a critical-democratic pedagogy for self and social change. . . . It approaches individual growth as an active, cooperative, and social process, because the self and society create each other" (p. 15).

Human service practitioners should pursue a goal of empowerment, while remaining alert to the possibility that teaching techniques can also be used to inculcate in learners the acceptance of oppression (Freire, 1970a, 1970b, 1973). Thus, in effect, teaching can also be used as an instrument of disempowerment.

In exploring this possibility, Paulo Freire (1970b) has stated that learning should achieve what he has termed "education for liberation." He contrasts this with "education for domestication," in which people are educated, or "domesticated," to behave in ways that benefit the needs of the most dominant and powerful people in a society. Freire believes that liberating learning occurs through a process that he terms "conscientization," or consciousness-raising, in which people come to a conscious awareness of the social forces that lie at the root of their oppression. He also believes that learning and critical reflection should be linked with collective action; he uses the term "praxis" to describe this fusion of reflection and action.

Freire voices concern over how the term "empowerment" has come to be used. This is reflected in the following excerpt from a dialogue he had with Ira Shor (Shor and Freire, 1987):

> **Ira:** Do you feel that "empowerment" gives us too easy a way out? Does it lead us to think of the teacher as a kind of lamplighter?
> **Paulo:** You understand my feeling. It may make the situation seem too easy when it is not. . . . For me education is always directive. . . . I don't believe in self-liberation. Liberation is a social act. Liberating education is a social process of illumination. (pp. 108–109).

A final definition of empowerment may help pull together some of these themes: "In essence, 'empowerment' is the process of increasing one's capacity to define, analyze and act upon one's problems. The sense of mastery and control inherent in this process is also fundamental to physical and mental health . . . and is mediated through a process of social support" (Labonte, 1988, p. 10).

In a later publication, Labonte (1989) cautions that "we cannot 'empower' anyone; to presume so strips people of their capacity for choice. . . . Groups and individuals can only empower themselves" (p. 87). Throughout the balance of this book, the term "empowerment" will be used to describe the process by which individuals and groups increase their capacity for critical reflection and reflective action.

As noted earlier, empowerment is closely related to the process of enabling people to achieve increasing levels of self-efficacy. This is reflected in the following observation by Bandura (1977a): "The strength of peoples' conviction in their own effectiveness is likely to affect whether or not they would even try to cope with given situations. . . . They get involved in activities and behave assuredly when they judge themselves capable of handling situations that would otherwise be intimidating. . . . Efficacy expectations determine how much effort people will expend and how long they will persist" (pp. 193–194).

Conger and Kanungo (1988), in a discussion of some of Bandura's work, indicate that empowerment is a process through which an individual's belief in his or her own efficacy is enhanced. Empowerment may result from a strengthened sense of personal efficacy or a weakened belief in personal powerlessness. An attempt to promote these processes should infuse all teaching in the human services.

Critical Reflection

Effective teaching relationships are characterized by a continuing effort on the part of teachers to foster the development of critical reflection skills, both in themselves and in others. Critical reflection enables us to correct distortions in our beliefs and errors in our problem-solving techniques. Critical reflection involves a critique of the presuppositions upon which our beliefs have been built (Mezirow, 1990, p. 1).

Critical reflection may also be directed outward, to a critique of external social forces. Freire describes the process of becoming critically aware as "conscientization" (Freire, 1970a): "the process in which men, not as recipients, but as knowing subjects, achieve a deepening awareness both of the sociocultural reality that shapes their lives and of their capacity to transform that reality" (p. 27). Freire suggests that this level of critical consciousness cannot be achieved through the traditional "banking" approach to teaching, which he likens to depositing knowledge into an empty vessel (the student). Rather he sees learning as an outgrowth of problem posing, in which learners pose problems and the teacher becomes a coinvestigator into the nature of reality.

Others, including Jack Mezirow (1990), describe profound shifts in understanding as changes that require the transformation of perspective, which involves the reconstruction of paradigms or points of view. Mezirow and a number of his colleagues are particularly interested in the kinds of dramatic, second-order changes that can transform the way people view themselves and the world around them. This should not obscure the fact that critical reflection can also produce subtler, incremental shifts that may also result in important learning and change over time. The practitioner's goal should be to create an environment that encourages praxis, the constant succession of action, reflection, and action.

In seeking to promote this kind of critical reflection, practitioners need to remain alert to the constraints that imbue their own perspective. An individual's unique worldview is in part an outgrowth of his or her own life experiences, as well as the worldviews of others they come in contact with. The individuality of each person's perspective means there can never be a faithful correspondence between the teacher's perspective and that of the learner. It is therefore important that, in building learning relationships, professionals respect the perspective of the learner—a person who has developed different meanings out of different life experiences. Narayan (1989) underscores this point by using the term "epistemic privilege" to describe the respect professionals should accord people with direct, personal experience with an issue: "The claim of epistemic privilege amounts to claiming that members of an oppressed group have a more immediate, subtle and critical knowledge about the nature of their oppression than people who are nonmembers of the oppressed group" (pp. 319–320).

In effect, she says practitioners should recognize that people who have experienced oppression have a unique perspective based on what she calls their "insider" status with regard to these experiences. This applies in particular to those who have had direct experience with classism, racism, sexism, ageism, heterosexism, or other forms of oppression; however, the notion of epistemic privilege can also be extended to those with direct, insider experience with events such as physical or psychological illness, bereavement, the loss of a valued social role, or the collapse of a relationship. Practitioners need to respect this kind of experiential wisdom if they are to help learners affirm and value their own perspectives. To the extent that practitioners are willing to learn about and from the learner's viewpoint, they may be less likely to project their own views onto these people. The following examples reflect the voices and viewpoints of those who have developed meanings from an insider's perspective:

A woman quoted in Women's Ways of Knowing: "There's a part of me that I didn't realize I had until recently—instinct, intuition, whatever. It helps me and protects me. It's perceptive and astute. I just listen to the inside of me and I know what to do" (Belenky, Clinchy, Goldberger, and Tarule, 1986, p. 52).

A member of a self-help group: "The ideal professional respects my dignity as a human being, treats me as a colleague, not as an authority over me, . . . values my experience and my point of view and consults me as to anything that may affect my life" (Cardinal and Farquharson, 1991, p. 5).

A client of a marriage counselor: "The first time we went there we were both dissatisfied with the counselor. She was very young, had never been married, acted like a trainee. She didn't seem to understand what we were going through" (Maluccio, 1979, p. 130).

A self-help group member: "When two alcoholics speak they can communicate like nobody else—we are experts and can talk freely.

There's an empathy there that you couldn't get anywhere else in the world" (Farquharson, 1975, p. 92).

This last comment effectively illustrates the kind of mutual affirmation of insider perspectives that can occur when a group of learners gathers together to exchange shared experiences. In effect, similar experiences contribute to the construction of like meanings that are not readily understood by the outsider. This is just one of the ways group learning can be so influential; it also explains why a report given by the members of a learning group is often not very meaningful to those who were not part of the discussion.

Self-Directed Learning

Another ingredient in effective teaching is the cultivation of increased learner self-direction (Knox, 1990). Malcolm Knowles (1975) defines self-directed learning as "a process in which individuals take the initiative, with or without the help of others, in diagnosing their learning needs, formulating learning goals, identifying human and material resources for learning, choosing and implementing appropriate learning strategies, and evaluating learning outcomes" (p. 18).

Brookfield (1986) particularly stresses the need to look critically at Knowles's central concern with self-directed learning. Brookfield is concerned that those who teach should not lose sight of the factors that can act to constrain the ability of learners to be self-directing. He notes that "within most formal educational contexts, full self-directedness on the part of the learners is likely to be an unattainable, if seductive, chimera" (p. 67).

Self-directed learning is in fact very much a part of the fabric of daily life; but it is all too easy for human service professionals to lose sight of the fact that many citizens pursue their own needs with only limited recourse to any formal services. People identify their needs (some of which can be met through learning activities) and then actively seek out ways to meet these needs. Along the way they may choose to access human service professionals, but even in these cases, the people who are most self-directed tend to preserve a good deal of autonomy.

The work of Allen Tough (1979) reveals that most people are much more actively engaged in self-directed learning than they realize. The average person he studied spent more than seven hundred hours annually on major learning projects of seven hours duration or more. Consider the number of hours devoted to the following self-directed learning project. A young woman who had been sexually assaulted was referred to a private therapist. She did not find this to be an effective way to deal with her pain and fear, however, so she began to read exhaustively on various pathways to recovery. She arranged to attend a professionally led workshop, where she met members of a support group for people who had suffered similar experiences. The young woman joined this group for two years, during which time she learned to find further meaning for what had happened. Finally she went on to become a volunteer at a local women's center.

To the extent that people become increasingly self-directed in the way they manage their learning, they will be able to learn more effectively. This is true even in those situations in which the learning is to a significant extent directed by another, as is frequently the case in more formal and didactic teaching situations. For example, parolees who are more capable of self-direction will tend to engage more proactively with what their parole officer and other learning resources have to offer. This will be more difficult for those who have been more thoroughly institutionalized, because their capacity for self-direction has been stunted.

Brookfield (1986) provides a summary of two different aspects of self-directed learning: "It is useful to distinguish between two forms of self-direction: . . . techniques of self-directed learning [and] a particular internal change of consciousness [that] occurs when learners come to regard knowledge as relative and contextual . . .

and to use this altered perspective to contemplate ways in which they can transform their personal and social worlds" (p. 47). In effect, Brookfield sees that self-directed learning consists of both a set of skills and a perspective that views learning as an active, constructive process.

It may seem idealistic to promote the notions of empowerment, critical reflection, and self-direction given the mundane, pragmatic, directive teaching that frequently occurs in human service practice. This is evident in such basic activities as teaching patients how to care for their own surgical dressings, teaching adults how to prepare for a job interview, or teaching a group of citizens about the Landlord and Tenant Act. While these teaching interventions may seem to be quite straightforward, practitioners would do well to bear in mind that in the majority of teaching situations a guiding principle should be to help learners make choices and increase their capacity for self-direction. The challenge is to teach and facilitate learning, not just with content (such as the Landlord and Tenant Act) but with a process that makes the learners capable of increased autonomy in their learning. Thus an implicit goal in all human service teaching is to act in ways that increase the capacity of the learner to learn and reduce unnecessary or confining dependence on teachers and teaching.

The Teaching-to-Facilitating Continuum

Promoting learner self-direction dictates the need for continuing change in the nature of the relationship between teacher and learner. There are two related ways to think about these changes. First, it is possible to conceive of a continuum of practitioner activities that extends from didactic teaching all the way to pure facilitation of learning. Second, associated with this shift are changes in the locus of control of the learning process. The information-dissemination approach is more teacher centered, while facilitated learning or learning through problem solving tends to be more learner centered.

The continuum of teacher-as-information-giver to teacher-as-facilitator-of-learning is reflected in Figure 3.1.

At the left-hand side of the continuum are those situations in which the practitioner transfers information to learners—either directly, through face-to-face teaching, or indirectly, through print and other media. As teaching shifts toward more active engagement of the learner, the teacher tends to become involved in both imparting information and in encouraging learners to share and apply their own understanding. At the right-hand end of the continuum lies the pure facilitation of learning. In these circumstances the practitioner becomes involved in coaching or in facilitating inquiry rather than relying solely on didactic teaching. The following examples illustrate some alternative teaching roles:

> *Giving information:* A physician who is an expert on the burden carried by those caring for relatives or friends with Alzheimer's disease shares with a group of these caregivers some indicators that they

Figure 3.1. The Teaching-to-Facilitating Continuum.

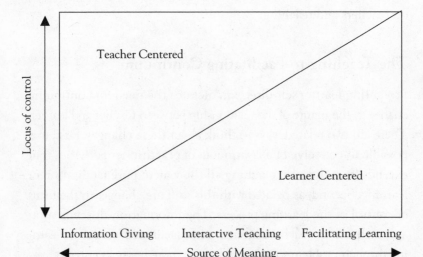

might use in order to assess their own stress levels and their potential need for outside assistance.

Interactive teaching: A nurse helps a group of people who have had cancer of the larynx explore how they might use a new piece of technology to help them swim with less discomfort. This teaching intervention involves a blend of disseminating information and engaging in active experimentation.

Facilitation of learning: A community development worker facilitates the discussion of representatives from several different community groups. These people meet together to reflect on their shared perceptions and concerns and to find ways they might work together to address issues they hold in common.

This understanding of the differences between information-giving and the facilitation of learning may also be used to reflect about the kinds of teaching and learning activities that may lie beyond the two polar ends of the continuum shown in Figure 3.1. For example, instruction that completely excludes any form of learner input might lie beyond the left-hand end of the continuum. (And it might be viewed as indoctrination if it actively constrains any critically reflective thinking by the learner.) Beyond the other polar extreme, fully learner-directed, or autonomous, learning may be evident in self-help and community groups as they address shared concerns. It should be noted that multiple points on the continuum can be represented at different times within a single teaching intervention.

It is not easy to conjure up an example of indoctrination that might find its way into human service practice, but in the past some of the more coercive ways of working with the poor, the mentally ill, and other powerless groups have had the character of indoctrination. Today the extent to which many North American professionals are constrained by Eurocentric perspectives can lead some of them to perpetuate racist, classist, or sexist attitudes. Paulo Freire might be inclined to argue that this is inevitable in the very nature of positivist or "banking" approaches to teaching.

On a more positive note, exciting examples of autonomous learning are evident in the following:

> A public health nurse, the lone professional in an isolated Arctic community, was able to access the Internet by satellite. She set out a number of goals for her own ongoing professional development, and she established a network of contacts who could support her continued learning.

> A new self-help group was formed by retiring professional athletes. Several of the initial core group were people who had run into psychological and financial difficulty making the transition after their sports career had concluded. The members learned from one another how to reestablish a sense of identity, how to cope with chronic injuries, and some ways in which they might ensure their future financial security.

Self-help or mutual-aid groups like this provide an important example of autonomous learning. They can form a powerful complement to the activities carried by human service professionals. For example, a health professional requires technical/positivist knowledge to perform a mastectomy, but women who have gone through this experience can construct experiential knowledge about how to live with the condition. The preferred relationship of the practitioner working in collaboration with such groups is captured in two self-help slogans: "Professionals should be on tap and not on top" and "Professionals should be the guide on the side and not the sage on the stage." These maxims reflect the desire of self-helpers to define when and how professionals become involved with the learning activities of the group. Group members want practitioners to respect the experiential wisdom of the insider, while sharing professional knowledge that is current and useful (Cardinal and Farquharson, 1991).

Situational Teaching

An alternative way to conceptualize the variety of teaching roles available to practitioners is through what may be described as the situational teaching approach. This conceptual framework is a modification of the situational leadership model (Figure 3.2) developed by Hersey and Blanchard (1988). These authors studied how effective managers interact with their employees, isolating four key kinds of management interventions: telling, selling, participating, and delegating. In specific situations managers might simply *tell* an employee the correct behavior and indicate sanctions that could be mobilized in the event of a failure to comply. They describe selling as *instructing* the employee in the how of the required behavior and helping him or her understand why it is important. *Participation*, for Hersey and Blanchard, denotes the manager's providing participatory support to employees until they feel confident and competent to carry out new behaviors on their own. Managers feel they can *delegate* a task to an employee who has demonstrated that he or she has both the motivation and the know-how to perform a specific activity.

Hersey and Blanchard, unlike some other management theorists, do not assume that there is one optimum or "bionic" style of managerial leadership. Rather, they advance the idea that any one of these four modes of intervention—telling, selling, participating, or delegating—might be the action of choice given the specific capacities of an employee in responding to the demands of a specific situation. Hence the term "situational leadership." These authors suggest that, given one such specific challenge for a particular employee, the way to select from among the four alternative methods is to determine the level of motivation and know-how (the "readiness") the

Figure 3.2. The Situational Leadership Model.

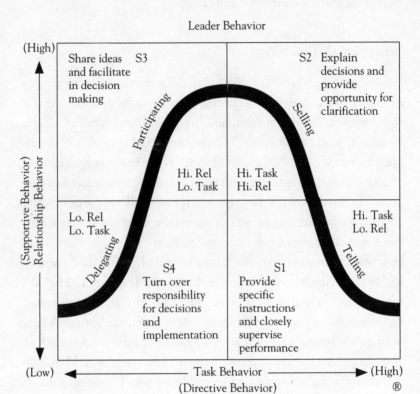

Reprinted with permission from Paul Hersey and Kenneth Blanchard (1988), *Management of Organizational Behavior: Utilizing Human Behavior*, Escondido, CA: The Center for Leadership Studies, p. 182.

employee can bring to the task in question. On the basis of this assessment, one of the following interventions is selected:

R1 = low motivation and low know-how = Tell

R2 = high motivation and low know-how = Instruct

R3 = low motivation and high know-how = Participate

R4 = high motivation and high know-how = Delegate

In choosing telling as a teaching strategy, the practitioner is in effect saying that he or she *requires immediate compliance* with a specific change in behavior, even if this may carry the danger of undermining the relationship with the client. This may be the intervention of choice when the practitioner has the statutory power to prevent such things as child abuse and neglect or abuses of public health codes.

Instruction (selling) is selected as a teaching strategy when the client appears to be motivated to learn but needs a good deal of direction about the actual content of what is to be learned. Participation equates with what has previously been described as facilitation. This is the teaching approach of choice when the learner has some knowledge or skill that can be liberated if the practitioner offers support and encouragement.

Finally, delegation implies that the practitioner determines the client has both the knowledge and the motivation to learn in a largely independent fashion, although there is likely to be continuing periodic contact with the practitioner. This contact is planned in order to ensure that gains are maintained and that the learner is continuing to be successful with coping tasks.

Thus, Hersey and Blanchard's model may be reframed to reflect the situational teaching approach, in which instructing equates with selling. The utility of this revised model is that it offers practitioners a way to assess what sort of teacher-to-learner relationship will be needed to promote learning for a specific learner confronting a

specific learning task. Alternative teaching paradigms are reflected
in the following examples. All involve a form of teaching, but there
is a shift from teacher-centered telling toward learner-centered
participation and delegation as higher levels of knowledge and
motivation are judged to be present.

Telling: There was poor compliance with health and safety procedures
at a forestry camp for young offenders. The counselor responsible for
safety reviewed the procedures and outlined sanctions that would be
applied in the case of future violations.

Instructing: A speaker from a community AIDS agency was invited to
a junior high school to instruct students about HIV and safe sex practices. It was a fairly didactic presentation, but it was spiced with a
good deal of humor to sustain student motivation.

Participating: A social worker consulted with a support group for
women experiencing menopause. The goal of the members was to
maintain their self-image and self-esteem during a difficult change.
The social worker helped the group's leaders learn group-manage-
ment skills, by providing them with modest coaching and support.

Delegating: A nurse in a diabetes clinic was involved in a long-term
teaching relationship with a diabetic woman. The woman had taken
a long time to stabilize her diet and to learn how to manage her
insulin. Eventually the nurse was able to give her some protocols to
guide her at home, and the patient was encouraged to return to the
clinic at regular intervals for "learning checkups."

The situational teaching approach may also be used to understand how an ongoing learning relationship might evolve over
time. As learners become increasingly willing and able to assume
more self-direction in their learning, the teaching relationship may
progressively shift from telling to teaching to participation and
eventually to delegation. In effect this represents a progression

from teacher-as-giver-of-information to teacher-as-facilitator-of-learning.

Promoting this kind of evolution in the practitioner-client teaching relationship fits with the ideal of promoting increased self-direction. To the extent practitioners become locked into a particular stance—that of telling, for example—they will find that learners will remain dependent on them. In order to prevent this from happening, practitioners should "aim to the left." That is, when professionals are unsure about which developmental level they should teach at, they should assume that the learner has greater capacity and motivation than has been noted. In other words, they should move at least one stage to the left on the development continuum illustrated in Figure 3.2. Therefore, if faced with a choice between telling and instructing, for example, the practitioner is encouraged to opt for instructing.

The situational leadership model is obviously not a precise instrument, but it does provide a way to reflect about the kind of teaching/learning relationship that may be required in specific situations.

Another, more elaborate adaptation of the situational leadership model has been developed by Gerald Grow (1991). He applies the four stages of the model to the communication of both teachers and learners in order to predict whether the teaching style of the teacher is likely to fit the learning style of the learner. This approach neatly marries the situational teaching approach with material on learning styles.

Interpersonal Skills

It is crucially important that practitioners recognize the repertoire of existing helping skills they bring to their teaching interventions. Among many other interpersonal skills, the ability to communicate understanding, to offer support, to clarify needs, and to facilitate problem solving are at the core of effective teaching, just as they are in other kinds of helping interventions. It is not possible within the scope of this book to review all of these professional counseling skills, but readers may wish to refer to some key authors in this field, including Ivey (1988), Corey (1990), and Egan (1990). These authors spell out, in practical detail, a repertoire of important interpersonal and group-facilitation skills. In addition, a competency profile has been included at the back of this book, in Resource A, which practitioners may use as a self-assessment tool in evaluating their existing range of interpersonal and interviewing skills. This profile outlines ten stages of the helping process and fifteen helping skills; the practitioner can rate his or her proficiency according to five levels of performance for each stage and skill.

Attributes of Effective Teachers and Facilitators

The literature on effective teaching abilities—particularly those interpersonal skills associated with the facilitation of adult learning—is rich and varied (Brookfield, 1986, 1990; Cranton, 1992; Daloz, 1986; Mezirow, 1990, 1991; Schwartz, 1994). Likewise, there is a good deal of material that addresses the attributes required of those who teach adults (Apps, 1981; Knox, 1990; Weimer, 1991; Cranton, 1992). However, some of these ideas apply more directly to learners in formal settings, and given the context for much of the teaching that occurs in human service practice, the attributes described by Raymond Wlodkowski (1991) may apply more directly. Wlodkowski suggests that teachers need to demonstrate the following attributes:

- *Expertise: The Power of Knowledge and Preparation*

  connecting material to learner's life experience

  adjusting content to allow for spontaneity and creativity

  preparing teaching materials that build on motivation

- *Empathy: The Power of Understanding and Consideration*

  checking out learner needs and expectations

  shaping teaching to the learner's capacities

  constantly considering the learner's perspective

- *Enthusiasm: The Power of Commitment and Animation*

    having a personal investment in what is taught

    expressing emotion, animation, and energy

- *Clarity: The Power of Language and Organization*

    ensuring that learners understand the logical connection of ideas

    continuously checking learner comprehension (adapted from Wlodkowski, 1991, pp. 16–43)

Building Learning Relationships

Successful teaching and learning is heavily dependent on the kind of relationship that develops between the parties involved. The goal is to try to establish clear working agreements that spell out the roles and goals of the various parties in the learning process. Sometimes referred to as the "contracting" phase of the helping process, this may involve the explicit negotiation of learning processes and outcomes, or it may evolve from more implicit and ephemeral agreements. These more tacit agreements about the teaching-learning relationship may be necessary when explicit agreements are not possible or appropriate. Also, a practitioner may spot a teaching opportunity before an explicit helping relationship has been established. This might occur, for example, in the course of a public health nurse's initial contact with a mother at a well-baby clinic; the nurse may find an opportunity to do some informal, implicit teaching about how to limit or prevent diaper rash. Alternatively, implicit teaching might be required if a client appears to be unready to explicitly accept the formal role of learner. For instance, in early interviews with an adolescent client, a probation officer might use role-reversal strategies to help the client get in touch with some of the ways his behavior might affect his parents.

In most situations it is more respectful, more ethical, and more effective if teaching relationships can be established that are explicit and mutually agreed upon. This ensures that the rights of the client are respected, that his or her energy for learning is optimally engaged, and that the roles and goals in the learning relationship can be renegotiated when necessary. To the extent that teaching and learning relationships are mutually agreed upon, learners are empowered to become active partners in the learning process. Conversely, if teaching and learning agreements remain implicit and unstated, it can be difficult to negotiate changes in the relationship between the practitioner and the learner. This difficulty is further exacerbated if one of the parties in the relationship—typically the practitioner—retains all the power to make and change the rules that govern the learning contract. This is entirely possible in the human services, where so much power is vested in professionals— it is evident in sometimes coercive attempts to change the behavior of involuntary or unaware "clients."

For all of the foregoing reasons, practitioners are encouraged to involve learners as much as possible in the process of building clear teaching and learning agreements. The term "transparent" might be applied to the process of making such contracts as visible as possible to the parties involved.

In order to appreciate the continuum from concrete, explicit teaching contracts to ephemeral, implicit learning agreements, it may be helpful to consider the following examples:

An explicit, concrete agreement: A counseling psychologist employed by a large industrial firm was asked to run a smoking cessation group in the workplace. Time off with pay was negotiated for employees who wished to participate, and these individuals were required to sign an agreement to attend a specified number of sessions. Later they developed individual written learning goals in consultation with the practitioner.

An implicit, somewhat ephemeral agreement: A youth counselor worked with a group of homeless young adults to help them learn about their shared needs and some ways they could work together to improve their circumstances. She felt that these young adults had such negative associations with school that she would not refer to her activities with them as a learning process.

In those situations where it is possible to build clear learning agreements through mutual negotiation, it is easier to include ways to monitor learning progress. This kind of continued scrutiny can generate data that may be used to keep the teaching and learning relationship on track.

The ingredients of effective teaching and learning contracts in human service practice include the following:

Clarification of what the learner expects and hopes the practitioner will do: A marriage counselor clarifies with a young couple that they hope that she, the counselor, can rekindle all the feelings they had for one another during their courtship; but they also expect that not much can be done to stem the deterioration of their relationship.

Mutual agreement on the issues to be addressed: The counselor and the couple agree that the main focus of their work should be to identify times and activities when the couple can be alone with each other.

Clarification of what the practitioner can and will do: The counselor stresses that the couple need to be prepared to work hard as they attempt to renegotiate their relationship. She will help support and facilitate this process.

Agreement on what each party will do to support the learning process: The counselor agrees to hold one session with the parents of both partners, and the couple agrees to carry out some agreed-upon activities between sessions.

Shared framing of explicit and attainable learning goals: Among the goals they agree upon is a set number of hours the couple will aim to spend together each week.

Establishing methods to assess teaching effectiveness and learning progress: The counselor indicates that she would like to conclude each session by asking the couple to summarize what they have learned, and to commence each subsequent session with their report of how successful they have been in transferring these learnings into their relationship.

Reciprocal accountability for progress toward these goals: At the start of each session, the counselor shares her view of the couple's progress after they have reviewed the extent to which they seem to have transferred their learning into their relationship.

Built-in methods by which the learning agreement can be revised: The learning contract spells out their agreement that the learning relationship will be reviewed at the conclusion of the fifth session.

It is important to note that in the first step of this process a distinction is made between hopes and expectations. Hopes reflect the outcomes the learner might earnestly wish for, but these may be at odds with what the practitioner is realistically able to do. Hope can provide an important motivational pull for learning, but in unrealistic excess it can lead to impatience with the slow pace of change or failure to accept the amount of effort required by the learning process. Expectations, on the other hand, can sometimes be quite pessimistic and can be colored by previously unsuccessful attempts to learn. This can likewise reduce the energy required to achieve the desired learning outcomes. For example, a physician started to teach a woman some techniques for helping her severely asthmatic son. The mother clearly, and unrealistically, *hoped* these methods would eventually alleviate his condition. However, she also had low *expec-*

tations of her ability to effectively learn the methods that were to be taught. The practitioner found it necessary to reduce a little of the unrealistic hopefulness while at the same time building up some of the client's low expectations, through support and encouragement.

Sources of Influence

Teaching by its very nature is a process of wielding interpersonal influence. In the human services, practitioners try to shape the perceptions of others through a process of adding to, or altering, the meanings learners assign to their life experiences. This reinforces an observation made earlier: teaching is not neutral, and all teachers need to remain alert to the personal values and biases they bring to the learning process. Given that the teacher/facilitator is an "agent of influence," the next task is to understand the sources of this influence and the way in which interpersonal influence can be accumulated and deployed.

One of the difficulties in any discussion of the nature of interpersonal influence is that the terms "power" and "authority" are quickly introduced into the debate. Unfortunately, few authorities share the same definition for these two terms. In this discussion of sources of influence, the term "influence" is used to include both power and authority. Power, in this context, refers to the kind of influence that is ascribed to certain individuals by the social systems they represent. Those persons who are given this type of influence can use different forms of power to ensure that others comply with their dictates (Richardson, 1982; Hepworth and Larsen, 1990). An example of the use of power in practice might be a situation in which a person is required to enroll in an alcohol education program as a condition of their probation. The message is clear. The individual must attend such educational sessions if they wish to avoid a period of incarceration.

In contrast to this conception of power, the term "authority" may be applied to the influence practitioners are able to exercise because others perceive them as authorities, and so grant them that influence.

For example, a group of people may decide to be influenced by the teaching of an individual who has already earned their trust and respect. This might be a trustworthy, valued family physician or a reliable, honest community worker—either of whom may have earned or achieved influence in the eyes of those they serve. Thus authority is the influence granted these kinds of practitioners. But just as it is voluntarily given, so too can it be voluntarily withdrawn if this confidence becomes eroded. Figure 3.3 illustrates a continuum of types of influence, extending from ascribed power to achieved authority.

The value of this schema is that it reveals a variety of different sources of influence; thus it moves beyond a simple bipolar distinction between power and authority. These five potential sources of influence have the following characteristics:

Coercive Influence

This is the ability to influence others through the application of direct sanctions, possibly including physical restraint. The telling mode of teaching (outlined in the situational leadership model) certainly requires access to some of the forms of influence found at this end of the power-to-authority continuum; otherwise a telling type

Figure 3.3. The Continuum of Influence: From Power to Authority.

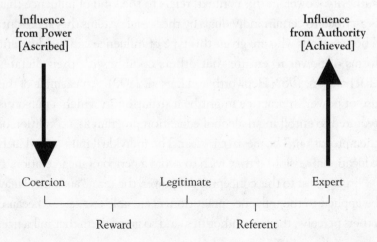

of intervention might be blithely ignored. The danger in resorting to this kind of direct control is that it can be overused: the exercise of power then becomes the only form of intervention that is likely to have any effect. An additional concern is that compliance under threat of coercion does not necessarily mean the required behavior has become internalized. Finally, if there is insufficient coercive influence available to produce compliance, then this source of influence will thereby be diminished. (This is a lesson that is often painfully learned by parents of children entering adolescence.)

On a rather more positive note, coercive influence can be used merely to require a certain amount of contact with a reluctant client until more benign—and potentially more potent—forms of interpersonal influence can be established. This beneficial use of coercion can be seen in the effective use of legislated influence (coercive power) by human service workers who are in a position to exert statutory power. This would include probation officers, medical health officers, child protection workers, and others. For these professionals, statutory power can be used to coerce clients into making the initial contact. During this time of contact-under-duress, the professional can work hard to develop other forms of influence. The following examples illustrate the use of coercive influence to support teaching interventions in the human services:

A child welfare worker, as part of a plan to return an abused child to her mother, requires that the mother participate in an eight-session anger management program.

A young offender is required to attend an Outward Bound–type outdoor education program in order to learn some skills in cooperation and leadership.

The value of coercing people into participating in educational programs is very much in question. This concern has led some people to express reservations about the value of court-ordered participation in mutual aid learning groups such as Alcoholics Anonymous or self-help groups for men who batter.

Reward Influence

In this case, professionals have the potential to exercise influence through their ability to control clients' access to certain rewards. These rewards may consist either of various types of material resources or of human resources and relationships. The potential for this type of influence exists because of the strategic gatekeeping function carried out by many who work in the human services. For instance, human service professionals can control access to financial assistance, job opportunities, and medical services. Controlling a client's access to these things is clearly a strategy that lies toward the coercive end of the influence continuum; but again, it can be used to sustain a minimum level of contact while other forms of influence are established. The following are some examples of how practitioners might use material resources to influence learning outcomes:

> A vocational counselor in a sheltered workshop for mentally handicapped adults uses a system of rewards to influence the performance of the participants in the program.

> A public health nurse builds her influence with a group of new mothers by her ability to direct them to various free and reduced-cost services for parents of newborns.

It has already been noted that professionals are strategically located to influence the client access to other resource persons. These further examples illustrate practitioners' exercising influence through the facilitation of access to these kinds of human resources:

> A counselor teaching in an employment retraining program develops a comprehensive and current list of potential job opportunities for

participants in the program. In the early days of the course this helps
to establish her credibility with this group of learners.

A community psychologist employed by a public housing authority
sets up a referral service in the lobby of a new building. His ability to
link newcomers with other helpful people in the community helps to
establish his influence with this group of new tenants.

Legitimate Influence

This is the type of influence professionals gain by virtue of the
formal position they occupy or through their educational qualifica-
tions. The degree of legitimacy accorded a particular professional
position or title varies, as is evident in the levels of hierarchy that
exist within the human service professions. Legitimate influence
may be thought of as the blend of power and authority associated
with a particular "cloak of office." Some professionals tend to draw
heavily on this type of influence, while others may downplay their
legitimate influence in favor of developing other forms of credibility. The following situations exemplify the exercise of legitimate
influence to support practice teaching:

A man with AIDS participates in a powerful series of educational television programs about living with HIV and AIDS. In addition to some
sterling personal attributes, the fact that he is a physician gives added
legitimacy to his account of his experiences.

A clinical social worker engaging in marital counseling has her various degrees and diplomas framed and hung on the walls of her
office. The social worker's experience with her predominantly middle-
class clientele affirms that clients seemed to accord her credibility on
the basis of her educational achievement.

Parenthetically, it is also interesting to note that the way in
which human service professionals prefer to be addressed by their

colleagues and clients often gives a clue to the degree to which they rely on legitimate sources of influence.

Referent Influence

To the extent that one person admires another or identifies with that individual, he or she tends to invest that person with referent influence. This type of attractiveness in another may be based on perceived similarities such as those based on gender, class, or culture. Alternatively, this type of interpersonal influence may derive from a perception that the influential other shares similar views, or that influence may be granted on the basis of a desire to develop capacities or qualities that are admired in the other. Referent influence should not be confused with types of influence that effect compliance because the subject fears ridicule (coercion) or seeks praise (reward). The key to determining referent influence is that it lies toward the achieved authority end of the continuum.

Referent influence is voluntarily granted the practitioner by the client. A note of caution should be added, though, regarding this contention: there are certainly situations in the human services in which a charismatic practitioner can disempower the unwary. A well-known and controversial example of this is provided by what has become known as the "Dr. Fox Effect." A study by Naftulin, Ware, and Donnelly (1973) addressed how a teacher's personality can influence learners' ratings of his or her instructional ability. In this case, a professional actor was asked to teach a group of physicians while exhibiting charm but offering little of substance. The participants gave favorable ratings and valued the examples, the organization, and the stimulation of the presentation. This study sparked much controversy; but in the context of this discussion, it does sound a warning about the potential for the misuse of referent influence. The following are some examples of more appropriate uses of referent influence in human service teaching:

A pediatrician conducting ward rounds with a group of medical students lets his natural sense of humor emerge. In this way he helps the students relax, and he also models an effective way to engage and teach their young patients. The students' evaluations of this teaching experience stress the attractiveness of this physician as a role model.

A former wheelchair athlete gets a degree in social work. Her reputation for courage and tenacity travels with her, and she becomes an important figure in educating the public about the needs of people facing a variety of physical challenges.

Expert Influence

Expert interpersonal influence derives from the perception that the influential individual has a demonstrable expertise of some kind. It is important to stress that this expertise is in the eye of the beholder: it is achieved authority and should not be confused with the kind of credentialed ability associated with legitimate influence. The person who grants expert influence to another person already sees that person as demonstrably helpful. Just as expert influence is earned through perceived helpfulness or usefulness, so too it can be withdrawn if the person holding that influence subsequently does something to undermine the perception of expertise. The following are some examples of achieved expert influence:

A dietitian associated with a wellness program for seniors is able to build a good deal of expert influence with her colleagues and her clients. This influence is derived from the perception on the part of these people that the dietitian appreciates the social and physical realities that confront older people and the various losses they tend to experience. Some of her expertise is derived from the experiential know-how she developed from time spent caring for her own aging mother.

A police officer on a youth squad is assigned to do outreach work
with youth who frequent a downtown shopping area. He manages to
develop expert influence with this group by informally offering suggestions about temporary work opportunities, emergency housing,
and tips for preparing for court appearances. He also comes to be
respected as someone who can, and will, follow through on what he
says he will do.

It is strategically useful for practitioners to assess the quality and
quantity of different types of influence that may be available to support a particular teaching intervention. This evaluation can enable
professionals to calibrate teaching interventions to the types of
influence that exist or that could potentially be developed. For
example, a community worker involved in a street outreach program for the homeless might achieve much expert credibility based
on his evident resourcefulness and his acceptance of the people he
works with.

Building Credibility: Increasing Achieved Influence

From the preceding discussion it is evident that practitioners frequently work hard to increase their level of achieved authority. The
accumulation of this type of influence is an incremental and sometimes slow process that unfolds in three stages: achieving maintenance credibility, achieving organizational credibility, and, finally,
achieving credibility as an agent of change.

Maintenance Credibility

One place to start the process of developing achieved credibility is
to detect opportunities to perform low-key, useful activities for people who may become learners. The goal is not to spring into the role
of change agent, but rather to identify chances to perform tasks that
make life easier for an individual or group in the immediate present.
To the extent that practitioners perform these apparently mundane

tasks with sensitivity and effectiveness, they may over time earn maintenance credibility. The following are some examples of the way in which human service professionals might take advantage of opportunities to earn this kind of credibility:

A parole officer helps a young parolee learn some of the skills he needs to carry out a systematic job search. He also drives the man to two job interviews that are not readily accessible by public transit.

A community development worker trying to build a relationship with a group of new immigrants to Canada is able to establish credibility by learning about their religious and social customs. He is careful to incorporate respect for these traditions in the way he plans and conducts community meetings. He also arrives early at these sessions to help with setting out chairs and organizing refreshments.

A heart surgeon takes the time to participate in writing an information booklet for families and friends of heart patients. The booklet is based on a question-and-answer format, and it tries to address some basic questions, ranging from hospital parking to post-operative procedures. The material also contains the names and photographs of all the people family members might encounter during their loved one's hospital stay.

There are at least two obstacles that can make it difficult to engage in these kinds of maintenance activities. The first has to do with what might be termed "the proliferation of professions." There is an apparent tendency in the human services to constantly create new subprofessions to deal with the less attractive aspects of a particular professional domain. In effect, a new profession is created to take care of the dirty work. The problem with this kind of process is that the so-called dirty work very often includes important activities that address the maintenance needs of human service consumers. These are often low-key, low-status activities; but they are nonetheless perceived as manifestly useful by those who benefit from them. Examples include such things as arranging for or providing child care, changing dressings, and locating a place for meetings. The danger for professionals who avoid or discard too many of these basic functions is that this may cut them off from opportunities to be perceived as practically and immediately helpful.

On the other hand, a second obstacle can arise if the professional becomes too invested in these kinds of maintenance activities. This can detract from the time they have available for other important professional activities. Likewise, there can be negative consequences if the practitioner fails to gradually transfer maintenance duties to the learner as his or her capacity to assume these responsibilities develops. Locking oneself into a position of constantly doing things for a client or patient actually disempowers that person. Many who are drawn to the helping professions have an admirable desire to help, but if this need becomes too strong it can exclude people from learning how to take action on their own behalf. In the above example of the parole officer, for instance, it is easy to see that a person in this role might become involved in driving the client to more than just inaccessible appointments.

Organizational Credibility

Once a teacher or practitioner has earned respect as one who can reliably pay attention to the maintenance needs of learners, he or she is positioned to begin work on developing organizational credibility. That is, he or she can begin to offer suggestions about minor changes in procedures or organizational approaches that might make the client's problem solving or learning more effective or efficient. The key to the successful use of this approach is for the practitioner to already have some degree of maintenance credibility or other form of influence available. The following examples illustrate the subtle nature of some of the activities that enhance organizational credibility:

A family therapist who has already established a floor of maintenance credibility begins to involve family members in learning from one another about ways they might reorganize some of their more fractious household routines, which provoke conflict. These points of contention include mealtimes, doing laundry, and use of the TV.

A community worker successfully establishes maintenance credibility with a group of migrant farmworkers, mainly by working with them to get the toilets fixed in their bunkhouse. He then begins to help them learn ways to organize themselves to begin lobbying for some other minor improvements in their living conditions.

To reiterate, it is important that the practitioner is able to gradually disengage from these activities as his or her credibility becomes progressively strengthened. This frees the practitioner to begin to earn legitimation as a change agent.

Change Agent Credibility

The practitioner who has built a platform of credibility at the two earlier levels is now positioned to have a greater potential influence over the learning process. This carries with it a greater responsibility to limit the unconscious imposition of personal values and perspectives onto the learner. Human service professionals, as noted previously, can overexercise their influence in a sincere effort to act in what they perceive to be the best interests of their clients. Practitioners can also use their accumulated influence to promote important learning:

A community educator employed by an international development agency establishes considerable credibility with members of an agricultural cooperative in a developing country. She engages community members in a popular education exercise involving the dramatic representation of power relationships. The exercise enables these learners to reframe their view of the way they are locked into servitude by landowners.

A correctional counselor working in a medium security federal peni-
tentiary arranges for inmates to work as companions and mentors to
young adults who have some mental disabilities. Some security difficulties are encountered, but a significant proportion of the prisoners
begin to indicate that this experience has helped them learn to be
less self-centered and more concerned for the welfare of others who
are more vulnerable.

This incremental model of influence development makes
it apparent that building credibility is not an easy process. In
situations where helping professionals find themselves with
large amounts of potential influence at their disposal, there are
concomitant responsibilities to act from a learner-centered, ethical perspective.

In summary, this review of some of the important aspects of
teaching relationships in the human services has stressed the pursuit of three ideals: empowerment, critical reflection, and self-
direction. There may be restraints on the extent to which these can
be achieved in a given situation, but they remain guiding values in
building teaching relationships in professional practice. It was also
noted that the demands of a particular teaching or learning
encounter will to some extent determine the kind of teaching relationship that needs to be cultivated. Finally, five different ways to
exercise influence were explored, together with some approaches
for increasing the credibility of the practitioner. In Chapter Four
the focus shifts to teaching relationships that develop in the facilitation of group learning.

. . . .

4

Becoming Skilled at Group Facilitation

Developing the skills required for the effective facilitation of group learning is a lifelong project, but fortunately the majority of human service professionals are already equipped with many of the basic requisite skills. (A checklist of personal group facilitation skills is included at the back of this book, in Resource B.) For this reason this chapter will not review the extensive literature on teaching and learning with groups (see, for example, Egan, 1985; Corey, 1991; Tiberius, 1990; Schwarz, 1994), but instead will focus more selectively on several conceptual frameworks that practitioners can use to reflect on the progress of their work with learning groups. The ongoing task of honing skills for the effective facilitation of group learning is an exercise that can be full of excitement, but also full of pitfalls; likewise, it can be full of creativity, but also full of lost opportunities. It represents a worthwhile investment of effort and reflection, because groups are one of the most potent ways to influence learning.

The focus in this chapter is on teaching with small groups of from two to a dozen learners, but much of what will be discussed can be readily applied to teaching with much larger numbers of people (teaching in community development projects, for example, or public education programs). Once again, teaching activities may not always be explicitly recognized by the members of a learning group—teaching may occur in more subtle and ephemeral ways, within a family interview or team meeting, for example. The following are some examples of these kinds of embedded teaching and learning opportunities—in groups in which learning is not necessarily the members' primary focus:

A family therapist finds that she needs to help two generations of a family learn more effective ways to deal with interpersonal conflicts that arise during the course of their counseling sessions.

A psychologist uses opportunities that arise during team meetings to help colleagues from other professions learn about the strengths, limitations, and potential class or cultural biases of certain psychological tests.

A child care worker becomes concerned that her organization's weekly staff meetings are becoming a shapeless mass of inconclusive and often bitter debate. She offers to plan the meetings' agendas, and she uses this opportunity to identify items that might require decision-making, problem-solving, or information-giving skills. Her system, while not perfect, does ensure that teaching items are correctly identified and therefore dealt with more effectively.

A social worker finds it desirable to establish a weekly telephone conference between a group of isolated and homebound elderly people. His goal is to provide an opportunity for these people to learn from one another how to cope with some of the common challenges they face.

This last example illustrates how new communications technologies can be used to create "virtual learning groups." These technologies make it possible to incorporate some of the benefits of group learning in the absence of face-to-face contact (Madara, 1993).

Reasons for Working with Groups of Learners

Teaching in human service practice often involves groups of learners for at least three important reasons: the learners may be members of an existing social support system or work group, the learners can benefit from potent influences that are particularly present in group learning situations, and there may be economies of scale that can be achieved through working with several learners at the same time.

Teaching with Existing Groups

In practice, professionals frequently find it necessary to work with groups of learners who may already be part of a family, community, professional association, or work-based team. In these situations practitioners recognize that an individual member's learning (and its associated changes) is inextricably linked to the learning of the other members of that learner's social network. In effect, if each individual's learning is to be reinforced, then learning also has to take place for all other members of the group. To the extent that all group members are involved in the learning process, they will be increasingly committed to implementing changes that flow out of their shared learning experiences. This kind of group participation in the learning process is not just a strategic consideration: it also respects the right of individuals to participate in shaping events that will ultimately impact on their lives.

The following examples illustrate practitioners' teaching with these types of groups:

A worker in a needle exchange program engages in some subtle, implicit teaching on safer sex practices with a group of teenaged prostitutes who had formed a supportive network to spot "bad dates."

A family counselor works with three generations of a family that has recently arrived in North America. The learning projects he engages in with them involve understanding the school system, teen pressures for conformity, and ways to gain positive acceptance from friends and neighbors.

A practitioner who has developed particular expertise in the promotion of team development facilitates learning and growth among members of various interdisciplinary work groups at the large human service organization where she is employed.

A nurse is awarded a contract by her professional association to design continuing professional development programs for association members living in her area.

In each of these examples the practitioner recognizes that it is difficult to achieve individual learning without the concurrent involvement of those who belong to the learner's work or social support groups. Involvement of these other people is most likely essential if learning is to result in changed behavior. This represents one of several strategies used to promote what is known as the process of learning transfer (Fox 1984), which will be discussed in Chapter Eight.

Using Groups to Enhance the Impact of Teaching

Group teaching is particularly helpful in situations in which learners have to achieve higher-order abilities that involve the evaluation, synthesis, and application of ideas. Group discussion and group experiential learning exercises can provide a useful way to grapple with new concepts, attitudes, and skills, and group learning can help learners understand the material from multiple perspectives. This contrasts with situations in which learners are only exposed to the perspectives of a single authority—the teacher.

In ways that are often less explicit, some learning groups offer people an opportunity to learn from successful and less successful models provided by the thoughts and behaviors of other group members. This process, known as social learning (Bandura, 1977b), is particularly evident in self-help groups such as those for people with addictions and other personal difficulties. In these situations, learning from the experiences and examples of others is a powerful influence. Here are some illustrations of the added impact of group learning:

A practitioner is involved in helping a group of colleagues in supervisory positions understand the full implications of their organization's new equity policy. In order to support her staff development workshops, she develops a videotape containing a series of dramatized situations that, if handled incorrectly, could provoke charges of inequity. She recognizes the subtleties of much of what needs to be learned, and she feels that the video vignettes and group discussions on the tape will stimulate some of this higher-order learning.

A medical doctor is invited to serve as an arms-length consultant to a self-help group for women experiencing postpartum depression. She observes that some of the veteran members—as well as some of the more successful newcomers—provide powerful examples for others in how they handle their feelings on a day-to-day basis. And the members who do remain mired in depression, although they to some extent represent negative models, nonetheless serve as a salutary reminder to other members of the group of their need to work hard.

A vocational counselor working in a job retraining program finds that she is investing a great deal of time in teaching individual new participants about the alternative aspects of the program. Her response is to develop some video and print materials to facilitate group learning, and she uses this to work with groups of new trainees.

Working with groups may also serve to strengthen the voice of learners and thus redress some of the inherent power imbalances that can exist in formal teaching relationships. The support of other learners in a group can build the confidence of individual members. This kind of empowerment process gives learners an opportunity to shape the direction of their learning, and thus to increase their stake in actually implementing what they learn. This effect may be most evident in certain community education and development programs, in which learners build confidence and problem-solving ability through group problem solving. The concluding section of this chapter addresses popular education, an approach to group learning that aims to harness these benefits.

Using Groups to Engage More Learners

A third reason for using group teaching in the human services is, obviously, to achieve economies of scale. In many situations it is simply not either cost- or time-effective to teach on a one-to-one basis. This is particularly true of staff training and development programs, family life education programs, and public education programs, as the following examples illustrate:

Large numbers of volunteers are trained in basic communication and referral skills before being assigned to shifts on a telephone crisis line.

A pastor arranges a six-week marriage renewal course for couples in his congregation.

An international development agency becomes involved in a program to promote condom use in a country in Southeast Asia.

The Types of Groups Encountered in Practice

There are several different types of groups that are becoming involved in the teaching interventions of human service professionals, and some theoretical distinctions may be drawn between them. This is not just an academic exercise—while many groups may have a mixture of features, a guiding theoretical framework for a given group can offer the practitioner a way to think about the nature of the group and to work purposefully to best further that group's interests.

First of all, it is possible to distinguish between the kinds of *existing* groups discussed previously and various *emerging* groups that either coalesce of their own volition or are brought together by a human service professional. The second distinction has to do with the way in which the boundaries of a particular learning community are determined. Some groups form on the basis of the shared *functional* interrelationships of their members. These relationships might include work ties, family bonds, or a shared social or health concern. Other groups are defined in *geographic* terms, because the members live within a defined locality. In practice there is frequently a good deal of overlap, with people in a given group belonging to both a functional and a geographic community. The utility of these distinctions are that they provide a way for the practitioner to characterize the nature of a learning group. For example, a public health nurse might decide to create a temporary learning group on nutrition for people living in a small rural community. Such a group would be characterized as emerging, concerned with a shared functional issue, and located in a defined geographic area.

Understanding the Development of Learning Groups

Many group theorists have directed their attention to the stages groups pass through as they progress from formation to action to dissolution. There are several different theoretical models of group development (Tuckman, 1965; Jones, 1973; Johnson and Johnson, 1982), and practitioners can use these conceptual tools to guide their work with learning groups. Groups can vary in their approach, focusing more on achieving specific learning objectives (task-oriented groups) or on maintaining positive relationships between group members (relationship-oriented groups) (Bennis,

Benne, and Sheets, 1948; Bales, 1950; Deutsch, 1960). For example, in the case of the child care worker who plans her organization's staff meetings, she might plan the meetings to focus particularly on accomplishing specific tasks. In contrast, a mutual aid group for people experiencing manic depression might be more concerned with sustaining supportive relationships between the members. Whatever the character of a particular learning group, if it is to continue to exist and make progress, the members need to direct some attention to both (1) getting on with the job (accomplishing the required task) and (2) relating interdependently with each other (fostering the necessary relationships).

Human service professionals are likely to be familiar with the contribution of Bales (1950) and others to developing an understanding of how group members differentially assume task-accomplishment and relationship-building activities. That is, members have individual styles of contributing to the life of the learning group. Some members tend to be more concerned with helping sustain relationships among members, while others are more invested in task accomplishment. Finally, there are those members who focus on both task-accomplishment and relationship-building activities. For a group to continue to exist and thrive, it is necessary for the collectivity to address both of these types of activities, although the weight given each type will vary depending on the character and purpose of a particular group.

A range of specific task-accomplishment and relationship-building activities are spelled out in a number of sources (Nylen, Mitchell, and Stout, 1976; Johnson and Johnson, 1982). These different kinds of group roles are the basis of the group facilitation checklist mentioned earlier (see Resource B). Practitioners can use this competency profile to reflect on their group facilitation style and identify areas that might be strengthened. This resource can also be used to explore what different learners contribute to the group. Awareness of different member roles and contributions can help the facilitator strengthen the group's effectiveness.

A Situational Teaching Approach to Group Facilitation

The situational teaching model introduced in Chapter Three (p. 70) may be used as a reflective tool to help learning group facilitators assess the general capacity of an existing or emerging group and the kinds of facilitative interventions that may be required in specific situations. The four alternative interventions identified in that model are telling, instructing, participating, and delegating; for groups, however, task-accomplishment and relationship-building activities are used to inform the desired character of a particular teaching intervention.

Low Relationship, High Task Emphasis (Telling)

In some situations practitioners (or their employers) believe that mastering certain tasks is a crucial and to some extent nonnegotiable outcome for a given learning group. Learners are required to reach a prescribed level of competence in these tasks, or face a variety of sanctions. It is understood that this kind of teaching intervention may have adverse effects on the teaching relationship, but this consideration takes second place to ensuring that learners have the ability to perform the required task. In the human services there tend to be relatively few circumstances in which this type of group learning situation is encountered; the following example illustrates a situation in which it might be called for:

> The director of an outdoor-education mountain climbing center for young offenders is very directive in his teaching of the fundamentals of mountaineering safety to a group of new residents. He indicates to them that *any* breach of these protocols will result in that person's being returned to prison.

High Relationship, High Task Emphasis (Instructing)

In some situations the practitioner determines that the learners need the support of a strong interpersonal relationship with the teacher as they address valued learning tasks. In such cases the role of the professional is to engage in active teaching:

> A family counselor joins the staff of a camp that offers family vacations for single mothers and their children. The counselor leads the camp's parenting course, utilizing a lot of active learning methods, including role-playing, to make the experience meaningful and fun.

High Relationship, Low Task Emphasis (Participating)

This method is used for groups in which the exchange of social support among members may be more important than the achievement of specific tasks. Because many professionals in the human services tend to be quite task oriented, they may have difficulty controlling their desire to intervene in groups that appear to put more emphasis on developing group relationships than on learning tasks. For example:

> A physiotherapist notes that, in a teaching program for new amputees, the members like to take time out from the group's structured training exercises to socialize and share life experiences with one another. Controlling her initial impatience, she eventually recognizes the importance of this informal, participatory learning. In response she increases the amount of time in which this subtle sharing of information, support, and mutual aid can occur.

Low Relationship, Low Task Emphasis (Delegating)

This type of teaching relationship characterizes situations or stages in the life of a learning group in which members are ready to take on many of the roles previously carried by the practitioner. Delegation does not necessarily signal the end of the teacher-learner relationship, however, as there may be sporadic continued contact to ensure that learning gains are sustained:

A medical doctor runs a workshop for a number of patients living with multiple allergies. The group develops guidelines outlining effective ways to cope, and the doctor suggests that the members meet with her six weeks later to check on their continuing learning progress.

The need to terminate a group may become evident when members exhibit little focus on either shared task accomplishment or maintenance of group relationships. This may indicate that the group members are ready to disband, and the practitioner should check this out with them.

The following example illustrates the conclusion of a group learning experience:

Attendance begins tapering off at the meetings of a support group for people providing care to dependent relatives. After consulting with group members, the professional facilitator suggests they hold one concluding meeting to review and celebrate what they have achieved together.

One other alternative is that the members may wish to continue to meet, but would prefer to function autonomously, without the professional present. Human service professionals have needs for recognition, and they can be reluctant to see learning groups disband or to dispense with their services even when the members themselves feel ready for them to do so.

The foregoing discussion focused on the general character of different kinds of learning groups. However, as noted previously, practitioners need to gauge their interventions to the know-how and capacity of the group members in relation to specific situations. Over time the group may pass through enough developmental stages that the practitioner is eventually able to delegate all the learning tasks to the members of the group.

A Stages-of-Development Approach to Group Facilitation

There is a good deal of variation among the various models of the process of group development, but Tuckman (1965) provides a particularly practical way to consider the evolution of learning groups. The progressive stages in this particular conception of group development are: forming, storming, norming, and performing. Other theorists include a fifth stage, variously described as adjourning, re-forming, or re-norming. The Tuckman model has the additional advantage of having a certain cadence that makes it easy to recall.

Having a way to conceptualize the developmental phases of a learning group offers the practitioner at least three advantages. First, a model such as Tuckman's enables a group facilitator to act purposefully to promote optimum evolution of the learning group. Second, this model enables the professional to speculate about the stage of development of an existing group he or she might be asked to facilitate. Third, when a group runs into difficulty performing a learning task, this model may shed light on problems arising from earlier phases of the group's development. For example, a group might be hampered if it is composed of incompatible members or if some group norms interfere with the learning process.

In the first stage of development, *forming,* practitioners become involved in identifying who should be included in the learning group. For example, in some situations a more homogeneous group might be selected so that learners share similar entry-level abilities and motivations. In other circumstances the practitioner may deliberately create a group composed of people with varying degrees of ability so that members can learn from each other and through reciprocal teaching. The facilitator may include people who are in a position to influence whether what is learned in the group is practiced after the group disbands. Examples include managers, family members, and community opinion leaders.

Other forming-stage activities include helping the learners get to know one another and beginning to establish the learning climate. Clarification of an explicit learning agreement tends to be associated with the norming (contract or working agreement) phase, but mutual expectations and aspirations are shaped from the moment of initial contact among members.

The *storming* phase is the period during which learners begin to test out their relationship with one another and with the practitioner. At this time there are either explicit or implicit struggles about the level of shared commitment to the group's learning goals and to the roles various members will assume. Typically, in more structured, task-oriented learning groups this phase is either quite brief or entirely overlooked. This can produce difficulties later on if it becomes evident that group members have a wide variation in their expectations about the purpose of the group and the roles they are to play in the learning process.

Storming moves into *norming* as group relationships, roles, and goals become more established. The norms that come to influence a learning group tend to consist of a blend of explicit, publicly acknowledged agreements and implicit rules or patterns governing the way group members function together. This mixture of norms affects the group's productivity and influences the roles members play, including that of the facilitator. (A method for identifying and assessing adherence to desired group norms is discussed in Chapter Eight.)

To the extent these working agreements are clear and fit well with the group's purpose, they contribute to effective learning during the *performing* phase. The role of the practitioner now becomes one of helping to sustain interpersonal relationships, keeping the group moving forward on learning tasks, mediating differences, and providing summaries to sustain the group's momentum.

The termination of a learning group is also an important phase. It is at this time that the facilitator engages the members in summarizing what they have learned, dealing with feelings generated by the end of the group experience, and conducting evaluations of both the content of what was taught and the process of learning. It is also the time to make certain that measures have been taken to ensure that what has been learned will continue to be used once the group disbands.

The following examples illustrate some of the difficulties that can arise at each stage of the group development process:

Forming phase: A community psychologist is in the process of creating a support group for former patients from a local mental hospital. However, he includes a number of people who have been in highly dependent relationships with their therapists. It quickly becomes evident that these people lack the core strength needed to engage in the reciprocal, mutual provision of aid. As a result, in a relatively short time the group begins to disintegrate, and eventually it disbands.

Storming phase: A probation officer is asked to run a day-long workshop for police officers on mediation and conflict resolution. However, in his eagerness to get started, he fails to allow time for the participants to express some of their reservations about the topic and his plan for the workshop. This undermines the development of effective learning relationships and fosters learner resistance to some of the experiential learning exercises he had wanted to use.

Norming phase: A public health nurse working with a group of recent immigrants wants them to become actively involved in exploring ways to use Canadian food products. However, she fails to explain to them and to reach an agreement with them on the need for active participation by the learners. They sit still and silent, obviously puzzled and frustrated by her constant requests for their ideas and opinions. The expectation of the participants is that the practitioner will tell them exactly what they should do.

Performing phase: A family counselor runs a series of marriage preparation classes for a group of engaged couples. She does not do any kind of ongoing evaluations at the end of each session, and she is surprised to learn after the series ends that several of the participants took away some misinformation. This happened because they had not fully understood some of the things the counselor thought she had taught.

Adjourning phase: A group of Catholic priests attends a three-day workshop on counseling youths involved in the criminal justice system. This is a powerful and positive experience for them. The final session consists of a content-driven presentation by the practitioner; when this session ends, the group quickly disbands in order to make the facilities available for another workshop. As a result, the learners have no opportunity to acknowledge the importance of the new relationships they have forged with other participants or to thank the facilitator.

In Chapter Eight there is a discussion of strategies to involve learners in a discussion of the desired norms for their group. These are used to construct what is known as a group norms scale. This is a custom-made assessment tool that allows learners to monitor their adherence to their desired norms on an ongoing basis.

Experiential Approaches to Group Learning

Much of the learning that takes place in the context of human service practice has to do with learning from and about life experiences connected with economic, health, and social factors. In daily practice this learning from experience happens in conjunction with the kinds of teachable moments that were discussed earlier. This kind of learning, stimulated by the ebb and flow of life events, is defined by Houle (1980) as "the education that occurs as a result of direct participation in the events of life" (p. 221). Pfeiffer and Jones (1980) are rather more specific about this process: "Experiential learning occurs when a person engages in some activity, looks back at that activity, critically abstracts some useful insight from the analysis and puts the result to work" (p. 3).

This latter definition identifies stages in the experiential learning process and leaves open the possibility that learning can be a natural outgrowth of reflection about both spontaneous life experiences and planned learning activities. The product generated through this process of action and reflection has been previously identified as experiential knowledge (Borkman, 1976).

In the discussion that follows, the focus is on two types of experiential learning in groups: one that is more planned and positivist in nature, and another that is more emergent and constructivist.

Planning for Experiential Learning

Human service professionals find it necessary to incorporate structured experiential learning activities into their teaching for several reasons. A teachable moment may not be present, and it may be necessary to promote motivation among a group of learners through the use of role-playing or simulations. Learners may need to view a simulated problem from multiple perspectives in order to construct an appropriate course of action. Learners may need to rehearse complex sets of skills in a group setting, which offers many sources of feedback. And learners may need to bring to the surface self-limiting beliefs and assumptions that act to constrain their coping efforts. In sum, experiential learning strategies may be used to stimulate motivation, to plan future action, to practice complex behaviors, and to clarify values and assumptions:

Motivating: A counselor in a transition house for abused women involves a group of residents in role-playing how they might deal with a variety of potentially abusive encounters.

Planning action: A recreation worker in a racially diverse neighborhood uses a simulation game to help a group of young people explore how they could work more effectively with one another.

Practicing complex skills: A trainer in a peer counselor training program helps a group of adolescents develop their listening and responding skills by videotaping their efforts and encouraging group feedback.

Clarifying values: An outreach worker for a young offenders home uses a values-clarification exercise with a group of neighbors who are willing to explore their beliefs and assumptions about such homes.

The process of experiential learning can be understood to involve several stages (Kolb, 1984). A way of conceptualizing this process is illustrated in Figure 4.1.

Figure 4.1. The Cycle of Experiential Learning.

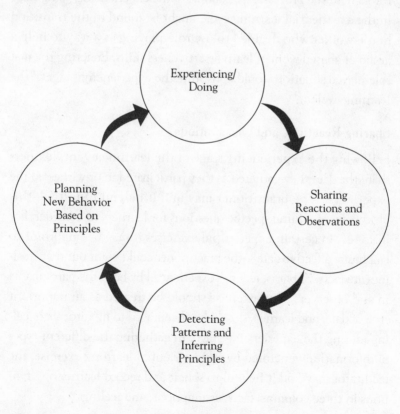

Experiencing/ Doing

Sharing Reactions and Observations

Detecting Patterns and Inferring Principles

Planning New Behavior Based on Principles

Experiencing/Doing

This is often the phase of the experiential learning process that receives the most time and attention from teachers. It is the stage when experiential learning tasks are designed or selected, and learners are actively engaged in these experiences. There must, however, be equal attention directed to the other phases in the cycle of experiential learning, or the benefits of this approach are unlikely to be fully realized. An experiential learning exercise is a means to an end, not an end in itself. For this reason, practitioners may find it helpful in more formal learning situations to outline the stages of the experiential learning cycle prior to the experience so that learners will have a clear understanding of what will be expected of them throughout the process. An example of the experiencing/doing stage in the experiential learning cycle might be found in the transition house worker who decided to use role-playing as a way to help a group of abused women learn assertiveness skills. Enacting the first role-played situation would constitute the experiencing stage of the learning cycle.

Sharing Reactions and Observations

Following the experiencing stage of the learning event, learners share the data they gathered as they participated in or witnessed the experience. The practitioner may find it helpful to initiate this process by providing specific questions for learners to consider. For instance, in certain experiential exercises it may be important to emphasize affective data—the practitioner could point out that "feelings are facts." That is, feelings experienced by both the participants in and observers of an exercise should be treated as an important type of data, and learners should be encouraged to monitor such feelings during the experiencing stage. In gathering the different types of information generated by an experiential learning exercise, the facilitator may find it helpful to solicit and record learner observations in three columns: facts, assumptions, and feelings.

The value of this approach is that it helps the participants to sort out more verifiable information from assumptions they may have made about the events they experienced. This approach gives legitimacy to personal affective responses as sources of data for learning.

In a previous example, role-playing was used to help a group of abused women prepare to deal with potentially abusive future situations. In such a case, following the role-playing phase, all participants would be asked to reflect on and record not only what they observed, but also what they thought and felt during this experience.

Detecting Patterns and Inferring Principles

The next stage in processing the initial experiential learning exercise is one that involves learners in looking for patterns and connections among the data gathered in the preceding phase. Learners are encouraged to look for overarching principles, concepts, or theories that might account for what they have reflectively observed. In effect they are encouraged to construct a meaning perspective to account for what took place during the experiencing phase, and to use this perspective to generate principles for future action.

Returning again to the transition house example, participants might be divided into pairs to tie together the data they gathered into theories that might suggest possible effective courses of action.

Planning New Behavior Based on Principles

In this final stage learners are asked to take their most robust theories from the previous stage and plan new activities to check out the validity of the principles they derive from these theories. The testing of these new behaviors will in turn generate further experiential grist for the learning process. In the transition house example this stage of the cycle might involve the participants' replaying the role-play situation in order to test the effectiveness of the actions they planned.

Examples of the use of experiential learning exercises with two different groups of learners illustrate this process:

A college counselor leads an assertiveness training group for female students. The group's current focus is on preventing date rape. The counselor asks the group members to give examples of potentially hazardous dating situations. Among the ideas contributed is a situation in which a young woman accepts an offer of a ride home from a party, only to be driven in the opposite direction from her apartment. The person who volunteers this experience agrees to role-play the male driver, and another group member agrees to represent the young woman. The other ten group members functioning as observers form a circle around the members playing the two roles. Following the role-play encounter *(experience),* the observers report on what they observed, including their own assumptions and feelings *(data).* The group members all add their observations and begin theorizing about what these observations might suggest. They speculate about how this type of harassment can arise and how women can effectively respond *(concepts and principles).* Finally, the group members develop ways to test the utility of these principles *(active experimentation).*

A practitioner is asked to design and deliver some management training materials for new front-line supervisors in a large human service organization. In order to raise matters related to workload management and decision making, he uses a simulation exercise involving the contents of an "In" basket that might confront a manager returning to work after a short vacation. One participant volunteers to sort the various letters, phone messages, and reports into a perceived order of priority *(experience).* The other participants listen to this person's comments as he performs this task, and they make notes on what they observe *(data).* The members then all try to categorize these observations in order to arrive at patterns and theories, and thus principles for deciding on priorities *(concepts and principles).*

Finally, the members use these concepts to sort out the contents of another simulated "In" basket *(experimentation)*.

Experiential learning can be extremely potent, but a great deal of the potential value depends on the skill of the practitioner in facilitating this process of mining an experience for transferable principles. It is crucial that sufficient time and structure are assigned to the latter three stages of the experiential learning cycle: data collection, concept development, and the checking of practice principles. All too frequently the potential value of an experiential learning exercise is not realized because too little time and attention are given to the phases that process the experience and thereby lead to learning that will translate beyond the immediate learning situation.

Popular Education: Facilitating Emergent Learning

Popular education is a comprehensive approach to learning from experience. This method is now being applied in a wide range of human service contexts. It has been defined by Arnold and Burke (1983) in this way: "Popular education . . . is a collective or group process of education, where the teacher and students learn together, beginning with the concrete experience of the participants, leading to reflection on that experience in order to effect positive change" (p. 7).

Popular education grew out of the pioneering literacy programs of Paulo Freire in Latin America in the 1960s. He taught his students to read and write by encouraging them to discuss pressing local problems such as a lack of drinking water and the loss of arable land. Freire noted that as students developed literacy skills they also began to reframe their understanding of the conditions under which they lived. Through their shared reflections, students came to perceive that their problems were in part the result of an oppressive political system and could only be addressed through collective action. This development of critical awareness and a continuing cycle of action-reflection-action is at the heart of the process Freire terms "conscientization" (Freire, 1970b).

Freire distinguishes his approach from the traditional "banking" approach to education, in which participants are treated as empty vessels that must be filled with information. He says that in such an approach, "people learn to distrust themselves, their own knowledge and intuitions, and this can lead to confusion" (GATT-Fly, 1983, p. 13).

During the mid 1980s this approach to community education and development spread to Central America and later to North America. Popular education draws on many of the more familiar and structured experiential learning exercises, including role-playing, visualization, sculpting, and values clarification. But in the popular education approach, learning outcomes are determined by the participants themselves. "What distinguishes popular education from traditional education is that people participate in creating the conditions and the content of their learning" (Women's Self-Help Network, 1984, p. 25). In the case of popular education, experiential learning is not just one component of the learning process, it *is* the process—and learning activities are not contrived, but are rooted in real life.

The popular education process may extend over a single day, but more typically it involves a series of three or more workshops of this duration over a span of months. It is also possible to apply the popular education process within a much more compressed time frame. Arnold, Barndt, and Burke (no date) describe using the popular education method to explore participatory research approaches in a workshop lasting less than two hours.

The process of critical reflection is determined by the participants and shaped by the issue they choose to address. Typically the process contains the following elements, which parallel the phases of the experiential learning cycle (see Figure 4.1). Learning begins with an accounting of the learners' experience with the topic in question. Participants move to deepening their shared analysis of the issue, then develop theories to account for their experiences, and finally develop plans of action.

This approach to learning has been used with a variety of groups of adult learners, and it is no longer confined to work with the oppressed and the marginalized. There is a good deal of practical literature on popular education, and this philosophy and its supporting methods can provide an effective way to generate community animation around public health and social welfare issues. The following example offers a brief illustration of the way in which a popular education project might develop:

A public health nurse works with residents of a public housing project to help them identify and take action on their health concerns. The meetings of this group of women take place during a Take-a-Break program, when child care is provided by the local YMCA. These meetings lead to a day-long program involving many of the housing project's residents. Several different experiential learning methods are used, and through these processes participants identify as a priority concern the fact that children from the project must cross a busy street in order to get to their school. While more affluent neighborhoods have crossing guards, their crosswalk has none. This leads to collective action in the form of demonstrations and lobbying, which eventually produces the desired result.

Additional examples of the use of popular education approaches may be found in the handbooks produced by the Women's Self-Help Network (1984). Also, a book by Vella (1994) includes a broad range of case studies of popular education projects undertaken in a variety of international contexts.

5

Assessing What Needs to Be Learned

The next four chapters focus on four key elements of the teaching process: assessing learning needs and learning resources, developing ways to facilitate learning, selecting or creating activities and materials to support the learning process, and selecting ways to assess learning progress and results. Laid out in this way, these steps may suggest a tidy linear progression from one stage in the learning process to another, but in reality teaching and learning tends to involve a much more dynamic interplay among these various elements. An appreciation of these ingredients does at least afford a way for the practitioner to sort out where in the process he or she may be at a particular point in time.

The term "assessment" is used to describe a variety of different activities that occur throughout the cycle of learning. Assessment may involve pre-formative evaluation of the needs to address in a particular teaching episode. Formative assessment embraces a range of methods used to adjust the character of the teaching, as it unfolds. Finally, summative assessment evaluates the extent to which learning outcomes have been achieved.

Pre-formative Assessment

In this chapter the focus is primarily on the pre-formative assessment of learning needs that takes place at the very beginning of, or prior to, a teaching intervention. Parallels in other forms of human service practice might include an intake or diagnostic interview or a team review of client documents as a prelude to some form of professional intervention. Assessment of learning needs refers to a systematic process of collecting and analyzing information about the educational needs of individuals, groups, or organizations (Moore, 1980).

In this case the focus is on situations in which practitioners— either alone or in concert with others—identify learners, their learning needs (felt, perceived, and real), and the available learning resources. Egan (1985) notes that "assessing needs critically involves discovering their causes, identifying the assumptions and values on which they are based, assessing the cost/benefit ratio in satisfying them, establishing priorities among competing needs, and making sure that needs are related to goals" (p. 82).

The elements of pre-formative assessment will be discussed in sequence, and, indeed, they may unfold in a linear fashion in practice when a logical-positivist approach to the learning process is taken. More frequently there is a continuing and emergent dialogue between the practitioner and learners as learning needs, learning resources, and learning opportunities are explored and refined. Nevertheless, it is useful to tease out the ingredients of this process.

Learning needs may be defined in the following way (Percival, 1993): "A need implies a discrepancy or gap between a desired condition or state of affairs and the actual or perceived condition or state of affairs. Educational programs are designed to close or narrow the gap between what is and what is desired" (p. 93).

Pre-formative assessment in the human services should not, however, be restricted just to an evaluation of the learning *needs* of individuals, groups, or organizations; it should also include an exploration of available learning *resources*. In the past, diagnostic assessments or intake interviews were too frequently preoccupied with the client's or patient's perceived inadequacies and limitations, and too little concerned with that person's capacities and strengths. In the case of teaching interventions, the resources and capacities of the learner and his or her social networks can contribute in important ways to the process of learning and change. For example, there is evidence that in the case of more autonomous or self-directed learning, such as occurs within mutual aid groups, there has to be a core of strength among the group members if they are to be able to affiliate and learn from one another. It is necessary for members to be able to participate as members rather than as patients, if they are to successfully build on their own strengths and resources and draw on the capacities of others in the group.

In the following example it is clear that the practitioner makes an effort to identify both learning needs *and* learning capacities and resources during the assessment process:

> A child welfare worker, employed by a First Nations community, meets with a group of elders to assess needs and resources that might affect child protection on their reservation. A number of needs were noted and some important resources identified, including the elders themselves, some indigenous healers, extensive networks of extended family members, some funds for educational programs, and an unused building.

An additional consideration in the needs assessment process is to include an evaluation of three other variables in addition to determining the content to be learned. These include an assessment of the learner's *motivation* to learn; the *capacity*, or entry-level ability, the learner brings to the learning task; and the learner's *opportunity* to implement what is learned within his or her social environment.

Vella (1994) suggests another formulation of the needs assessment process, based on what she terms the WWW question: "*Who* needs *what* as defined by *whom?*" (p. 52). Her emphasis is on the need to be clear about who the learners will be, what their learning needs are, and who will make these two determinations.

Finally, Knox (1990) indicates that, along with needs assessment, there needs to be what he terms "context analysis" (p. 66), a more comprehensive assessment of the factors that might impact learning (including, as previously noted, a lack of opportunity to implement what is learned).

This discussion now moves to an exploration of the following questions: Who determines what persons will be regarded as the learners, and who will determine what these learners need? How, in both general and specific ways, will needs and resources be determined? How can desired learning outcomes be stated so that they are most helpful in planning a teaching intervention?

Who Identifies Learners and Learning Needs?

The identification of who will be addressed by a teaching intervention is often made initially by the human service professional, based on needs the professional *perceives*. In other circumstances people may identify their own, *felt* learning needs and then seek out the required learning resources. In either of these situations it is important to be clear on who the learners are, who will determine their learning needs, and how the learning will be conducted. There is also a third possibility, that *real* needs are determined by the practitioner on the basis of some measurable gap between the current functioning of the targeted learner and some normative (Wlodkowski, 1991) or prescriptive (Monette, 1977) standard. For example, there may be baseline standards for typing or language proficiency for a particular job, or there may be tightly restricted normative margins of error for certain medical procedures.

The power and prestige invested in human service professionals makes it all too easy for them to fail to clarify who is the target of a given teaching intervention and to ensure that the felt needs of this group correspond with the practitioner's perceptions of their learning needs. A brief anecdote may serve to illustrate how a professional, as an outsider to a particular community or experience, may not be well situated to make an accurate assessment of that group's felt needs:

> The director of a family counseling agency was part of a group of practitioners, from a range of human service agencies, that decided to examine the needs of a large ethnic community composed of people newly arrived from Europe. Euphemistically known as the Committee for New Canadians, these professionals were in reality mainly concerned about their perceived needs for a group of Italian immigrants. Surprisingly, however, a preponderance of the committee members had names like Smith, Brown, MacDonald, and, yes, Farquharson. The agency director felt consoled by the fact that there was at least one professional present, a Dr. Karpati, representing a community health center, who had what the director assumed to be an Italian surname, and he confided his relief to this doctor that they had at least one member to represent the felt needs of the community in question. Dr. Karpati responded, "Interesting! That wouldn't be me because I'm in fact Hungarian."

There are other examples of situations in which professionals in positions of power are able to push ahead on the basis of their own perceptions of what others need to learn (Farquharson, 1975; Maluccio, 1979). In situations in which the needs the practitioner perceives are not felt by the person or group in question there is likely to be a disastrous mismatch between the teacher's and the learners' motivations. Indeed, even when the two parties have the same perceptions and feelings about a learning need, they may have quite different beliefs about the way in which this mutually perceived need should be addressed. One way to understand how people can develop such highly individualized health belief models is to combine an understanding of the epistemically privileged insider's perspective with an appreciation for the constructivist nature of meaning making. Together these processes can lead individuals, groups, and communities to construct disparate notions about what constitutes a need and about how a perceived need should be addressed. The potential for misunderstandings, particularly when there are cultural differences between the practitioner and the learning group, has been carefully documented in a number of interesting studies (Rogers, 1983; Timpson and others, 1988; Vella, 1994).

In concluding this part of the discussion on learning needs, it may be useful to review exactly what is meant by "learning needs." Learning needs may be needs and wants felt by the learner or they may be needs perceived and prescribed by practitioners. Practitioners perceive learning needs based either on their beliefs and assumptions or on some kind of normative assessment; such assessments may yield what are referred to as "real" needs. Brookfield (1986) argues for an approach that takes into account both felt needs and perceived and real needs: "It is my contention that a total subscription to a felt needs approach to program development condemns education to an adaptive reactive mode and turns educators into mere providers of consumer goods" (p. 222).

Assessing learning needs and resources, like other activities associated with teaching in the human services, may be done either formally and explicitly or informally and implicitly, depending on the context in which teaching takes place and the nature of the people in the learning group. For example, a professional development workshop might be planned on the basis of a specific, explicit process of needs assessment, while a needle-exchange worker might conduct a more informal and implicit assessment of the learning needs of a group of IV drug users.

A general principle for effective and ethical human service practice is that the practitioner should strive to enable the client, patient, or learner to become as fully engaged as possible in all facets of the helping process. This is particularly true during the initial needs assessment process; however, there are situations when the learning needs perceived by the practitioner and those felt by the learner will not correspond. In these situations it may be most effective for the practitioner to first attend to the felt needs of the learners. This may provide an opportunity for the professional to build some credibility and to establish a more effective, in-depth dialogue about the nature and context of the needs felt by members of the learning group. This process is evident in the following example:

> A Canadian community development worker accepts a contract to work with villagers in a country in South America. It is apparent to her that there are problems with health, education, and agriculture, but she embarks on a process that will involve the peasants in an assessment of their needs and resources. She is somewhat aghast when they tell her that their top priority is to build a swimming pool, but she comes to recognize that this need arises out of their desire to emulate what they see at the local landowner's hacienda. She is able, through strong lobbying, to get funds to launch this first project. The credibility she accumulates by responding to the felt needs of the citizens and through the critical dialogue she has developed with them eventually leads to a community-wide program of health education. Later the villagers use their newly forged skills of cooperation and shared learning to convert the pool into a grain storage facility.

The practitioner should consider that not all of the needs identified during the assessment phase may require teaching interventions. Teaching is indeed a potent form of intervention in the human services; but if practitioners become overzealous aficionados of this approach, there is the danger that teaching may be used in situations where other forms of intervention would be more effective. This danger is captured in the saying "Give a child a hammer and everything will start to look like a nail." Some assessed needs may require the exercise of statutory authority, others may need to be addressed through counseling and therapy, and still others may not need to be addressed at all, or not at the present time. In some situations it may be appropriate to wait for a more teachable moment to arise. Practitioners should be particularly wary of situations in which a third party identifies the need for a teaching intervention; in such cases they should build in an opportunity to verify the learning need. This might take place prior to accepting a teaching assignment or during the initial contact with the learners, when a more mutual appraisal can be undertaken. The following example illustrates a situation in which there might be an inaccurate perception of a need for a teaching intervention:

> The director of a chain of group homes for mildly mentally challenged adults is concerned that many of the residents repeatedly violate the rules against smoking inside the homes. His response is to ask one residence manager to develop and lead a series of workshops for the residents about the dangers of smoking inside the homes. The manager is reluctant to take on this assignment; she feels that such reeducation would be a long-term process and that the more pressing need is to enforce the existing smoking rules, for safety reasons.

Felt needs alone are generally not considered an adequate measure of the real needs of adult learners (Brookfield, 1986; Wlodkowski, 1991). Therefore, assessments of potential teaching needs are generally more accurate if triangulated from a variety of different perspectives (Knox, 1990), including that of potential learners, the practitioner, and various other stakeholders. "Stakeholders" are those people and institutions other than the learners themselves that are likely to be affected by the learning outcomes; they are one of the factors in Knox's context analysis. Stakeholders may include learners' family members, their peers, their employers, or leaders in their community. It has already been noted that there are several different aggregations of potential learners, including individuals, families, groups, communities, and organizations. Stakeholders may be powerfully situated to either block or support the implementation of what is learned. The extent to which such people play a role in the needs assessment process may affect their potential support (or their potential resistance). Thus the content and process of a proposed teaching intervention can be adapted either to harness support or to reduce opposition.

Who Perceives the Need?

There are two important tasks to perform in determining learning needs and resources: first, determine the extent to which needs are perceived by the practitioner, the learners, or both; then select a specific needs assessment strategy.

The conceptual model outlined in Figure 5.1 (Farquharson, 1978) offers a way for practitioners to think about the different vantage points from which they and prospective groups of learners may view learning needs. The basic dimensions of the model are derived from a model of self-disclosure known as the Johari Window, after the first names of the two authors (Luft, 1969). This matrix may be used as a tool in planning needs assessment strategies.

The first quadrant covers those needs (and resources) that are already recognized by both the learners and the practitioner. In effect, the felt needs of the learner coincide with the needs perceived by the practitioner; thus more direct assessment strategies may now be used to plan the teaching intervention. These strategies might include individual or focus-group interviews or surveys to tap learner and stakeholder opinions. These approaches can be used to confirm the shared perception of the need and to determine such things as the level of need, the number of potential learners, and the context in which the learning should take place. For example:

Figure 5.1. A Model for Learning-Need Identification.

	Need Seen by Learner	Need Not Seen by Learner
Need Seen by Practitioner	Quadrant 1 Shared Perceptions of Need	Quadrant 2 Outreach to Learners
Need Not Seen by Practitioner	Quadrant 3 Outreach to Professionals	Quadrant 4 Exploration of Needs Through Mutual Reflection

A family physician with a large caseload of elderly people is concerned that some of his patients are carelessly mixing different med-
ications and increasing dosages beyond prescribed levels. In
collaboration with a social worker from the local senior's center and
the chair of the center's advisory board, a telephone survey is
devised. Senior volunteers then phone senior citizens to check on
their interest in a course on managing their medication, their level of
understanding of the drugs they use, and the type of questions they
would like answered. These data help influence the level and nature
of the information given in the subsequent workshops.

The second quadrant in Figure 5.1 includes those learning needs
that are perceived by the practitioner but have yet to be perceived
as felt needs by the potential learners. In these types of situations a
needs assessment strategy needs to include a process for bringing
awareness of the need to the learners in a way that begins to engage
them in a process of critical reflection. For example:

A community psychologist involves a group of low-income single
mothers in a discussion of their needs and resources. She uses a
variety of popular education methods, including sculpting, which has
participants assume postures that reflect their sense of powerlessness. The teacher also asks small groups of the women to create
composite pictures of their daily lives and concerns. This enables the
participants to see their shared concerns, drawing them closer
together.

The third quadrant in the matrix, outreach to professionals,
includes situations in which a group of people have shared learning needs that have yet to be perceived by human service
providers. For example, people who are socially or geographically
isolated from human service professionals may experience difficulty communicating their learning needs. Assessment strategies
in these circumstances need to involve active outreach that offers

these people a voice to express what they require. Outreach tools might include consumer advisory groups, community surveys, and a review of needs identified in other, similar functional or geographic communities. This process is sensitively explained by Vella (1994) in describing a learner-driven approach to need identification with a group of indigenous relief workers in Ethiopia. A further example illustrates this approach in a North American context:

> The staff of a neighborhood family counseling agency is concerned that their caseload does not reflect the demographics of the neighborhood. They recognize that this might reflect a blind spot in the way they think about community needs. A daylong meeting of local citizen representatives is convened to advise the agency staff of the felt needs of community members. Among the identified needs are English-as-a-second-language programs and more Asian staff members who can speak several Asian languages.

This is a good example of how professionals from the dominant social group sometimes overlook the felt learning needs of minority groups.

The fourth quadrant represents those situations in which learning needs (and resources) are not recognized by either practitioners or potential learners. This may be a little difficult to visualize, but it can occur when a useful innovation that has been pioneered elsewhere remains unknown to another group of practitioners and to potential learners who could benefit from it. The lag time in moving AIDS and HIV educational programs out to rural communities provides a case in point. Monitoring a variety of sources of information—newspapers, radio, TV, journals, and computer bulletin boards—may reveal potentially helpful innovations that have been pioneered in other communities. Freire and other popular educators pursued a similar strategy as they sought to raise their critical consciousness and reframe their social situations through a process of intense, reflective dialogue between various parties.

There may also be situations in which neither practitioners nor the people they serve recognize that certain of their shared concerns may be addressed through education that reframes their experience and prepares them for collective action. This is at the core of the work of Freire (1970a, 1970b, 1973) and other popular educators (Arnold and Burke, 1983; Vella, 1994). For example:

A group of citizens, law enforcement officials, and representatives of social agencies meet to discuss problems of vandalism and other criminal acts perpetrated by young teens in their community. It gradually becomes apparent that once they are able to move past blaming, all the parties at the meeting share similar concerns. However, they cannot seem to move beyond harsh punitive measures as their preferred response. In the course of several more long and intense meetings, several new educational strategies are hammered out. These initiatives include the creation of a new community school; the development of a positive parenting course, to be sponsored by the local YMCA; and a storefront job-skills program.

In addition to such identifiable, community-based efforts, it should be recognized that much of this kind of mutual exploration takes place in interviews with individuals, families, and small groups. This occurs as practitioners and the people they work with name feelings and perceptions as they struggle to achieve a shared understanding that will set the stage for new learning. This kind of mutual needs assessment is at the core of much human service practice.

Assessment Strategies

There is a large and useful body of literature on alternative strategies for assessing learning needs, resources, and contextual factors (Kemp, 1985; Knox, 1990; Barnsley and Ellis, 1992; Cantor, 1992). Practitioners should start with an understanding of the whole continuum of needs assessment strategies. Some strategies, such as interviews and surveys, involve direct contact with individual respondents; others involve contact with focus and nominal groups. There are also needs assessment approaches that rely on more indirect approaches, such as reviewing available data. One way to organize this brief review of assessment methods is to consider them as lying along a continuum, from methods that are more convergent and positivist to methods that are more emergent and constructivist. For example, in the assessment model illustrated in Figure 5.1, checklists, questionnaires, or structured interviews are various ways to gather additional data about needs perceived by both the practitioner and the learner (Quadrant 1). In situations where the potential existence of needs is to be explored through mutual reflection (Quadrant 4), it may be necessary to promote consciousness-raising and critical dialogue through some of the verbal, nonverbal, and visual methods associated with popular education (Barnsley and Ellis, 1992). Figure 5.2 outlines four different types of needs assessment strategies. First, data may be collected by using surveys, questionnaires, or psychological tests (Gordon, 1980). These may be either mailed in or completed in an interview with potential learners. Sometimes a practitioner will develop these kinds of instruments himself to suit a particular purpose. Or practitioners may use an existing normative test.

A second cluster of needs assessment strategies includes a variety of interviewing approaches that rely on direct or telephone

Figure 5.2. Needs Assessment Strategies.

Questionnaire	Interview	Focus Group	Popular Education

Positivist → Constructivist

Predetermined → Emergent

contact with the learner or with people familiar with the learning task. This latter approach is known as task analysis (Cranton, 1989). It involves interviewing people who understand a particular learning task in order to determine the competencies required for successful performance.

A third set of approaches to needs assessment relies on the use of groups to identify learning needs. Focus groups (Kreuger, 1988) offer one approach, but there are other kinds of advisory group processes, including the nominal group method (Ford, 1975) and the Delphi technique (Bunning, 1979), which involves informants in successive rounds of anonymous debate.

The right-hand end of the continuum in Figure 5.2 covers the most active and emergent approaches to needs assessment, represented by the wide variety of methods used in popular education. As noted earlier, these include sculpting, drama, drawing, and role-playing. The objective is most frequently to identify and name shared experience, to identify needed changes, and to take collective action. Emergent assessment is also found in the daily practice of human service professionals as they work with learners, through progressive approximations of communicated understanding (see Resource A), to clarify feelings and desired outcomes.

Embedded Assessment

There are a number of situations in which the realities of practice require that the practitioner commence teaching without data from a pre-formative assessment of learning needs (Draves, 1984). For example, an unanticipated teachable moment may present itself in the midst of a therapeutic interview with an individual, family, or group. Similarly, it is often not possible to do a precise assessment of learning needs in advance of a professional development workshop. In these kinds of situations the practitioner will find it useful to conduct what might be termed an "embedded assessment," which has some of the same characteristics of an emergent assessment.

This process is introduced as the first component of the teaching intervention; it involves the use of one of several strategies that can yield data on the entry level needs and resources of learners. Introductory activities, often referred to as icebreakers or warm-ups, are used to help learners get to know one another during the forming and storming phases of group development. These same opening activities, if carefully designed, can also give the professional important information about the motivation and entry-level skills of the learners. This approach differs from emergent assessment to the extent that it is more heavily influenced by the practitioner.

The most direct approach is to begin the session by asking the learners what they hope to achieve by the conclusion of the learning event. This process may be made more lively by using brainstorming techniques or by inviting the participants to imagine what their thoughts and feelings might be at the conclusion of a positive learning experience. The alternative learning goals generated from the group members can then be gathered into categories. Finally, the various goals can be ranked by assessing each goal according to defined criteria or by a condensed version of the nominal group method.

An alternative way to assess learning needs and resources and entry-level skills is through the use of "critical incidents" (Brookfield, 1986). This technique is similar to posing hypothetical challenges in the course of a helping interview. In the critical incident technique the process is more formal, however. Participants are asked to consider brief written vignettes of human service practice situations that relate to the topic in question. They then discuss how the described situation should be addressed. The practitioner can observe the discussion in order to gather data about the motivation and know-how of the learners. In turn, this can yield some potential learning goals to be shared and negotiated with the learners. The creative practitioner can also devise additional emergent assessment exercises that will reflect the entry-level abilities of the learners.

In concluding this introduction to the assessment of learning needs in human service practice, there are several questions that can guide the deliberations of practitioners as they conduct pre-formative evaluations:

- To what extent are the felt needs of learners and the needs perceived by the practitioner reflective of real needs that can be verified by a more objective analysis?

- Are the identified needs really learning needs, or do they require some different kind of intervention?

- Have the needs and resources been correctly framed and named?

- Can the needs be verified using additional needs assessment measures (triangulation)?

A last consideration is the place of intuition in the process of needs identification. Experienced practitioners should not reject their own subjective assessment of learning needs: as Schön points out, "Skillful action often reveals a 'knowing more than we can say'" (1983, p. 51). The intuitions or hunches professionals experience about learning and about opportunities for teaching (Denis and Richter, 1987) can usually be verified either by other forms of assessment or by trying a tentative teaching intervention and then observing the results.

Clarifying Learning Outcomes

"Learning outcomes" is an umbrella term used to describe the products of learning. These may include the achievement of narrowly defined, predetermined learning objectives, evidence that more general desired learning outcomes have been achieved, or documentation of the changes that result from emergent and dialogical learning activities that are evolutionary in nature. Concrete and fully measurable learning objectives are possible in only a limited number of specialized practice situations. The importance of understanding this approach is that it clarifies the value of specifying learning outcomes whenever it is appropriate and possible.

Learning Objectives

Learning objectives are written statements describing the observable behaviors that result from a teaching intervention. Bob Mager (1984), an early authority on the development and use of learning objectives, defines them in the following way:

> An objective is a description of a performance you want learners to be able to exhibit before you consider them competent. An objective describes an intended result of instruction rather than the process of instruction itself [p. 3].

In more teacher-centered and performance-driven interventions these objectives may be largely prescribed for the learners. The early enthusiasm for this approach has begun to decline somewhat as its applications to learning in the human services have come to be recognized as somewhat limited. In part this is due to the relative difficulty of specifying learning objectives of three different types: the acquisition of specific types of knowledge (cognitive objectives), the development of discrete skills (psychomotor objectives), and the development or clarification of values and attitudes (affective objectives).

A second important variable in the classification of instructional objectives involves specifying the level of achievement of cognitive objectives. One learning outcome might require the simple recall of a piece of factual information, while another might ask the learner to provide a sophisticated analysis and synthesis. The full range of levels in the cognitive domain are spelled out in the work of Bloom and others (1977) and are developed in the following progression: knowledge (list or recall factual information), comprehension (describe or explain), application (demonstrate or interpret), analysis (distinguish or compare), synthesis (propose or diagnose), and evaluation (assess or select). These fine distinctions between different levels of objectives are rather too precise for many practice teaching situations, in which a basic differentiation between lower- and higher-level learning is more useful. In this case *lower-level* objectives are those that require recall, recognition, or the restating of information, while *higher-level* objectives require the learner to be able to deconstruct an issue, to combine information in unique ways, or to use criteria to arrive at judgments. In addition to this elaboration of the cognitive domain, Harrow (1972) has identified six levels of objectives in the psychomotor domain (skill development), and Krathwohl (1969) has identified five levels of affective (attitude and feeling) objectives.

The following example illustrates how objectives from the cognitive domain might guide training in a sheltered workshop for mildly mentally challenged adults in which a more behaviorally based teaching approach might be appropriate:

Knowledge: Learners are able to identify three power tools used to trim wood in the assembly of planters.

Application: Learners are able to select the correct jig to safely cut planter ends to size.

Evaluation: Learners are able to select knot-free wood for planter sides.

Even these statements are not precise enough to satisfy true adherents to behavioral objectives. Such people would expect to find the following elements in a satisfactorily stated learning objective:

Who?   Identify who the learners are.

Will do what?   Specify the desired behavior (using an action verb).

Under what conditions?   Describe context in which the behavior will be exhibited.

To what level?   Specify the required level of ability or success.

The following example illustrates this type of learning objective, developed for use in training crisis telephone volunteers:

> Volunteers (who) who have completed their training for work on a telephone crisis line will be able to correctly (level) select from five alternatives the appropriate place to refer a client in crisis (performance) whose telephone call has been recorded on audio tape (conditions).

The following objective might be developed for a learner who is working to ensure he or she maintains a controlled and self-conscious pattern of moderate drinking:

> A person (who) who is learning to maintain a moderate pattern of drinking will, in social situations (conditions), be able to keep an accurate count of drinks consumed (performance) and will be able to consistently (level) alternate nonalcoholic with alcoholic drinks (performance).

Advantages of Explicit Objectives

There are several advantages in clarifying desired learning outcomes and in sharing these with learners in explicit teaching situations. Clearly stated objectives empower learners by creating opportunities for mutual renegotiation of planned outcomes to better meet the learners' felt needs. Objectives can also serve as goalposts that enable participants to see where learning activities are intended to lead them. This has the effect of reducing some of the learners' dependence on the teacher, which returns a measure of control to the learner. Learners benefit from the unmediated positive feedback they experience when they are able to concretely measure their own success. This occurs because self-evaluation of learning progress tends to be more potent than positive feedback from human service professionals. The perception of some consumers is that professionals are "paid to say such things; they are paid to be positive."

The clarification of learning objectives also offers important benefits to practitioners. Objectives provide a guide for developing a teaching plan, they are an anchor point for monitoring group processes, and they are the foundation of formative and summative evaluation. Lastly, in an age of increasing accountability, the demonstrated achievement of learning objectives provides important data to employers and funding organizations.

Limitations of Performance-Based Objectives

One of the first limitations of tightly worded objectives is that they may simply not fit with the dynamic way in which teaching in the human services unfolds in the majority of practice situations. Unanticipated teaching opportunities need to be exploited as they arise, and a more mutual appraisal of desired outcomes is generally preferred and possible. Brookfield (1986) also points out that it is more difficult to develop statements of objectives in relation to certain kinds of learning tasks: "It is much easier to specify beforehand the acquisition of psychomotor skills than it is to outline objectives regarding the development of affective, esthetic, or insightful capacities, [thus] these latter domains run the risk of being neglected" (p. 212).

It is also possible that practitioners will tend to opt for lower-level outcomes, which are easier to measure, rather than higher-level outcomes, such as synthesis and evaluation, which can be more elusive. A more general concern is that a reductionist approach that relies on performance-based objectives will fail to capture the complexity inherent in certain types of learning. A comprehensive and skillful learning outcome may require more than the sum of its parts (that is, its constituent learning objectives). A final concern is that the determination of highly structured learning objectives can become a largely practitioner-centered activity, limiting learner input.

Alternative Ways to State and Measure Outcomes

An alternative approach to framing learning outcomes has been suggested by Whitman (1993). His approach has the advantage of being less arduous than the approaches proposed by Mager (1984) and others (Gagné, 1985; Gagné and Driscoll, 1988). Whitman describes an approach that involves the development of what he terms "impact statements." His suggestion is that teachers should apply the following simple formula to the development of objectives:

> What do you want your learners to be able to do as a result of the teaching intervention? [C]
>
> What do you want your learners to know? [A]
>
> What do you want your learners to feel? [B]

The impact statement is then created by combining the teacher's responses using the following formula: A + B so that C. For example:

> A speech therapist has certain skills he developed working with special needs children who have difficulty swallowing. To guide his work with parents, he develops the following impact statement:

Learners (the children's parents) will

[C] be able to insert a gastrostomy tube into their child's stomach

[A] know the anatomy of the throat, esophagus, and stomach and know sterilization techniques

[B] feel confident cleaning and inserting a gastrostomy tube

Impact Statement (A + B so that C): Parents of children with swallowing disorders will know the anatomy of the throat and stomach and feel confident cleaning and inserting a gastrostomy tube.

As described above and as illustrated in this example, the development of impact statements is largely instructor-driven, but there is no reason why this general process cannot be followed with the mutual involvement of the practitioner and the learners.

Another alternative is for the practitioner to accept that in very many practice situations the development of a sense of what is to be learned and of what constitutes the desired learning outcome is a joint process. Egan (1990) captures this approach in the following way: "Very little [work] has been devoted to determining what payoffs these methods [psychological tests] have for clients. . . . Assessment is the ability to understand clients, to spot 'what's going on' with them, to see what they do not see and need to see, to make sense out of their . . . behavior and help them make sense out of it . . . a kind of learning in which both client and helper participate" (p. 164).

In this approach to the assessment of needs, the practitioner and the learners engage in a continuing, deepening reflective dialogue about needs, resources, and desired outcomes. The agenda of the mutual teaching and learning shifts as the process unfolds. This is very much the character of the partnership and the critical dialogue that is representative of emergent and constructivist learning.

6

Teaching Effectively—
Spontaneously and By Design

The creation of ways to promote learning has been termed an exercise in design, because it involves both structural and aesthetic considerations. In Chapter Five it was established that learning objectives are sometimes derived from a process of rational, positivist deduction, carried out primarily by the practitioner. However, it was also noted that learning objectives might emerge as the product of critical, inductive, mutual reflection on the part of both the practitioner and the learners. In a similar fashion, development of a teaching format and mode of delivery that will achieve the desired learning outcomes may follow either a linear, predictable pattern or a process that is more collaborative, emergent, and dynamic. There are occasions when structured presentations and formal workshops are the most appropriate method for teaching in human service practice, but some questions should be raised about this approach: Is it a useful method? Does it conform to the way people actually learn? Does it fit with the realities of professional practice in the human services?

Teaching is frequently an embedded aspect of human service practice. It usually consists of relatively brief and spontaneous teaching episodes requiring the active engagement of both teachers and learners. These encounters tend to require more emergent, constructivist learning formats. This chapter will begin with an examination of structured teaching interventions, offering a definitive map of the path to follow in planning such events. Insights from considering these formal approaches will then be used to understand the elements of teaching interventions based more on mutual, inductive, and evolving approaches to learning. In this way the elements of the more deductive, structured learning designs can serve as a compass to help practitioners position themselves and learners within the more turbulent world of inductive, emergent learning. Thus structured design concepts can be used to locate a starting point for the journey of emergent learning, rather than offering a prescriptive map.

In the real world of practice there is no clear dichotomy between deductive, linear design strategies and those that are inductive and cyclical. Rather, there are various points along a continuum between these two polar extremes. These alternative design approaches include presentations, structured workshops, guided inquiry, and emancipatory learning. There is seldom a tidy distinction between these various approaches.

Selecting a Delivery Method

Data from the assessment phase is used to help the practitioner choose a delivery method, given his or her understanding of the situation at hand. In addition to the familiar mode of direct, face-to-face instruction of individuals or groups, one alternative is to use "interactive distance education." In this model, teachers and learners that are not in the same location are nonetheless able to interact via computers, telephones, or television. A third option is for practitioners to use materials that simulate human interaction. This kind of approach can be supported by powerful new learning programs available on CD-ROM. Finally, there is learning at a distance without interaction. This is facilitated by distributing print-based learning materials such as learning kits (Farquharson, 1985), educational brochures, and self-help manuals.

The following examples illustrate ways these different modes of teaching may be used in human service practice:

Face-to-face teaching: A respiratory therapist teaches a group of patients and their families how they can manage home oxygen equipment. The group setting allows for questions and discussion.

Interactive distance education (person-mediated): An experienced support group facilitator establishes a program of conference calls for people in several remote northern communities who are recovering from major cancer surgery. In the monthly telephone conferences the participants are able to exchange support and practical tips to promote optimum wellness.

Interactive distance education (program-mediated): A specialist in cataract surgery develops a CD-ROM program to help people in small communities prepare themselves for the procedure before traveling to a large, urban medical facility for treatment.

Non-interactive distance education: A specialist in childhood sexual abuse develops a printed manual with advice on developing support groups for survivors. This manual is developed using a great deal of input from members of an existing support group. This material proves to be effective in guiding the development of several new groups.

The latter approach to instruction has been most fully developed by Keller (Keller and Sherman, 1974) with what he terms the personal system of instruction (PSI). In this behaviorally oriented approach, learners follow clearly defined learning processes in order to achieve highly specific learning outcomes. The bonus of this approach is that learners are able to adapt their pacing and methods to their own learning abilities in order to achieve mastery of the material.

Increasingly no clear-cut distinction is made between these different modes of teaching, as various methods of instruction are linked together synergistically. In the future more permutations and combinations will become possible with the emergence and integration of increasingly powerful forms of educational media. That said, at the present time the bulk of current teaching in the human services still occurs in the form of face-to-face interaction between teachers and learners.

When direct contact between learners and practitioners is selected as the appropriate mode of teaching, decisions need to be made about the appropriate format for that encounter. The term "format" refers to the alternative ways in which teaching and learning can be organized. The alternatives range from didactic presentations to the facilitation of learning groups to emancipatory learning (unobtrusive teaching embedded within a therapeutic interview or community work). The variables that govern choice of teaching formats include the number of learners involved, the implicit or explicit nature of the learning contract, and the degree to which the experience is to be teacher-centered or learner-centered (see Figure 3.1). One caution should be introduced with regard to formats: the practitioner may find that an unsuitable teaching format has been chosen. The format may be at odds with the character of the learners, the nature of the topic, or the time available, and if these things cannot be changed then the practitioner would do well to decline involvement.

Formal Presentations and Didactic Workshops

One characteristic of formal presentations and didactic workshops is that both learning outcomes and the learning design are made quite explicit. In the context of human service practice this raises some important questions: Is this linear and rational approach useful? Does it conform to the way people actually learn? Does it really fit with the way human service professionals approach their teaching? Skirting these questions for the moment, what is the case for developing an explicit and detailed plan for a teaching intervention? First of all, there is the argument that such an outline permits the practitioner to design a teaching intervention that takes full account of what is known about effectively promoting adult learning. As Cantor (1992) notes: "Regardless of your experience or educational background, you need a blueprint for success. A good lesson plan assists you in your task of assisting learners to achieve the instructional objectives. . . . It enables you to remember what you might otherwise forget" (p. 105).

Furthermore, such plans provide a structure for evaluating the effectiveness of the teaching episode: Did the plan prove helpful in guiding the teaching and learning process? Should the plan be modified in subsequent teaching interventions?

The key decisions to be made in more structured teaching situations include the following:

- Selecting a teaching/learning format

- Sequencing learning activities

- Planning a teaching episode

- Selecting teaching methods

- Developing learning resources

- Proofing the plan

These last two activities, developing learning resources and proofing the plan (checking the overall soundness of the learning design), are dealt with in Chapter Seven. The first four are addressed in the following discussion. More emergent design processes will also be discussed later in this chapter.

Practitioners are frequently invited to make formal presentations to professional gatherings and community groups. These events may be described as lectures, speeches, talks, panel discussions, colloquia, or symposia. There are other, more subtle, kinds of presentations that are not assigned a descriptive term. These occur, for example, when a presentation is called for within the agenda of a regular meeting of an interdisciplinary team. These various forms of more didactic teaching have been subsumed under the general category of "presentations." It is important for the practitioner not to lose sight of the fact that all of these forms of presentations are intended to help the participants learn something. This means that information is not simply transmitted, but also becomes internalized and can be recalled in the appropriate circumstances. It follows therefore that there are better ways and worse ways to construct a presentation. Many of the ideas presented thus far can be applied to the design of effective presentations (Verderber, 1988).

In circumstances that allow for presentations to be planned in advance, it is possible to construct and conduct them so that they yield the optimum learning outcomes. The following examples illustrate the types of presentations that might fall to the practitioner:

A social worker is asked to make a presentation to the annual meeting of a foster parents' association about new legislation regarding children's rights. She prepares handouts and graphics for overhead projection, and she develops a number of anecdotal stories to illustrate the major points she wishes to emphasize in her presentation.

A senior manager in a human services ministry is asked to give a speech to officials in a related government ministry on the impact of a new piece of legislation the manager had helped to write. She recognizes that she needs to do more than talk *at* the participants, and so she carefully crafts her presentation to promote understanding the intent of the policies and their implications for joint ventures between the two ministries.

A public safety officer at a local police department designs a particularly well-crafted presentation to introduce neighborhood groups and tenants' associations to the concept of "neighborhood watch".

The advantage of presentation formats is that they allow for the presentation of information to large groups of people. The limitation is that frequently there is only one-way communication, which can limit the practitioner's ability to clarify ideas and to address psychomotor and affective learning needs that involve skills, feelings, and values. A presentation format should be selected when large numbers of learners need to be addressed, there are time constraints, a skillful presenter is available, and there is an appropriate, comfortable facility with good acoustics. A key way to improve the effectiveness of presentations is to precede them with an advance organizer (Ausubel, 1960). This is a conceptual framework, or what Ausubel calls an "intellectual scaffolding," into which learners can fit the ideas to be included in the presentation. For this reason, advance organizers are not a popular method with those who espouse a constructivist and emancipatory approach to learning.

It should be understood that assigning teaching formats to just three categories is quite artificial. In reality there are many different formats that fall at different points on the continuum from presentation to facilitation. For example, at a conference for professional helpers and nonprofessional caregivers there might be keynote speeches, workshops, problem-solving groups, and a variety of other learning formats. The practical value of recognizing different learning formats is that this permits the practitioner to make a more purposeful decision about the format that is best suited to a particular learning situation.

Workshop Formats

There is a subtle shift in the role of practitioners as they move from a predominantly teacher-centered style of teaching to facilitating what are commonly called workshops. This shift usually involves a greater emphasis by the practitioner on the design of an active learning experience, but workshops can vary widely. In some cases workshops are still primarily concerned with information transmission, while in other cases they involve the generation and exchange of learning through the use of more flexible teaching and facilitation strategies. Sork (1984) offers the following definition: "The term *workshop* refers to a relatively short-term, intensive, problem-focused learning experience that actively involves participants in the identification and analysis of problems and in the development and evaluation of solutions" (p. 5).

A more succinct observation might be that a workshop is a place where learners "*work* hard and *shop* for ideas." It is useful to share such a definition with workshop participants, to help convey the expectation that they are to be proactive participants in the learning process. Learners are encouraged to engage in the struggle to construct meaning, by interacting with the material to be learned and by taking full advantage of the contributions of their fellow learners. The value in stressing this kind of active participation is that it can offset some of the passivity people may have learned in educational settings that use more instructor-centered learning formats. An explicit discussion of the requirements of workshop-based learning can lead to the development of clear group norms that will facilitate the learning process (see the discussion of structured formative evaluation in Chapter Eight).

Among the salient characteristics of workshops are that they tend to be relatively short-term, intense, and problem-focused. Workshops can vary widely in quality and in the extent to which they are successful in translating learning into new behaviors. Examples of the types of workshops that occur in connection with human service practice include the following:

A nurse practicing in the field of gerontology conducts a study of the factors that contribute to falls suffered by elderly people. She designs two workshops of different duration (two hours and one day) and intensity to help family caregivers and volunteer visitors learn from some of her research.

A community worker develops a two-day workshop for elementary school principals to help them learn ways to increase parent involvement in school activities and school involvement in the community.

A college counselor develops a workshop on date rape for student peer counselors. She wants participants to learn about the nature and prevalence of the problem, ways to extend support to victims, and ways to facilitate referral to additional sources of help.

The advantages of workshops include the fact that they tend to foster high levels of learner involvement, they are of relatively short duration, and they frequently focus on practical problem-solving skills. The limitations of workshops are that the brevity of the experience may limit the extent to which learning is fully internalized, and there is a danger of overloading the learners with too much material too quickly.

The following guidelines may help the practitioner design workshops that achieve the maximum payoff in terms of participant learning and change. In order for workshops to achieve their full potential, it is important that the participants possess adequate skill in group problem solving (Bergevin and McKinley, 1970), that a skillful facilitator is available (Renner, 1983), and that the learning demands problem solving rather than a simple prescriptive solution (Sork, 1984).

Sequencing Learning Activities

"Sequencing instruction" is a more elaborate way of describing the process of making decisions about what should be taught, and when, within a sequence of learning activities. In Chapter Five task analysis and subject analysis were discussed as alternative activities that might take place during the assessment phase. In the event that these types of analysis have already taken place, then it is likely that a good deal of information is available about the components of the learning experience. In the absence of a prior assessment process, some of the component elements of the learning task may be established by the creative design of a warm-up or icebreaker activity. For example:

> At the start of a short workshop series on parenting skills a family counselor uses an exercise to assess priority learning issues and learner-preferred sequences for the learning activities. He lists each topic on a separate self-adhesive note. Participants in groups of three then sort the topics in two ways, ranking them first in terms of perceived importance and then according to preferred learning sequence.

Even when the optimal sequence for performing a task is understood, it does not necessarily dictate the order in which the component elements should be taught. Designing the structure of a learning episode is particularly challenging because the practitioner is continually confronted with understanding how learners will construct the material presented to them. This is not easy; the practitioner is likely to assume that the teaching plan should reflect the way he or she originally learned the material. For example, a family therapist might try to explain a skill in expressing feelings by suggesting a general principle and then helping family members apply this to a variety of specific situations. However, the family might find it more helpful to consider a specific situation of concern to them, and then move to the generation of general guidelines. It is helpful if practitioners can place themselves in the learners' shoes, developing a learning design that fits with the way the learners are likely to develop their understanding of the material. In a word, practitioners need to be empathetic, to develop an understanding of the learners' perspective.

There are many considerations that can be used to shape a learning design; this can be done during the pre-formative assessment process. Factors that should be considered include the nature of what is to be learned; the entry-level knowledge, skill, and motivation of the learners in relation to the learning tasks; the learning and teaching styles of those involved; the required level of learning achievement; and the time available.

The most basic version of this approach involves the practitioner's noting each learning subtask on a separate card or self-adhesive note. This makes the data easier to manipulate, and the challenge then becomes one of sequencing and resequencing the tasks until an arrangement is arrived at that promises to promote the optimum learning.

There are no hard-and-fast rules for selecting the right sequence for the elements in a teaching design, but there are some useful alternatives to consider when making a decision about ways to construct a flow of learning activities. These options include

- Proceeding from simple to complex

- Using an established sequence

- Using a historical sequence

- Proceeding from most important to least important (felt or real needs)

- Proceeding from most familiar to least familiar

- Proceeding from general to specific (or vice versa)

- Proceeding from concrete to abstract

Some of these alternatives are evident in these examples of sequencing decisions:

Simple to complex: A nurse in a residence for mentally challenged adults wants to teach these people how to go to the store to purchase basic items. The first skill the participants are taught is how to select a specific item on a shelf close to the cashier. A later, more complex task requires the learners to select the correct amount of bills and coins to make payment.

Established sequence: An admitting nurse plans to teach a group of interns the sequence of activities and decisions that are made in the hospital emergency room when a new patient is admitted for service.

Historical sequence: A legal aid lawyer helps his client learn about courtroom procedures by tracing the historical precedents that shape current courtroom practices. He selects this approach because he recognizes that his client's learning style relies heavily on a need to understand the basic data that inform actions.

Most important to least important: A nurse teaches a new group of assistants the correct method for lifting patients. She begins by identifying the three most common mistakes that are made when lifting. She gives the participants a handout that describes correct lifting procedures and outlines ways to avoid the common errors.

Most familiar to least familiar: A person training volunteers for a telephone crisis line begins by eliciting the learners' ideas about people in crisis. She adds one or two items to this list of familiar characteristics, and then proceeds to more complex material dealing with ways to assess the seriousness of suicide threats.

General to specific: A counselor training volunteers who would be working for an immigrant agency first helped them to learn about some of the general problems faced by refugees from Central America. Later she went into more specific detail about the adjustment difficulties of people who were relocating from Guatemala.

Concrete to abstract: A school counselor was working with the parents of children in the primary grades who had severe behavioral difficulties. Her first task was to help them work through some concrete guidelines for dealing with things such as homework and bedtime routines. She then had them consider written vignettes of some more complex behavioral problems to help them develop the conceptual skills necessary to respond appropriately to diverse situations.

Selecting a sequence of teaching tasks is a creative enterprise, and it is possible to involve learners as partners in this process. There are several practical references that offer additional guidelines for sequencing learning activities (Cranton, 1989; Cantor, 1992). A common pitfall for many practitioners is attempting to teach too much material within a restricted period of time or to teach more material than the learner is motivated to absorb. In these circumstances there is a danger of extinguishing learner motivation by overloading the teachable moment. One way to avoid this situation is to borrow a technique often used by trainers in business and industry. Once these trainers have identified a number of constituent learning tasks, they sort them into two categories, separating "need to know" items from "nice to know" items. In the results-oriented, cost-conscious environment of the private sector it becomes essential to focus training only on those competencies that are essential to the required performance. In the human services it is less common for teaching to have to be conducted with quite the same level of precision and economy. Nonetheless, this approach can still be helpful in selecting priority learning tasks and in identifying ancillary learning tasks that may be less crucial to the achievement of the central learning objective.

Planning a Teaching Episode

Teaching episodes are relatively discrete teaching interventions that can vary in length from ten minutes to an hour or more. In longer-term teaching interventions several teaching episodes are linked together. One model that can be used to guide the process of designing such a teaching intervention is known by the acronym EDICT. In some respects this is an unfortunate abbreviation, because it may conjure up an image of highly teacher-centered, directive teaching.

This is not the case, however. As this discussion unfolds, it will become evident that the EDICT model may be used in situations that require widely varying degrees of learner and teacher involvement. The value of this particular planning model is that it contains five important elements that can be used to shape more structured teaching interventions. It is particularly important to understand that the five elements do not need to follow the sequence suggested by the letters in the EDICT acronym:

E = Explain

D = Demonstrate

I = Involve

C = Coach

T = Test/Terminate/Transfer

Explaining

Practitioners who opt to use the EDICT approach start by selecting the main ideas to be presented in a particular teaching episode. They then proceed to make decisions about the best way to sequence the explanation in order to facilitate learning of the ideas to be presented. The sequencing alternatives identified previously may be considered during this stage of the EDICT approach to planning.

Demonstrating

The next step is for practitioners to think about how they can help learners make connections between the more conceptual ideas presented in the explanation phase and how these concepts connect with events in the real world. That is, the teacher looks for ways in which they can powerfully *demonstrate* the operational effects of the ideas previously presented. This may be accomplished using a vivid anecdotal story that brings the concepts alive, by means of a brief video segment, or through a computer simulation that demonstrates the ideas in action. Resource persons can also be used to demonstrate how the conceptual material comes alive in practice.

Involving

The third step is to select a way for learners to be involved in actually using or applying the ideas. There are many alternative ways to do this, but typically some kind of experiential learning exercise is appropriate. For example, learners might be encouraged to reflect on a higher-order question through a think-pair-share exercise. This exercise asks learners to spend one minute engaging in individual reflection about a question, then spend several minutes sharing their conclusions with a partner, and finally participate in a plenary discussion of the issue. Alternatively, an experiential learning activity might involve learners in role-playing, simulation, or another problem-solving activity (see Chapter Seven). The important aspect of this stage of the planning cycle is that it should *involve* the learner actively in the construction and application of meaning (Meyers and Jones, 1993).

Coaching

On the basis of observations gathered during the involvement exercise, the practitioner can now provide some coaching or corrective feedback. This usually occurs during a debriefing discussion following the involvement exercise. Effective coaching requires that the practitioner have some way to gather data about learners' performance during the involvement phase. This might mean that the practitioner circulates to observe the content and process of small group discussions. Alternatively, observers or recorders might be delegated to take notes on the process within small learning groups.

There are also situations in which the involvement and coaching phases need to be more structured. For instance, highly specific corrective feedback may be necessary when there are clearly right and wrong answers to the involvement exercise. An example would be the kind of feedback needed when teaching people how to use a potentially hazardous piece of medical equipment. In giving feedback during the coaching phase, practitioners should consider the following guidelines:

- Check the learners' self-appraisal of their performance.

- Give feedback as soon as possible after the performance.

- Avoid overload. Give feedback in manageable quantities.

- Give more positive than negative feedback.

- Give feedback only about those things that the learner can change.

Testing

The final phase of the EDICT model involves testing and transfer of what has been learned and/or termination of the teaching relationship. Testing is an important stage, at which the practitioner checks to see if what was taught was in fact learned. Testing may also involve checking at a later date to see whether this learning has been transferred into changed behavior back in the "real world." Alternatively, the letter T might also stand for termination, which is the case when a cycle through the EDICT model concludes the learning relationship. In such a circumstance it may be necessary to design a way to conclude the experience so that feelings are addressed and learning is reinforced.

It is important for practitioners to use a good deal of flexibility in ordering the phases of the EDICT model. Different situations may call for teaching designs in which the component activities take place in a different sequence from the one suggested by the acronym. The practitioner may wish to engage learners' interest with an initial demonstration, for example, or energize them with an involvement exercise up front. For instance, a practitioner working with a group of prison inmates might try to engage their interest in an anger management course by starting the first session with a video clip demonstrating a person exercising self-control in a highly provocative situation. He or she might then proceed to explain the important elements in the scenario the learners have just witnessed, and then move on to other phases of the EDICT model. Almost any sequence can be followed; the model should be considered as a practical checklist of the elements that need to be included in an effective learning episode rather than a lock-step sequence. The following additional examples illustrate other applications of the EDICT model:

A community health nurse conducts a well-baby clinic for parents of newborns. She begins a session on breast-feeding by explaining [E] the different chemical composition of breast milk as compared to that of a typical commercial baby formula. She then demonstrates [D] the effects of the misuse of formula with a short film on a group of new mothers in Africa. She next proceeds to involve [I] the learners in an exercise in which they are asked to evaluate the relative merits of three different baby formulas. As the group members report their findings, the nurse provides some corrective feedback [C]. At the end of the series of sessions she includes an evaluative question asking the mothers to indicate the relative merits of breast milk and two different formulas [Test]. She also helps the learners to anticipate how they might deal with objections from relatives [Transfer]. She also arranges a modest celebration of what they have learned together [Termination].

A family therapist waits for a teachable moment to help a family learn about the indirect ways they communicate their feelings to each other. The moment is not forthcoming, so the therapist decides to precipitate a teaching opportunity by showing the family a brief video clip from a popular movie. This recorded segment demonstrates

[D] communication patterns similar to those apparent in the destructive interactions of the family members. The therapist then involves [I] the family in a discussion of what they regarded as problematic in these exchanges. As a result of her observations during this discussion, the therapist coaches [C] the family on some alternative ways these exchanges might be handled. In the following interview she observes closely to evaluate [Test] whether the insights from the previous session are reflected in the current interaction of the family members. This assessment reveals that there are some barriers [Transfer] to introducing change.

In more formal and structured teaching situations practitioners can select from several alternative planning protocols (Goad, 1982; Renner, 1988). A simple way to map out a teaching plan is to work with three columns: Time, Activity, and To Do (see Figure 6.1).

Typically the planning process begins with the identification of items for the middle column, Activity. These notes should spell out in as much detail as necessary what the practitioner and learners will be doing at each phase of the teaching episode. Indeed, some practitioners may find it helpful to add an additional column in

Figure 6.1. Planning Sheet: "How Self-Help Helps."

Time	Activity	To Do
9:00	Intros and learner goals	Name tags
9:10	Objectives and agenda	Handouts
9:15	Warm-up: Clarify values [Involve]	Copies of exercise
9:30	Lecture: How mutual aid works [Explain]	Overheads with data
9:50	Study from self-help member [Demonstrate]	Contact Sue T. from A.A.
10:05	Discussion: Think-Pair-Share [Involve and Coach]	Question on overhead tran.
10:30	Coffee Break	Order coffee, juice, and muffins

order to distinguish between activities that are teacher tasks and those that are learner tasks. In this way the planning sheet can reflect what both teachers and learners will be doing at any given point in time.

The right-hand column provides a place for the practitioner to jot down all the preparatory tasks that need to be completed in order to support each phase of the teaching episode. These tasks might include preparing overhead transparencies, printing up hand-outs, contacting resource people, securing materials such as audio-visual equipment and flip charts, and so on.

The left-hand column is frequently the last one to be completed, but it is the most important. This column allows the practitioner to establish a schedule for the teaching event. In all likelihood there may be some deviation from this projected schedule, but the guidelines serve as a warning of impending time constraints. Many beginning teachers tend to both overestimate the amount of teaching material they need to prepare and to underestimate the time required to engage learners and promote active reflection. There is also the possibility that teachable moments will arise that will take up extra time. For these reasons teachers must be prepared to let go of nonessential material when necessary due to a lack of time or waning learner interest.

Practitioners should review their outline and flag items that can be skipped if necessary. The criteria of need-to-know/nice-to-know might be applied to this review process. This way, if practitioners find they are running short of time, they will know which elements of their plan may be jettisoned without seriously damaging the integrity of the overall teaching intervention. It is often helpful to include some additional nice-to-know items in the teaching plan in case the opposite problem—excess time—is encountered. These superfluous elements can help allay the novice teacher's fear of running short of material, and they can be always be discarded if there is a lack of time.

Critical Thinking: Inquiry Formats

The final two learning formats to be discussed are inquiry learning and emancipatory learning. These approaches both rely heavily on the use of critical thinking strategies. Inquiry learning most frequently involves a structure similar to a workshop. The process of learning through inquiry (Joyce and Weil, 1986; Bateman, 1990) has many parallels with the problem-solving process described by Knox (1990): "Inquiry methods come closer to problem-solving as participants [and resource persons as well] seek to discover answers, instead of receiving them from an organized presentation" (p. 96).

Inquiry learning is often selected when experiential learning appears to be the most appropriate learning method (for instance, when it is possible for a group of people to learn from one another by creating new meanings through a process of mutual problem solving [learning]). This mode of learning is distinct from self-directed learning (Brookfield, 1985; Candy, 1991), a process that may be entirely managed by the learner or group of learners. Inquiry methods are most frequently used with groups of learners, but the skillful helping professional can also promote this kind of critical, reflective inquiry in individuals.

Group learning is frequently embedded in the process of group problem solving or inquiry. Problem solving is a form of learning that involves the *generation* of meaning, in contrast to forms of learning that involve the *transfer* of meaning. (The continuum that lies between these different approaches to learning is illustrated in Figure 3.1.) Thus, in addition to teaching, the practitioner is often called upon to facilitate learners' solving of problems. Interestingly enough, this very concept of problem-based learning is now being used to replace more traditional teaching methods in a number of educational programs for human service professionals.

Group facilitators who understand the strategies and stages of creative problem solving can help make the process of meaning making, or learning, more productive. There are many different sources of ideas about the learning and problem-solving process, including the growing literature on creative problem solving techniques (Parnes, 1981; de Bono, 1984; Isaksen and Treffinger, 1985; von Oech, 1986). A unifying theme among these authors is the understanding that both divergent thinking (generating ideas) and convergent thinking (selecting ideas) are needed at different stages of the creative problem-solving process. Divergent thinking is important in the process of framing problems, because the way a problem is stated can limit or expand the search for its potential solution. Also, lateral, or divergent, thinking can enrich the process of generating multiple potential solutions and alternative problem-solving strategies.

Convergent thinking is particularly helpful when choices need to be made between several alternatives (for example, when describing a problem to be solved, selecting the optimum solution to the problem, or choosing the best way to implement that solution).

Learning—that is the product of creative problem solving—occurs over seven stages, with each stage relying on a predominance of either divergent or convergent thinking (see Figure 6.2). The first stage in this problem-solving cycle has been termed "problem sensing," although it is sometimes referred to in a more colorful way as "mess finding" (Isaksen and Treffinger, 1985). In a teaching intervention, this stage involves learners in the identification of vague discomforts or dissatisfactions that may indicate some kind of underlying problem. The next stage involves framing a statement of the problem that has been identified. It is particularly important for the problem to be stated in a manner that does not in any way prejudge how it might be resolved. (This can occur in the human services when diagnostic labels are carelessly applied to situations that have not yet been thoroughly assessed.) Problem solving then proceeds to the generation of multiple potential solutions. The role of the facilitator is to ensure that ideas are not prejudged, either by their originator or by other participants.

Figure 6.2. Divergent and Convergent Thinking in Problem Solving.

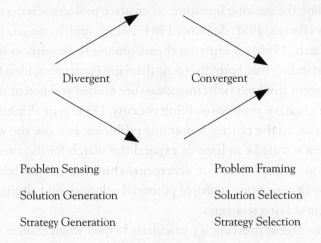

Divergent   Convergent

Problem Sensing   Problem Framing

Solution Generation   Solution Selection

Strategy Generation   Strategy Selection

The next stage involves a return to convergent modes of reasoning, as criteria are applied to the selection of the optimum solution. The process of learning through problem solving then proceeds to the generation of many alternative implementation strategies and the selection of a preferred strategic approach to guide the next problem-solving process. The change process concludes with the implementation and evaluation of the selected method of problem solving.

Emancipatory Learning: The Design Is in the Dialogue

The term "format" coupled with the descriptor "emancipatory" is in many respects an oxymoron. Emancipation, by its very nature, is a dynamic, unfolding process of action and reflection (called praxis by some). In contrast, "format" carries with it a connotation of stability and predictability. The essential task here is to begin the process of inquiry at an earlier stage that involves mess finding and problem framing.

At the stage where the practitioner and learner become bonded into an emancipatory learning partnership, they have in fact become a small group in which power is more equally distributed. At the core of emancipatory learning is dialogue, which, as Senge points out, is drawn from the Greek word *dialogos,* which means "a free flow of meaning through a group, allowing the group to discover insights, not attainable individually" (Senge, 1990, p. 10). Building on this point, Shor and Freire (1987) state:

It is part of our historical process in becoming human beings. . . to the extent that humans have become more and more critically communicative beings. Dialogue is a moment where humans meet to reflect on their reality as they make and remake it. . . . To the extent that we . . . communicate to each other as we become more able to transform our reality, we are able to know that we know, which is something more than just knowing. . . . We human beings also know that we don't know. Through dialogue, reflecting together on what we know and don't know, we can then transform reality" [pp. 98–99].

In this case dialogue is understood as a particular type of learning format that permits learners—sometimes in partnership with professional practitioners—to examine the question, "Are we the creators of or created by our social reality?" Paulo Freire tends to promote critical dialogue by beginning with the first part of this question (subjectivist radical humanism), and then he uses this as a springboard to address the larger issues related to social structures (objectivist radical structuralism). It is important to appreciate the interrelationship between these two types of analysis, as noted by Mullaly (1993): "Subjective reality and objective reality are irrevocably locked into a dialectical relationship. We are conscious creators of our surroundings, using thought, information, and emotion to act and choose. At the same time, we are created by our surroundings" (p. 148).

The other component that is coupled with the reflection stimulated by dialogue is action, and the two are linked through another Greek term, *praxis*, which describes a continuing process of action, reflection, and more action. One issue that emerges is the role of professional helpers in this process. Do they lead? Are they partners? Do they follow? Some critics of Paulo Freire (Elbow, 1986) suggest that in promoting critical awareness (Freire's "conscientization") he falls into the trap of many traditional helpers who were prone to taking the view that insight is manifested when a patient makes a statement about himself or herself that agrees with the therapist's notion of what is the matter with that patient: "Hidden elitism hovers behind any theory of false consciousness; he who understands the dimensions of true consciousness, whatever they are, must necessarily—however temporarily—play the role of an elitist guiding the unenlightened to their proper destiny. Freire appears to accept this elitism for his educator. . . . 'Conversion to the people requires a profound rebirth. . . . This allows [the] teacher to bask within the historical after-image of the dedicated missionary'" (Stanley, 1972, p. 44).

Freire is aware of the dangerous dilemma of needing to respect the learners' analysis while also trying to raise their consciousness during teachable moments. He states, "In the liberating moment, we must try to convince students and on the other hand we must respect them, not impose ideas on them" (Shor and Freire, 1987, p. 33).

The decision to engage learners in dialogue and praxis is often inescapably a choice that is initiated by the practitioner and can later be modified or rejected by the learner. This decision essentially involves a choice about the learning format—the way in which learning will emerge—but it does not predetermine the complete nature of what that learning will be. The decision to pursue a path of critical reflection means that the emancipatory dialogue is likely to reveal paradigms that contain self-limiting beliefs about one's self and social structures: "We see the world not as it is but as we are—or as we are conditioned to see it. When we open our mouths to

describe what we see, we in effect describe ourselves, our perceptions, our paradigms. . . . The more aware we are of our basic paradigms, maps of assumptions, and the extent to which we have been
influenced by our experience, the more we can take responsibility
for those paradigms, examine them, test them against reality, listen
to others and be open to their perceptions, thereby getting a larger
picture" (Covey, 1990, pp. 28–29).

In human service practice, emergent and constructivist design
through reflective dialogue might emerge in the following ways:

A psychologist counsels a woman who is concerned with what she
describes as the way in which her mother "encroached" on her marriage and family life. Through an intensive reflective dialogue, client
and therapist explore the woman's meaning for "encroachment," the
mother's possibly culturally derived assumptions about her role in
the lives of her adult children, and expectations about boundaries in
middle-class Canadian families. The client eventually frames the
issue as developing her need to learn how to communicate with
greater clarity and assertion. This becomes the focus for an agreed-
upon series of five counseling sessions.

An example of the results of critical reflection in community
development work is evident in the following situation:

A group of parents opposed to the placement of condom machines
in schools approaches a public health nurse for assistance in promoting their point of view. She agrees to meet with them, with the
understanding that in the initial meeting they will explore the broader
context in which action is being contemplated. The underlying need
of the parents is revealed to be their desire to prevent their children
from engaging in premarital sex. The nurse suggests that the group
might begin their analysis by exploring the data on the rate of sexually
transmitted diseases and unwanted pregnancies in their community.
It is not always easy to gather this data, but it has become evident

that local teens are already considerably sexually active, and there is little evidence that easy access to condoms will increase the frequency of premarital sexual contacts. The parents gradually reach the conclusion that condoms might be useful for a number of secondary preventative reasons, and they agree to work on some more primary preventative initiatives. These include an abstinence support group and a media-monitoring task force.

Questioning and Critical Thinking

An important element in both facilitated inquiry and emancipatory learning is the practitioner's skill in engaging learners in question posing and question framing (Long, Paradise, and Long, 1981) as aids to critical thinking (Meyers, 1986; Brookfield, 1987; Kurfiss, 1988; Mezirow, 1990, 1991; Paul, 1992). It is important for practitioners to be able to help learners frame questions that have personal relevance and pursue answers to those questions. Questioning is not an easy skill to develop, and it is even more challenging to teach the art of learning through question framing. In part this situation is the result of a culture of formal education that tends to be driven by the search for answers, as reflected in the anonymous observation that "students come to school as question marks and leave as periods." The unfortunate result of this answer-driven culture is that many people are uneasy in the presence of "really useful questions"—that is, questions they cannot answer at once. It is precisely the ability to generate unanswerable questions, to live for some time with ambiguity while seeking potential solutions, that is at the core of meaning making and the construction of new understandings. Thus question framing is a core strategy for both inquiry learning and emancipatory learning.

A distinction has already been made, in Chapter Five, between higher- and lower-order questions. In more formal teaching situations it is possible to structure teaching so that it proceeds from one level to another, by means of a teaching strategy that moves from simple recall of information toward questions that promote synthesis and evaluation. The following four-stage approach can be used to guide this process:

1. *Cognitive questions:* Use to check that learners understand basic information. (For example, What are the five elements of the EDICT model?)

2. *Convergent questions:* Use to relate, compare, and combine information. (How does the EDICT model compare with Kolb's stages of the learning cycle?)

3. *Divergent questions:* Use to apply knowledge creatively. (How could you use the EDICT model to design a unit of instruction on basic budgeting?)

4. *Evaluative questions:* Use to assess values and judgments. (What are the strengths and limitations of using the EDICT approach for planning?)

In preparing for informal teaching encounters, it may also be helpful to think through the level and type of questions to be asked, in order to calibrate the teaching information to the entry-level knowledge of the learners. A provocative opening question can also be an effective way to gain the learner's initial attention, and it models the message that question framing is one of the core skills in critical thinking.

Promoting Critical Thinking

Human service professionals have taken two slightly different approaches to the related questions of why and how to promote critical reflection in adult learners. Richard Paul (1992), the director of the Center for Critical Thinking at Sonoma State University, says: "Critical thinking is that mode of thinking, about any subject, content or problem, in which the thinker improves the quality of his or her thinking by skillfully taking charge of the structures inherent in thinking and imposing intellectual standards upon them" (p. 4).

This perspective tends to focus on the individual and puts the emphasis on logical reasoning abilities. Habermas (1979), a German social theorist who believes any critical dialogue should take into account the power relationships present and the way statements are justified by those in power, prefers the term "emancipatory learning" to "critical thinking." The definition of transformative learning suggested by Jack Mezirow (1991) is derived from Habermas. Mezirow states: "Emancipatory education is about more than becoming aware of one's awareness. Its goal is to help learners move from a simple awareness of their experiencing to an awareness of the conditions of their experiencing . . . and beyond this to an awareness of the reasons why they experience as they do and to action based on these insights" (p. 197).

There is a good deal of teaching or coaching skill involved in promoting the process of critical reflection. At times professional helpers may find themselves helping an individual think through an important life decision. In other situations the practitioner may need to facilitate the reflections of a learning group or help a community group think through their options for future development. The Mezirow definition describes the type of community learning that tends to be promoted through the popular education process.

There is a growing literature on the critical thinking skills that differentiate the thinking of novices and experts in a number of professional disciplines (Schön, 1983; Benner, 1984), and some excellent references on ways to enhance critical thinking skills (Meyers, 1986; Brookfield, 1987; Stice, 1987; Mezirow, 1990, 1991). The reader is encouraged to explore these references for a more in-depth discussion of this important topic.

The following examples illustrate a few ways in which inquiry teaching and learning formats may be used in human service practice:

A group of people representing a range of health professions decides to hold regular meetings to share what they have learned about effective health regimes for people with HIV. These shared learnings are derived from the research literature, from reflections about their own practice experiences, and from encounters with HIV-positive people and their families, friends, and lovers. The discussions are facilitated by the practitioner who convened the group.

A probation officer facilitates a group consisting of parents of children who have been in trouble with the law but have been diverted from the criminal justice system. These parents are interested in learning alternative ways of responding to their children. Their goal is to help reduce some of their children's acting-out behavior.

An employee-assistance counselor runs a group for frontline supervisors, to help them learn more effective ways of responding to employees with a variety of chemical dependencies. The counselor recognizes that these are very experienced supervisors who have the ability to learn a good deal from one another, particularly about forms of progressive discipline.

To summarize, the design of a teaching intervention involves deciding on the general format for teaching, the mode of delivery, the sequence of learning activities, and the type of facilitation that will best support these processes.

Proofing the Plan

This chapter concludes with a review of some of the ways the practitioner can double-check a teaching plan to make sure it has taken most considerations into account. No plan can be foolproof on all occasions; this is what makes teaching continually interesting, and it is one reason why practitioners need to constantly involve their learners as partners in the process. To the extent that both teachers and learners feel a measure of shared owner-ship over the process and outcomes of learning, even the occa-sional glitches can become occasions for comradely, creative problem solving.

There are two ways to double-check plans for a teaching inter-vention: first, ensure that the design has taken into account some of Malcolm Knowles's principles (1985) for working with adults as learners; second, verify that the design has included some of Ray-mond Wlodkowski's ideas (1991) about ways to gain and sustain the learner's attention and motivation to learn.

Knowles's assumptions about adult learning were introduced in Chapter Two. The following questions, based on the principles sug-gested by Knowles, provide a way to check a teaching design against his guidelines. The first set of questions has to do with respecting the self-concept of the learner:

- Is the plan free of factors that might make the learner feel threatened or inadequate?

- Does the assessment of the entry-level knowledge and skill of the learners seem reasonably well founded? Remember the situational teaching injunction "If in doubt, aim to the left."

The second area to investigate is the extent to which the design effectively brings learners' experience to the surface and the extent to which it helps them learn from one another:

- Is there a way to check out what learners already know about the material to be learned, so the teacher can create ways to graft the new learning onto metaphors drawn from learners' prior experience?

- Does the design effectively draw out prior experiences that may contribute to learning the new material?

- Are there opportunities and structures that will encourage synergistic learning among the members of the learning group?

Knowles's third principle is that teachers need to pay attention to learners' readiness to learn:

- Is this the moment when the learners are ready to explore this material, and if not, what steps can be taken to enhance their readiness to learn?

- Why would *these* learners want to learn *this* material at *this* time?

- Given the assessed motivation of the learners, is the amount of material appropriate or is there a danger of teaching them more than they would ever want to know about this topic?

- Would there be any value in delaying this teaching intervention until a more potent "teachable moment" presents itself?

The final major guideline from Knowles is that, for the most part, adults bring with them a life-centered or problem-centered approach to learning. The learning design should enable them to find this kind of relevance and application in the material presented:

- Is there an element in the design that will let the practitioner know very early in the learning process what particular applications individual learners have in mind for the material they are learning?

- Are there formative evaluation systems in place that will keep the practitioner aware of the way in which learners construct meaning?

- How are learners applying what they are learning?

There is one final check to complete on the teaching plan. This involves checking the extent to which the design conforms to Wlodkowski's ideas (1991) about ways to gain and sustain learners' motivation to learn. He offers sixty-eight practical strategies, but he also suggests six key questions that can be used to review the teaching/learning design. To paraphrase (p. 258):

- What has been done to foster a positive attitude for this experience?

- Does the plan address the felt needs of the learners?

- What will stimulate and sustain learner motivation during the event?

- What has been done to maintain a positive climate for learning?

- Does the event increase and sustain the learner's sense of competence?

- How will this learning continue to be reinforced in the future?

7

• •

Selecting Resources and Activities
to Support Teaching

The umbrella term "teaching activities" includes a wide range of methods and resources that may be used to engage learners in active learning processes (Meyers and Jones, 1993). The most important learning resources are the accumulated experiential and technical knowledge, attitudes, and skills of the learners themselves. In large measure, teaching and other forms of practice in the human services focus on the mobilization of these kinds of learner resources. A second learning resource is found in human service practitioners—the professional expertise, teaching skills, and support they bring to their work.

There are many other kinds of resources that can be brought together to support a teaching intervention. These include the following:

- A wide range of structured experiential learning exercises

- Outside people who offer expertise, experience, or support

- Printed materials in a variety of formats

- Audiovisual materials, including film and video

- Computer-assisted learning, and other new technologies

These activities, which embrace a variety of experiential learning approaches, can be integrated into a sound overall learning design to offer potent influences on the learning process. For example, learning activities and resources may be included in phases of the EDICT plan to foster active engagement in the learning process. This is evident in the sample plan outlined in Chapter Six. This blending of strategies can be useful in the development of self-directed and distance-education learning materials. The process of developing an effective learning design is analogous to the process of planning for an important journey. Both select a destination (using a map) and have a way to track progress (with a compass). The itinerary or plan for the journey identifies places to stay en route, and it suggests a sequence for visiting these way stations. Learning activities and resources are the equivalent of the supplies that are gathered to support such a journey. These supplies include the guides and scouts, the food, the backpacks, the modes of transportation. Resources are as essential to an effective teaching intervention as they are to a satisfactory journey.

In this exploration of learning activities and materials, it will become evident that many of these methods and materials are already part of the practice repertoire of many professional helpers. Existing practice skills may be reframed as teaching strategies.

There are several terms that are used in an overlapping way to refer to different types of learning resources: learning "methods," learning "activities," learning "media," and learning "materials." Knox (1990) makes a distinction between learning activities and instructional materials, Cranton (1989) employs categories that refer to instructional methods and materials, and Lewis (1986) and Renner (1988) both discuss a variety of teaching techniques.

In this chapter the following distinctions are drawn: the discussion begins with an exploration of the kinds of learning *activities* that can be mobilized to support active learning processes, including role-playing, values clarification, and discussion of case studies and critical incidents. The exploration then shifts to the topic of learning *resources*. This discussion includes an examination of the use of resource persons as well as print and other media to support the learning process.

Developing and Using Learning Activities

Learning activities are structured exercises that promote engagement in the active generation of meaning and the practice of new behaviors. There are numerous collections of learning activities available (Renner, 1983, 1988; Brookfield, 1990; Knox, 1990; Meyers and Jones, 1993) and several books that describe exercises used in the process of popular education (Arnold and Burke, 1983; GATT-Fly, 1983). In the event that an existing learning activity is available, affordable, and appropriate (an "AAA" activity), it should be used for the application in question. In situations in which learning resources do not meet this triple A standard, because they either do not exist, are too costly, or are not tailored to the motivation and know-how of a particular group of learners, practitioners will need to create their own materials. It will become evident that once the general format for a particular learning activity is understood, it is relatively easy to customize existing exercises or develop original learning activities.

A definition of experiential learning exercises and a four-stage model for getting the most out of structured experiential learning were presented earlier. To recap some essentials: structured experiential learning exercises are planned activities that promote active learning through a process of action and reflection. The fact that they are approximations of real situations distinguishes them from field work, internships, and work experiences (which are also intended to promote experiential learning). The following discussion explores some common experiential learning exercises, including icebreakers, role-playing, cases, critical incidents, simulations, sculpting, visioning, mind mapping, and values clarification.

Icebreakers

Some of the more frequently used forms of experiential learning are the kinds of activities known as either warm-up exercises or ice-breakers (Zastrow, 1985; Pfeiffer, 1991). As their name suggests, these are group exercises used to speed up the process of members' getting to know one another. These exercises may also be used to prepare learners for the content that will be learned; in this way, thoughtfully crafted warm-up exercises can function as advance organizers. Also, icebreakers may be used as a way to conduct an emergent assessment of learning needs or as a means to conduct an embedded evaluation of entry-level knowledge and skills. The following examples demonstrate some examples of warm-up exercises:

At the first session of a Lamaze course, couples are asked to pair off with another couple to introduce themselves. The new partners are then directed to interview one another so that they can introduce each other to the other couples.

Participants in a professional development workshop on teaching as an aspect of practice in the human services are asked at the start of the first session to (1) paste a Polaroid picture of themselves at the top of a poster (this helps participants learn the names of others); (2) list their name and one of their learning goals for the workshop; and (3) record on the bottom of the poster their metaphor for their role as teacher (for example, teacher as gardener or architect, bee or butterfly). Learners then introduce themselves to the group and explain their learning goals and their metaphors. The facilitator links this information to the goals for the course.

There are many published sources of warm-up exercises, as noted previously, but practitioners will find that there is satisfaction in creating introductory activities to fit the needs of specific teaching situations. This may in fact be necessary, because novelty seems to play a role in the effectiveness of these icebreakers, and some exercises may gradually lose their impact if they are used too frequently. For example, the kind of icebreaker used in the Lamaze class may seem stale and stilted to people who have experienced this activity on numerous previous occasions.

Role-Playing

Role-playing is frequently used as a learning strategy in the human services because it offers a way to learn new behaviors, rehearse responses for future situations, and sort out the facts, assumptions, and feelings generated by a current concern (Joyce and Weil, 1986; Van Ments, 1989; Cranton, 1992). Role-playing activities may be either more structured or less. In more structured situations, participants are given written role descriptions or even tightly scripted roles to enact. In less structured role-playing, learners are assigned general roles to enact in free-form interaction with others. These kinds of exchanges are similar to improvisational acting. The following examples illustrate a variety of ways in which role-playing may be used to teach skills or to explore issues:

An employment counselor helps a young man injured in an industrial accident apply for a retraining course that will prepare him for a career in electronics. The man is very apprehensive about the application interview, and the counselor helps him develop skill and confidence by role-playing the interview situation. The counselor then provides coaching on some alternative responses.

A family sees a therapist to try and resolve conflicts between the parents and children. The family members agree that some of the worst fights occur just before dinner, but they are at a loss to figure out why. The practitioner helps them do some inquiry learning by having them role-play a simulation of their activities in the pre-dinner hour.

In a treatment program for men who have abused their partners, one member has difficulty declining requests from his common-law partner without becoming hostile and belittling. The professional facilitator

sets up a spontaneous role-play in which she challenges this member
to practice respectfully saying "No" to her in a variety of situations.

There is often some resistance to role-playing. Learners may perceive the activity as being too "touchy-feely," or they may fear public exposure of personal inadequacies. For these reasons the
practitioner needs to be thoughtful about ways to introduce this
activity so that learners will find the experience both useful and safe.
For example, in some situations it may help to relax participants with
some playful warm-up exercises prior to the actual role-playing.
Another alternative is to explain to learners that in a two-person
role-play, typically only one person is performing a role—the other
is *practicing* a role. The performer might feel some stage fright, but
the other party should recognize that he or she is practicing a desired
interpersonal skill. This interpretation may help a reluctant participant overcome his or her anxiety over performing.

In concluding a role play it is important for the practitioner to
make sure no unresolved feelings remain. This is necessary because
this kind of dramatic approach to learning can tend to surface some
deep-seated feelings, including anger or guilt. In situations in which
the anxiety of learners constrains their ability to learn from role-
playing, some alternative method should be found.

Case Studies

A teaching case should reflect "a well written, engaging description
of a real life situation that confronts a practitioner. . . . A case does
not present or assess final outcomes of a situation for the reader.
Rather, it offers the raw data about an actual situation [facts,
assumptions, and opinions of the participants] facing a [practitioner]
. . . [and] ends at a point where a professional judgment . . . has to
be made" (Cossom, 1991, p. 141). Case studies "emphasize inductive learning, with conceptual frameworks and strategic guidelines
being developed from the analysis of one or more real-world situations" (Lovelock, 1986, p. 25).

Many professionals have been exposed to the case method of teaching in the course of their professional education. Indeed, some medical schools use a largely case-driven curriculum. This is true at McMaster University medical school, which uses a problem-based learning approach (Neufeld and Barrows, 1985) and increasingly true at several other medical and allied professional schools. Cases are less frequently used in continuing professional or community education, but they can be very effective with these groups.

The benefit of the case method is that it can surface hidden values and assumptions that shape learner responses. The effective use of cases can encourage learners to generate a number of alternative solutions rather than a single answer, and they provide a forum for peer learning. Cases may also be structured so that they offer learners a list of potential interventions from which they can choose in dealing with a situation. Specified limits of time or money, for example, may be used to constrain the number or nature of available options. Cases may also be used creatively in teaching with individuals and in community education.

Critical Incidents

A critical incident is a condensed variation of the traditional case study; it provides a useful tool for learning about the nature of challenging situations and for developing action principles. Typically, these written incidents briefly describe a problem confronting a particular person and conclude with a question about how that person might think, feel, or respond under the given circumstances. These written vignettes are used to trigger learning and shared problem solving among a group of learners. In a workshop for professionals dealing with issues of confidentiality and the rights and responsibilities of human service professionals to intervene, the following kinds of critical incidents might be used to surface attitudes and develop practice principles:

A community development worker in a small northern town supports
a group of local citizens seeking funds for a project to repair the

homes of elderly people. To her dismay she discovers that the two leaders of this group used the initial five thousand dollars to purchase two snowmobiles, with vague talk of using them to haul wood from the bush to the local sawmill. Does she have a right or a responsibility to intervene in this situation?

A health professional learns that a certain self-help group focused on weight loss is using a diet protocol that recent research has proved to be ineffective but in no way physically injurious. Should he intervene in this situation? If so, in what way?

Written incidents may also be used to help learners develop parenting skills, become more assertive, or deal with situations that might trigger conflict. Critical incidents are particularly useful when learning to make decisions in highly complex or ambiguous situations. They provide a way for learners to examine a range of alternatives, to surface value positions, and to identify interpersonal styles of problem solving. Critical incidents may be written in the first person and used in the following way: in small groups, learners are given three or four different critical incidents to consider. One person reads aloud the first card and shares his or her immediate response to the situation it describes. This response is followed by more general group discussion, preferably following the stages previously outlined in the experiential learning model. Principles and values identified in the course of the discussion are recorded, and then the next person in the group reads and responds to a new incident.

Critical incidents can be developed quickly; thus, in an extended learning event they can be used to enrich the learning design by including some of the back-home concerns of the participants. Indeed, one useful activity during the assessment of needs and resources is to ask potential learners to write a description of a difficult situation they have faced. A little editing can often turn these descriptions into an important learning resource.

An alternative to written incidents are brief vignettes dramatized on videotape (Farquharson, 1993). These are sometimes
referred to as "trigger tapes." These too should pose an open-ended
challenge, so they will raise issues that trigger learning through
problem solving. The practitioner should be conscious of learners
who are concerned about receiving concrete, definitive answers,
however. These more dualistic thinkers can be frustrated by this
kind of learning strategy. This frustration can be reduced if sufficient
time and structure is provided to ensure that discussion moves to
the point in the experiential learning cycle at which concrete principles for action are generated. A clear summary of these principles
is also helpful.

Simulations

Simulations or simulation games are a method of facilitating learning that combines elements of both case teaching and role-playing.
One example of a familiar form of simulation is the board game
Monopoly, which encourages players to become ruthless real estate
tycoons. In the process they learn something about the dynamics of
the commercial real estate market.

A simulation game is a simplified version of a real-life situation
in which two or more parties struggle to achieve certain objectives
that may be mutually exclusive. Abt (1970) offers a simple definition: "any contest [play] among adversaries [players] operating
under constraints [rules] for an objective [winning, victory, or pay-
off]" (p. 4).

Simulations can be used to promote learning in three different
ways: by rehearsing behavior that learners anticipate they will need
in the future, by teaching decision-making skills, and as a stimulus
for inquiry learning (for example, exploration of perspectives). Here
are some examples:

Rehearsing behavior: A counselor in a vocational training program
uses a simulated supermarket checkout counter and some shelves

filled with groceries to help a group of mildly mentally handicapped adults learn some job-related skills, including ways to stock shelves and bag groceries.

Decision making: A computer program was developed to help probation officers understand why an objection might be sustained or overruled during a trial. The program presented a transcript of a court proceeding and whenever an objection was raised the probation officer, acting in the role of the judge, had five seconds to decide if this objection should be sustained or overruled. If the decision made was deemed by the software program to be incorrect, then the officer would be offered a chance to learn about the precedents that informed a correct response.

Inquiry learning: A group of representatives from a local antipoverty organization agree to lead a group of nursing students through a simulation known as "the poverty game." The students learn a good deal about structural inequality and oppression. The success of this learning experience is reflected by one student's observation that "the trouble with being poor is that it takes all of your time."

Simulations are increasingly computer-based and can be used to learn everything from typing to conflict management. This trend will no doubt continue, and simulations will be used extensively to promote learning in the human services (Meyers and Jones, 1993).

Sculpting

Sculpting, or sculpturing (Arnold and Burke, 1983), is a learning activity that involves elements of both role-playing and simulation. It can be used to help people frame and explore some previously unnamed experiences, and it can be used to help learners place their personal troubles within a broader context of public issues.

A sculpture is composed of a group of learners positioned in stances that visually express the essence of an experience. Frequently these silent human sculptures help people learn about issues of conflict, power, privilege, and oppression. This is why sculpting is often a favored learning strategy in popular education projects. Sculpting is also used by family therapists and other professionals to help people learn to name, and sometimes reclaim, some of their life experiences. Two examples illustrate the use of sculpting to promote learning:

> A family therapist encounters difficulty helping a family tease out the power relationships that exist between them. She asks each family member in turn to compose a sculpture using other family members, to express the sculptor's view of family relationships. The family members discuss each of these sculptures in turn, to learn how each person views power in the family.

> A faculty member in a nursing school wants her students to begin to move from being passive students to being active learners. First she asks for volunteers to create a sculpture that reflects "being a student." This sculpture is discussed, and then a second group sculpts "being a learner." The discussions following the creation of each of these sculptures yield the following descriptors of the two roles:

> | Learners | Students |
> |----------|----------|
> | Creative | Obedient |
> | Powerful | Parroting |
> | Curious | Obsequious |
> | Interesting | Poverty-stricken |
> | Risk takers | Overloaded |
> | Intuitive | Mind readers |
> | Involved | |

> This list is then used to identify group norms that promise to engage members as learners rather than as students.

Mind Mapping

Mind maps, or concept diagrams (Deshler, 1990; Meyers and Jones, 1993), provide a way to help learners integrate complex relationships between related principles and concepts. A mind map is a visual representation of the way learners construct links between the various elements they are learning (that is, the way they visualize the potential interconnection of the concepts, principles, values, and feelings revealed through the learning experience). Learners tend to enjoy sharing their mind maps with others, which opens up the possibility of learners creating collaborative mind maps. Learners may also be interested in viewing the practitioner's personal mind map of the relationship between elements of what has been taught. Mind maps can also be an important aid in fostering the transfer of learning.

In order to illustrate the use of mind mapping, Figure 7.1 indicates one way a learner might link some ideas presented in an introductory workshop on crisis intervention. In a series of workshops, participants might be asked to create a succession of mind maps so that they will get the reinforcement of seeing the progress and elaboration of their learning. Mind maps can also be used to consolidate learning in popular and community education projects.

Values Clarification

Values clarification exercises typically consist of either brief descriptions of situations that raise value dilemmas or statements that reflect value positions. The purpose of this type of learning exercise is to enable people to surface values and attitudes that may be deeply embedded within their personal perspective. Once surfaced, these value positions may be compared with the perspectives of others in the learning group. It is important for the facilitator to make it clear that there are no right or wrong answers in this kind of learning experience, and people should be reassured that they do not have to share their responses with others if they do not wish to do so.

Exercises of this nature can also be used during the storming phase

Figure 7.1. A Mind Map.

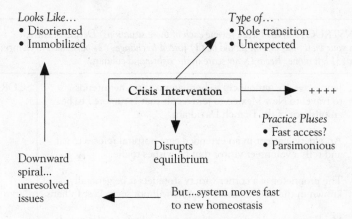

of group development, to clarify valued group norms. They also can provide useful information about the entry-level values of the learners in relation to the desired learning outcomes. The following is a typical values clarification exercise, which might be used to surface values regarding the right to control other people's behavior:

> A community liaison officer in a police department wants to organize a training program for citizens who have volunteered for a neighborhood watch program. He designs an opening exercise that might surface some of these volunteers' embedded values, particularly those beliefs pertaining to the rights and responsibilities of people to intervene in the lives of others. He devises a values clarification exercise, which enables him to tailor the balance of the workshop so that it addresses some of the personal values and attitudes surfaced by the exercise.

The type of values clarification exercise that the liaison officer might use is illustrated in Figure 7.2.

Problem-Solving Activities

There are many other different kinds of learning activities, but three merit discussion here because they can be useful strategies for

Figure 7.2. A Values-Clarification Exercise.

INSTRUCTIONS: *Please review each of these situations. Decide whether, in your view, this person should be (1) forced to change, (2) persuaded to change, or (3) left alone. Record your score in the right-hand column.*	
1. Jenny, age 16, announces to her parents that she intends to travel to New Mexico to join a cult that is rumored to be an offshoot of the Branch Davidians.	SCORE
2. An elderly patient in an extended care hospital refuses to eat and tells a volunteer visitor that he wishes to die.	
3. The proprietor of a corner variety store lets it be generally known in the neighborhood that he will not serve East Indians.	
4. Mr. Brown, an elderly man who may be a little senile, spends his day in the community park swearing with spectacular profanity at pigeons, children, and other passersby.	

promoting learning through problem solving. These three methods are visioning, brainstorming, and the decision matrix.

Visioning

An important way to help people learn and change, particularly if they have a more visual learning style, is to have them construct a picture of what a desired change might look like (Covey, 1989) and list the learning objectives that would lead to this change. The strategies used to develop such a vision of a desired future are referred to as imaging, imagining, or visioning exercises. Imaging is a way to jump-start the brainstorming process by helping learners break free of present constraints that may obscure alternative futures. In essence, the imaging process is a way of encouraging learners to contemplate their view of the ideal learning outcomes they would like to achieve. The role of the facilitator is to take the learners forward in time so that they can contemplate what things might look like if they were fully able to realize their hopes. This desired future might involve the resolution of problems or the real-

ization of learning goals. The facilitator of this forward-looking journey needs to spend some time planning how he or she will stimulate learners to envision the future; it is often helpful to write out a
script to guide this imaging exercise. A script typically encourages
the learner to try to get in touch with visual, auditory, and affective
responses—what the situation would look, sound, and feel like:

> A family therapist is working with a troubled family in which commu-
> nication difficulties become more extreme during holiday celebrations.
> It is only early in the fall, but she encourages them to close their eyes
> and journey forward in time to Christmas. They are encouraged to
> experience the sounds, emotions, thoughts, and visions each of them
> associates with a satisfying holiday together. The therapist then
> spends time helping the family members share what they saw, heard,
> and felt in their visions of this future event. This exercise makes it pos-
> sible for the family members to surface some faulty assumptions and
> reconcile some differences.

> A clinical psychologist with special skills in human resource develop-
> ment is contracted to help staff members in one department of a
> hospital develop a mission statement for their unit. He takes them on
> an imaginary trip by helicopter forward in time (five years) to visualize
> what their service might look, sound, and feel like if it were highly suc-
> cessful. The data from this exercise is used to generate a mission
> statement.

The value of imaging the future is that it clarifies long-term
objectives and also builds hope by helping the learner construct a
vision in which change is possible.

Brainstorming

In many group problem-solving situations, the process might be
enlivened if the group spends some time on the freewheeling generation of fresh ideas (Isaksen and Treffinger, 1985; von Oech, 1986;

Gelfand, 1988). Unfortunately, in all too many so-called brainstorming sessions the resulting discussion is quite desultory and may fade out before any notably vibrant new ideas have been generated. Factors that can contribute to this kind of outcome include learners with strongly convergent problem-solving styles and group norms that are so task oriented they do not permit divergent thinking. In order to promote the generation of more and better ideas, learners should be reminded of the following brainstorming guidelines:

Postpone judgment. Postponing judgment is at the core of brainstorming. Many people seem to have a strong need to rush to a hasty judgment on new ideas. In group learning situations this can mean that many potentially useful ideas are rejected before they have been fully explored.

Remember the spectrum. Likewise, people often do not recognize that within any single idea or suggestion there may be many sub-ideas that lie along a spectrum from more to less useful. In the rush to judgment, these constituent ideas may be lost because of a negative assessment of some other constituent element. The notion of a spectrum is intended to remind learners that each suggestion may contain a valuable kernel within a certain amount of chaff. The facilitator should therefore make a conscious effort to help learners focus on the positive end of the spectrum and to identify sub-elements that seem to be provocative or to have some intrinsic elegance.

Use metaphors. In the informal problem solving of daily life, people often use metaphors or analogies to solve problems. This process involves seeking analogous situations or illuminating metaphors that may shed light on a new challenge or problem. The following example illustrates how this process might be fostered within a helping interview:

A family physician helps a man learn new dietary practices following a heart attack. To encourage a broader search for ideas, the doctor asks the patient to think of examples from the world of nature of how animals or birds stick to their diets. The learner opts to look at the analogy provided by the feeding habits of a heron. This helps him generate ideas about the need for patience, discrimination, and caution.

Distortion. An alternative way to dislodge traditional patterns of thought is to encourage group members to consider a problem in either much greater or much smaller terms. In other words, participants can be encouraged to reverse the issue. Instead of "What can we do with the small proportion of children in an elementary school who have learning disabilities?" the group might consider "What could be done if 92 percent of the students had learning disabilities?"

Open problem statements. It has already been noted that the way a problem or challenge is couched has much to do with the resulting scope of creative problem solving. A poorly worded challenge may limit the search for a solution. One of the classic examples from the human services is the way the therapeutic outcome for a person with a drinking problem can be determined by the description given to the person's problem. A mental health professional might arrive at some convoluted Freudian diagnosis involving unmet infantile oral needs, maternal deprivation, and the like—clearly a statement of a weighty problem that requires professional attention and some form of long-term treatment. Alternatively, a member of Alcoholics Anonymous might conclude that the individual with the drinking problem is simply allergic to alcohol. The way in which this problem is framed can set up widely divergent avenues for problem solving.

Repetition and silence. A final guideline is to ensure that learners feel it is quite acceptable to repeat ideas contributed earlier or to remain silent. Often when an idea is repeated it reveals a different perspective, and silence may be an indication that people are thinking—a condition much to be desired in this kind of session.

Brainstorming and related techniques can be used to enable groups of learners to create multiple potential solutions to a particular learning challenge. However, some people may be overwhelmed by the challenge of choosing from among these alternatives. There are several practical strategies that can be used to facilitate this kind of decision making, including the nominal group method (Ford, 1975) and the decision matrix. This last approach offers a particularly robust and practical way to involve a group of learners in choosing between a limited list of alternatives.

Decision Matrix

In simple terms, the decision matrix (Figure 7.3), otherwise known as a valuing matrix, offers a way to separate the generation of decision criteria from the act of decision making. For example, this approach could be used to help a group of young people completing a preemployment program select a way to recognize their achievements.

Five steps are involved in using a decision matrix:

- Generating potential solutions
- Generating selection criteria
- Weighting selection criteria
- Evaluating options against the criteria
- Summing and ranking potential solutions

Generating potential solutions. Group members might be asked, for example, to brainstorm potential group-termination activities (a graduation ceremony, a potluck picnic, a fund-raiser for future groups). Several of the most attractive of these alternatives are then listed in the left-hand column of the matrix as potential solutions.

Generating selection criteria. The next step in our example would be for the facilitator to encourage participants to suggest criteria

Figure 7.3. The Decision Matrix.

CRITERIA ➡		Cost	Time	Purpose	Total	Rank	
Weight (max 5)		5	4	3.5	12.5	max	
S	Grad Ceremony	3	2	3	8	3	
O	Potluck picnic	5	3	3	11	2	
L	Fundraiser	5	3.5	3	11.5	1	
U	etc.						
T	etc.						
I							
O							
N							
S							

that might be used to select the most useful focus for the group-termination event. Factors might include the costs involved, the planning time required, and the fit with the purpose of the group. These criteria are recorded in the slanted columns across the top of the matrix.

Weighting selection criteria. Not all of the criteria will be equally important, so the next step is to rank their relative importance. In this example the maximum score for relative importance is 5. Thus, the affordability of a particular event might be awarded 5 (out of a possible 5), whereas the fit with the purpose of the group might be seen as less crucial and weighted at 3.5. (This is reflected in the numbers recorded in Figure 7.3.) The weighted scores are then recorded at the head of the column beneath the stated criteria.

Evaluating options against the criteria. The next task for the facilitator is to take each potential solution in turn and ask the participants to agree on a rating of the extent to which it meets each of the criteria. The maximum number of points for each criterion will be limited by the weighting assigned during the previous phase of the exercise.

Summing and ranking potential solutions. When each of the potential solutions has been rated, the accumulated scores for each of the criteria are summed, thereby establishing their rank order. The practitioner should be alert to the fact that new criteria and fresh potential solutions may surface as the rating process proceeds. These new ideas can be added to the matrix.

Learning Resources and Materials

A teaching intervention can often have greater impact and be more enduring if it is supported by print handouts, a running record of the discussion, or a variety of instructional media.

Printed Learning Resources

Print materials, including brochures, handouts, posters, and press releases, are used for personal and public education in virtually all human service organizations. Typically these print materials are used, in combination with other media, to explain agency services, describe treatment regimes, and inform the public about health and welfare issues. Many of these materials could easily be strengthened through a little more attention to the learning design process.

A practitioner who has identified a learning need that could be most effectively met with the help of printed educational materials is faced with a series of questions: What suitable materials already exist? Are they adequate as they stand, or will they need to be modified or supplemented? If modification is required, can this be done with supplementary materials, or can copyright release be obtained? (Incidentally, if copyright release is granted, it is possible to save a great deal of time by modifying existing materials for another purpose. This is particularly true if the original material can be obtained on a computer disk.) Here is an example of using printed materials in human service practice:

> The director of volunteers for a new residential facility for children with multiple physical and mental disabilities is confronted with the challenge of training large numbers of volunteers for a variety of roles. She hears of a volunteer training package and handbook developed in Florida, and she is able to negotiate copyright release at no cost by trading some software she had developed to track volunteer hours. The learning design of the handbook needs a lot of modification, but she still saves time because the original copyright holders give her a disk copy of their materials.

Creating original or supplementary printed educational materials need not be a daunting task. Rather there is a sense of creative achievement in developing print materials that not only look attractive but work effectively as learning tools.

The steps for building effective print-based learning materials are essentially the same as those for preparing materials for face-to-face instruction. The assessment of learning needs and resources leads to the development of clear learning objectives. These in turn shape the overall design of the print materials, the selection of additional resources, and methods of formative and summative evaluation. It is also possible to use elements of the EDICT model to create materials that are effective and learner-friendly.

There are some other important considerations in the production of printed learning materials. The first has to do with comprehension. Print is essentially a one-way medium, and it offers only limited opportunities to check learner comprehension. This makes it essential that all jargon is ruthlessly excluded and that necessary but unfamiliar terms are carefully defined. The practitioner also needs to be disciplined, to avoid including so much information that the teachable moment is overloaded or that excess detail obscures the important points. Need-to-know items should take precedence over nice-to-know items when space is limited. As the materials are being developed, it is important to get feedback on their utility—early and often. People who are representative of the readership should review the materials to ensure that the ideas are understandable and useful. This is particularly necessary for printed matter intended for lay readers. Technical information should be checked for accuracy by appropriate specialists.

In very general terms, the layout should mix print and graphics in a way that leaves a spacious feeling to the text. There are several books on this subject, and people in the business of desktop publishing can often give excellent advice on layout. In situations where an individual professional or employer own the rights to materials, it is possible to store them on a computer and then tailor them for particular applications. For example:

A family service agency finds that the demographics of its neighborhood are changing with the influx of many retired people. Thus the agency begins using a larger typeface in the various pamphlets it publishes, to make them more readable for the people in this population.

A physician, a specialist in rheumatology, is able to customize his informational brochures so that each patient is given material in which he or she is addressed specifically, by name.

This last example illustrates one way to try to offset the inherently impersonal nature of print communication. Another simple approach is to structure the text around questions and answers in a way that offers at least a semblance of dialogue. The advent of new ways to offer distance education and the emergence of potent new educational technologies are likely to uncover stimulating new ways to supplement print-based learning with other, interactive media.

There is one other type of educational text that needs to be mentioned—the press release. In the human services, information is given to the press in the hope that it will emerge in some form of publication and thereby influence (that is, teach) the public in some way. The effective press release, therefore, is one that succeeds in getting published or broadcast and does an effective job of teaching. There are several excellent resources available that describe the stages in this process; for a good introduction, the reader is directed to a practical booklet by David Reilley (1985).

Flip Charts

There is another resource that can be classified as print—the trusty flip chart. This has become an important resource in a wide range of teaching situations, where it may be used as a medium for presenting material (Bloomwell, 1983). The other value of flip charts, as mentioned in the chapter on group facilitation, is that they provide a way to track ideas generated in group discussions. Flip charts have the simplicity of chalkboards, but they are both more versatile and more portable.

There are one or two simple guidelines to ensure that this resource is used to its best effect. In preparing presentations to be delivered on a flip chart, it is useful to write in large block letters and to limit the amount of information on each page. Using more than one color can be helpful, but the practitioner should avoid colors like red and yellow, which tend to be difficult to see from even a short distance. In preparing presentations to larger groups it is helpful to avoid including material at the bottom of the page, as this may be obscured for those at the back of the room. A blank page may be left between each of the prepared pages, to record comments and questions from the learners. Masking tape can be used to post each of the presentation pages after they have been delivered. When using the charts to support presentations, the practitioner can write detailed notes in pencil on the margin of flip chart sheets. These penciled notes can serve as prompts for the presenter, while remaining invisible to the participants.

There are two additional ways this resource can be used to support teaching in practice. First, it can be used to chart the problem-solving or learning process during counseling sessions with individuals and families. This has the benefit of allowing the counselor and clients to sit shoulder-to-shoulder, facing the challenge together. This is an important symbolic gesture, signifying partnership in mutual problem solving. Another important role for flip charts is for recording issues and images generated when using popular education methods and other community development strategies.

Audiovisual Learning Materials

Audiovisual materials, including films, videocassettes, slide presentations, audiotapes, and overhead transparencies are frequently used as teaching resources in the human services. The appeal of these media lies in their ability to depict realistic situations. Video also seems to have a great intrinsic appeal for many younger adult learners, who tend to be accustomed to receiving information via this medium.

Videotape

Film is now used so infrequently for teaching in the human services that this discussion will focus on video, although many of the comments apply equally to the use of film. In fact, many useful films have now been dubbed onto tape. Videocassettes are attractive because the technology offers rapidly improving picture quality, is widely available, and is considerably more user-friendly that the old sixteen-millimeter film projectors and screens. These benefits of video are amplified by the fact that the majority of learners already spend significant amounts of time watching television and thus are attuned to learning from this medium. The downside is that most people have become accustomed to expensively produced commercial television and videocassettes, so they have a low tolerance for amateur productions.

There are two ways in which video recordings can be used as a teaching resource. The first is to use prerecorded, commercially made videos. The second is to use video equipment to give learners feedback about their learning performance or as a tool to promote reflection about challenging situations. In the first instance a videotape may be used to explain ideas or to demonstrate those ideas in action (phases from the EDICT model). Alternatively, video programs may be used to deliver images that stir feelings or pose problem-solving challenges. An example of the latter are videotaped critical incidents ("trigger tapes") used as an experiential learning tool. The practitioner needs to be clear about his or her purpose in using a videotape, and in most situations the learners need to be clear about why they are watching it. In the case of programs intended to convey ideas, a useful strategy is to outline the program prior to viewing, and then to encourage the viewers to generate questions that they might be able to answer after watching the program. In those situations where a videotaped program is intended to provoke subsequent problem solving, learners could be encouraged to generate questions as the material is viewed. This kind of advanced clarification and direction is important, because many people have learned to view television uncritically or to use it as a narcotic—hardly the desired effect in a teaching intervention! Incidentally, teachers should be particularly wary of showing videotaped programs directly after lunch, as this can amplify their soporific effect.

Improvements in video technology make it easier to produce segments of instructional material that require little editing. For example:

A family counselor uses teachers and students from a junior high school drama class to enact and videotape a series of vignettes depicting emerging conflicts between parents and young adolescent

children. These episodes are used to trigger problem-solving discussions in a family life education program.

The other educational use of video is to provide learners with
feedback. Applications include helping professionals improve their
clinical skills by observing their own performance and critiquing
that of colleagues, helping people develop job-related skills, and
helping citizens recognize shared concerns on which to base collective action:

> The head of the psychiatry department at a local hospital recruits com-
> munity psychiatrists to rotate coverage of the emergency room on an
> on-call basis. He organizes a series of orientation workshops in which
> the participants share feedback with their colleagues as they view
> videotapes of themselves responding to some emergency situations.

> Counselors in a vocational service for mentally challenged adults use
> video to give trainees feedback about their job performance. A
> remote-controlled camera is used to focus on one man, who on view-
> ing his behavior exclaims: "I'm just not paying attention to what I'm
> doing. Look at the mistakes I'm making!" This self-directed feedback
> is followed by a dramatic improvement in the man's job performance.

> A community development worker borrows a video camera for a
> group of tenants in public housing. The tenants take turns shooting
> segments of video showing what they regard as problematic aspects
> of their living situation. These include unsafe window screens, poor
> laundry facilities, and broken playground equipment. All the tenants
> in the project are invited to a screening of these segments, and after
> learning about their shared concerns, they form an effective advo-
> cacy group.

To conclude this discussion of the use of videotape, a word about
copyright and consent is in order. Virtually all prepared video pro-

grams are under copyright. This means that they may not be used in group teaching situations unless appropriate permission is obtained. This applies both to cassettes available from the corner video store and to personal recordings of broadcast television programs.

Photographic Slides and Audiotapes

Another audiovisual aid that is often used, particularly in continuing medical and patient education, is the slide-and-audiotape presentation. These have the advantage of offering high-resolution images and quality sound, while still being relatively cheap and easy to assemble. In some applications it may be effective to make a videotape of the completed slide show to facilitate ease of use. For example:

A physician who specializes in cataract surgery makes a slide show that explains the nature of cataracts and the surgical alternatives for remedying this condition. New patients are able to view a videotape of this presentation in the waiting room of his office prior to their initial consultation.

Overhead Projector

The overhead projector is a useful audiovisual aid in more formal teaching situations. Sheets or rolls of transparent acetate can be inscribed with a special type of felt pen, or graphics can be printed onto these sheets using a computer printer or a photocopying machine—but this is where a danger lies! The very ease of photocopying text onto an overhead transparency makes it all too easy to project whole pages of text, or intricate graphics. These overheads can be hard to read, time-consuming for the learner to transcribe, and, in a word, frustrating. This suggests two guidelines: first, only a limited number of key points should be included on an overhead transparency, and second, in the majority of cases what is projected on the overhead should also be available as a handout for the learners. To help with the process of preparing such overheads and handouts, a number of useful presentation software packages are now available. These offer a variety of templates that can improve the appearance of the presentation and can also shrink several slides onto a single page, to reduce the number of pages of handouts required.

Computer-Assisted Instruction

Software that supports the development of effective presentations and personalized brochures is just one example of how computers can be used to improve teaching in the human services. New teaching and learning applications for computer technologies are emerging at a bewildering speed, and it is not easy for most practitioners to keep pace with these developments. There are at least three other interesting ways in which computers are currently being used to promote learning in human service practice: computer-based simulations, learner-driven multimedia programs, and databases.

In the human services, computer-based simulations are most frequently used in programs for professional education. For example, there are programs that enable medical students to scalpel their way through the body of a simulated cadaver, and there are programs that offer practice in conducting a job search. In the future it is likely that there will be many more such simulations available, enabling people to learn skills as diverse as self-care, conflict resolution, parenting, and budgeting.

Multimedia

The term "multimedia," when used in a computing context, refers to "the integration of video, audio, graphics, and data within a single workstation" (Bates, Harrington, Gilmore, and van Soest, 1993, p. 120). Multimedia presentations are delivered via either CD-ROM or laser disc, and permit a uniquely learner-centered experience. On occasion multimedia is used to support elaborate simulations:

As a component of a training program for paramedics, a laser disc program on the function of the heart is developed. This includes video of

an opened chest, showing a pumping heart; graphics of heart cham-
bers and valves; and three-dimensional "wire" models of the heart that
can be rotated by the learner. This multimedia package was developed
so that the learner can decide how to progress through the material.

At present multimedia may be both more accessible and more
acceptable as a tool for promoting professional, rather than consumer, learning. In the future this is likely to change, as multimedia becomes a more generally useful tool for others involved in
human service systems. For example, computers might be routinely
available at the bedside of hospital patients, who could use CD-
ROM to learn more about their condition and self-care upon dis-
charge. The Internet could provide access to additional information,
as well as to other patients with shared concerns and experiential
know-how. This is a good example of how technology might enable
practitioners to take greater advantage of the learning opportunities that occur at teachable moments.

Finally, there is the ability of computers to facilitate communication and access to a wide range of information sources. Electronic
mail can facilitate closer collaboration, both between professionals
and between potential consumers of human services. In addition,
the Internet offers increasing access to a wide range of data, and it
already serves as a powerful resource for both lay and professional
learners. An example:

A woman who is both deaf and blind serves as facilitator for a self-
help group of people with disabilities who meet via CompuServe. She
is able to read output from her braille printer at phenomenal speed,
and she says that many professionals are the people who are really
disabled, referring to professionals and others who have not yet
learned how to touch-type.

These new technologies offer a great potential for liberation,
because, in the words of Kozma and Johnson (1991), they offer

learners "a more active role in constructing knowledge . . . the role of the teacher [shifts to] . . . coach or mentor, helping [learners] to solve problems" (p. 19).

In conclusion, it is important to stress that locating or developing learning resources requires practitioners to be resourceful and creative. As noted earlier, there are many existing materials, but these can be hard to locate, expensive to purchase, or not attuned to the needs and sensitivities of a particular group of learners. For these reasons it is helpful for practitioners to develop skill and confidence in developing customized learning materials.

There are two final cautions to bear in mind when choosing resources: first, beware of choosing a medium or media that overwhelm the message. Second, beware of selecting media without a clear sense of the purpose it is to serve. In the first instance there is the danger that very sophisticated technology can either intimidate or distract the learner. For example:

A birth control educator in India in the mid 1970s tried to use videotapes to support his presentations. He found, however, that rural villagers were distracted by this technology, which they did not understand. He therefore took an old bicycle frame—a very familiar piece of technology—and constructed a "viewing machine." He removed the rear wheel and linked the bicycle chain to a roll of paper containing images that could be advanced each time he turned the pedals. He gave his presentation perched on the bicycle seat, pedaling to scroll up each new image as required.

The other danger is that teachers, including human service professionals, can become so enamored of various instructional resources that the learning plan becomes weighted down with distracting bells and whistles. This tendency was described in a classic article, "The Woo Woo Factor" (Gordon, 1985). The aim in selecting resources is not to wow the learners with a mesmerizing mixture of sensory inputs, but rather to engage them in active learning. Practitioners are encouraged to remain flexible and inclusive in considering the mix of alternative resources that might complement a given learning design. A danger sign is when they start planning a learning event by choosing some piece of instructional media *before* they have given any thought to learning outcomes and learning design. There is a tendency to feel an attraction for one particular kind of instructional resource, and this makes it very easy to once again fall victim to the law of the instrument: "Give a child a hammer and everything starts to look like a nail." Draves (1984) offers some useful advice in this connection: "There is no best technique to use in teaching adults, and the only bad technique is the one that is used repeatedly with the same group. Try several new ideas every time you teach. . . . Some will not work while others will be a surprising success" (p. 61).

In the context of teaching in the human services, this means that a practitioner should avoid the seduction of using a single teaching resource in any and all situations.

8

....

Using Evaluation
to Enhance Effectiveness

This chapter begins with a consideration of some issues related to the formative and summative evaluation of teaching and learning in the human services. The focus then shifts to a discussion of a variety of strategies that may be used to increase the probability that what is learned during a teaching intervention will later become transferred to the appropriate social or work situations. These various approaches are all concerned with promoting what is termed "transfer of learning" (Broad, 1982; Fox, 1984; Suessmith, 1985).

The chapter concludes with an examination of the factors that should be considered when what is learned will influence people who are not part of the initial teaching intervention. The process by which teaching innovations flow out to influence other people is known as the adoption-diffusion process (Rogers, 1983; Rogers and Shoemaker, 1984; Edwards, Tindale, Heath, and Posavac, 1990).

Evaluation

The current push for greater accountability in the way human services are developed and delivered has been accompanied by a dedication to making many different forms of evaluation. In the past the following observation by Stephen Brookfield (1986) might have been accurate: "Attesting to the need for evaluation is somewhat akin to deciding to take exercise more regularly. Both are resolutions that are deemed important and necessary, but both are, for whatever reasons, rarely implemented" (p. 261).

Today there is an emphasis on evaluating all stages of the delivery of human services, including teaching. This evaluation takes the form of pre-formative assessment of needs and resources, formative evaluation of the emerging program delivery and teaching and learning processes, and, finally, summative evaluation of the program and of the learning and teaching outcomes. The purpose of formative evaluation is to provide feedback to human service professionals and learners about teaching and learning progress. This formative feedback can be used to change the focus of learning activities to achieve a better fit with the felt needs of teachers, learners, and stakeholders (Brookfield, 1986) and with the desired learning outcomes. Summative evaluation provides data on the effectiveness of teaching and the extent to which learning outcomes have been achieved. These data may be used to improve the quality of similar learning events in the future, to satisfy the accountability requirements of funding bodies, and to improve the future performance of practitioners and learners.

The central importance of these assessment processes is captured in this observation of a human service professional: "If you care you count" (Ricks, 1981). In other words, professionals who really care about the outcomes of their interventions will monitor their results by monitoring their clients' progress.

There are one or two general comments to make about evaluation procedures before embarking on a more detailed examination of the formative and summative phases of the assessment process. Cranton (1989) offers this overview of the nature and purpose of evaluation: "Evaluation . . . include[s] a wide array of activities, such as informal observation of [learner] reactions, tests, structured observations of performance and the use of discussions and anecdotal records or comments to provide feedback to the learner. . . . Evaluation implies a judgment of quality or degree; it may or may not include testing" (p. 136).

It is important to underscore Cranton's point that evaluative data on teaching and learning are gathered with a specific purpose in mind. This purpose usually involves using the information to shape some type of decision.

Human service professionals are likely to be more familiar with quantitative approaches to evaluation, which involve measuring the extent to which predetermined learning objectives have been achieved. The appeal of this approach is that it offers apparent scientific rationality, as a counter to much of the ambiguity that characterizes teaching in the human services. The downside to quantitative methods is that they do not take into account unintended learning outcomes and they do not gather information on learning that is more qualitative in nature. In a similar way, quantitative approaches to evaluation tend to be relatively inflexible—they are often insensitive to the experience of learners. Finally, quantitative methods of assessment can limit the extent to which evaluation is a collaborative effort. Thus they may not be helpful when used with constructivist research paradigms (Guba and Lincoln, 1989). Qualitative methods are the central approach in what is termed "naturalistic evaluation" (Brookfield, 1986). Naturalistic evaluation, or action research, places value on the perspectives of learners, and it seeks to present findings in an accessible way so learners can make sense of them.

The last point to stress is that this discussion of evaluation will be concerned not just with learners and learning outcomes, but also with assessing the effectiveness of teaching interventions and the teaching skills of practitioners.

Formative Evaluation

Formative evaluation is probably the single most influential way to maximize learning and to promote ongoing teaching improvement. It is easy for the teaching and learning processes to lose focus and effectiveness unless there is frequent formative evaluation that yields the necessary data to keep both processes on track. Feedback, particularly from the learners themselves, functions much like data gathered from radar or a depth sounder. This information helps the practitioner navigate, or make appropriate adjustments in speed and direction, during the learning process. The input of learner feedback is particularly important, given the unique way in which people tend to construct personal meanings from the material that is being taught. In the absence of some kind of learner input, the form of these meaning constructions remains uncertain to the teacher. Formative feedback is thus used in two ways: to provide information about what learners are actually learning, and to indicate the impact of the teacher and different teaching strategies on the learning process.

One of the most convenient ways to check what and how learners are learning is simply to ask them. Egan (1990), speaking about the need to conduct continuous formative evaluation during the counseling process, notes that "evaluation . . . means making sure that helping remains a learning process in which the counselor and client together learn about themselves and about the process of change" (p. 181). One way to evaluate these types of one-to-one teaching situations is to conclude the teaching event by asking individual learners how they would describe what they had learned to a close friend. This way of framing the question can be particularly effective, because learners will tend to be less inclined to respond with what they think the professional wants to hear. It also has the benefit of making the question seem slightly less inquisitorial. For example:

A woman approaches a male family counselor to complain about her husband's drinking. She has a clear desire for the counselor to phone her husband and tell him to "smarten up!" The counselor launches into a careful and exhaustive explanation of his role and the reasons why he doesn't think it would be productive for him to call the woman's husband. At the end of the interview, he asks the woman to summarize what she might tell a friend about what she had learned. She responded, "I'd tell her that you'll call Fred and tell him he has to come in, and you're going to have a man-to-man talk with him to straighten him out."

This kind of response is not unusual, because learners often bring with them very firm expectations of how their problems should be addressed. They may have a tendency to selectively learn only those items that fit with the expectations that flow from their existing set of health beliefs. It is therefore important for teachers to develop an understanding of the way learners will construct meaning on the basis of the teaching intervention. Strategies for formative evaluation are an important way to develop this kind of understanding.

Structured Formative Evaluation

In formal teaching situations, a wide variety of more structured strategies for formative evaluation may be used (Angelo and Cross, 1993). One very simple approach is to conclude each teaching session by gathering written feedback from the learners. For example, in a day-long workshop the practitioner might hand out cards at midday and ask participants to complete two statements in writing: "This morning I learned . . ." and "This morning I questioned . . ." These anonymous responses can then be reviewed during the break period. This technique can be enormously helpful in fine-tuning the design for the balance of the workshop.

It is useful for the practitioner to begin the next teaching session by indicating to the participants how their feedback has been used. This is also an opportunity to address common questions that were raised on the feedback cards. Alternatively, the cards can be handed out randomly, and each participant in turn reads aloud the comments on the card they received. This latter approach has the benefit of speeding up the re-forming phase of group development when there has been a delay between learning sessions. Feedback cards can also be used in conjunction with another formative evaluation system, the "feedback committee." This approach involves recruiting two or three volunteers from the learning group who agree to give and receive feedback on behalf of the other members. In longer-term learning events, the feedback committee meets periodically with the practitioner to share feedback from the group and to help identify appropriate future learning activities. The committee can also be used as a conduit for sharing teacher observations with the larger learning group.

The use of a feedback committee shows the group that teacher and learners have shared the responsibility for the success of a teaching or learning encounter. It can also help the practitioner avoid pitfalls or make an early recovery from teaching errors. In gathering any type of formative feedback, it is important that the practitioner act on at least some of the ideas contributed. And this should be drawn to the learners' attention, because if none of the feedback is ever used, or seen to be used, then the learners will soon lose interest in providing it.

Another practical way for the teacher to reinforce the integration of ideas and to gain a perspective on how learners are constructing meaning is through the use of mind maps, or concept diagrams (discussed in Chapter Seven). The way learners construct a visual representation of the links they perceive between items they are learning reinforces and clarifies what has been learned. It also provides the additional benefit of offering the teacher formative assessment data about how learners are constructing meaning. This data may suggest a need to alter teaching strategies, or it may reveal that corrective information is required. In an extended learning event, it can be useful to review early mind maps at a later date. In this way learners can see how their meaning making has become elaborated with the passage of time and further learning.

The group norms scale, illustrated in Figure 8.1, is another useful formative evaluation tool, which practitioners can use to sustain positive working relationships among the members of a learning group. This approach fosters active learning involvement in the storming and norming phases of group development. Later, this custom tool provides feedback that can help sustain productive relationships among the various group members while learning activities are being performed. A group norms scale is created in the following way.

After completion of the formation stage, when the learning group is created, members are encouraged to discuss the kinds of norms that they would like their collaborative work to be characterized by. They are encouraged to generate guidelines relating both to the relationships among members of the group and to the way their learning goals will be pursued. The practitioner, as a group member, is also free to contribute to this process. These statements of desired norms are then recorded in the right-hand (Desired Norms) column of a blank group norms scale (which includes a central series of columns constituting a simple five-point scale.

The facilitator then composes statements expressing the opposite of the desired conditions just described. These statements are recorded in the appropriate rows in the left-hand column (Norms Not Desired). The completed forms are then duplicated as handouts, and at periodic intervals learners are asked to anonymously check on the five-point scale the extent to which they think the group is adhering to the desired norms. These sheets are then collected, and the individual scores are recorded on a master sheet or overhead transparency. This yields a kind of scattergram, as reflected in Figure 8.1. These scores are shared with the group members, who are encouraged to identify results that seem less than satisfactory and to suggest ways in which the desired norms could be further reinforced. This evaluative discussion also provides the learners with an opportunity to add additional norms to the scale for the next time it is used. This kind of custom-made formative evaluation tool effectively models partnership in the relationship between practitioners and learners. Learners generate their own feedback data and arrive at their own decisions about how it will be used. Successive

Figure 8.1. Group Norms Scale.

Norms Not Desired	1	2	3	4	5	Desired Norms
A few members dominate much of the group discussion.	•	•	•	• • •	•	In this learning group everyone gets a chance to express their ideas.
The good ideas that are generated are not recorded.	• •	• • •	•			Members share responsibility for tracking the discussion.
Members do not share responsibility—they tend to see the practitioner as a scapegoat when the group fails.			•	• • •		The practitioner is not held solely responsible for the success or failure of the group.
Much of the group learning tends to be rather grim and earnest.			• •	• • •	•	The learning experience is mostly satisfying and sometimes fun.
Group members tend to be critical and competititve with one another.			• • • •	•		Group members build on the ideas of one another.

applications of the group norms scale can be recorded in different colors on the same master tally sheet. This gives learners a graphic representation of their performance over time. Typically, the norms will be increasingly highly rated with repeated applications of this instrument. This occurs as learners pay increased attention to norms that address both task and relationship components of the group experience.

More conventional survey instruments and other tools commonly used in summative evaluations can also be used to generate formative feedback. In some situations, however, these may need to be modified if learners are reluctant to invest the time required to complete lengthy formative evaluation instruments. In addition to information gathered from learners, the sources for formative evaluation data include observations of teaching by other professionals, teaching journals, and video recordings and review of the group.

Less Structured Formative Evaluation

Effective teachers are continually monitoring learners and the learning environment for both verbal and nonverbal clues to how the teaching and learning are unfolding. Inferences can be drawn from such things as seating patterns, the interaction of group members, or the way group members respond to questions. Any of these types of observations can provide formative information about the success of the learning enterprise, but these will usually need to be confirmed by some kind of more deliberate formative evaluation. In group and community teaching, the cohesiveness of the group, the clarity of working agreements, and the extent to which members work collaboratively to achieve shared goals are all informal formative measures of achievement. The converse of this is found when the work is not equally shared, when there is continuing conflict among the learners, and when the level of commitment to shared goals appears to be tapering off. Qualitative measures that tap the perspectives and feelings of the learners are an important source of data for formative evaluation, and fortunately they are very often part and parcel of the professional helping relationship. Once again, the slogan "Feelings Are Facts" very much applies to the value that should be accorded the subjective and affective responses of learners.

Summative Evaluation

Summative evaluation is concerned with both the process and the outcomes of teaching. It can be equated with the T (Testing) stage in the EDICT planning process (although very often evaluations that occur at the end of short teaching cycles are more formative in nature). The reality in human service practice is that the majority of teaching interventions are less structured than those conducted in professional education programs or professional development centers. Thus, while the achievement of learning outcomes may be checked, it is rarely done with norm-referenced measures that generate an evaluative grade, because the goal is seldom to compare individuals with one another. Rather, practice-based teaching is for the most part criterion-referenced and ungraded. The focus is on the ability of learners to achieve stated learning outcomes through repeated efforts, in a process known as mastery, or competency-based learning (Nored and Shelton, 1982; Cranton, 1989). This illustrates why clearly stated objectives can be important to the evaluation of teaching and learning, but Wlodkowski (1991) notes that competency and mastery can also be experienced by the learner as a subjective sense of accomplishment. This latter measure is of central importance in the human services, providing evaluative data to both practitioners and learners.

In developing a summative evaluation strategy there are several variables to consider. Data may be gathered from the perspective of learners, teachers, and others with a focus on the learning process and/or on the achievement of learning outcomes. In conducting a summative evaluation, it is possible to gather data from several perspectives: the views of the learners themselves, the judgments of the practitioner about the effectiveness of the teaching, and/or evaluations made by those who are involved with the learners after the teaching has taken place (these individuals might be family, friends, employers, or patients or clients in "back-home" situations). Summative evaluation is more robust when information is gathered from more than one of these sources, to contribute to a process of triangulation. This makes it possible to cross-check the data and to look for patterns or inconsistencies.

In seeking summative assessment data from a particular source, it becomes important to clarify the type of information that is being sought. One type of assessment might focus on facts regarding changes in the knowledge, attitudes, and skills of the learners. (Is there evidence to suggest that learning has taken place, and has this resulted in the desired changes in behavior?) A quite different assessment might be concerned with the extent to which the design of the learning experience was instrumental in producing the desired learning outcomes. (Did the learning design appear to be efficient and effective?)

In soliciting evaluative assessment data from the learners themselves, there are one or two key considerations to bear in mind. Many evaluations contain a question that asks them to rate their general degree of satisfaction with the learning event. This type of question is sometimes dismissed as a "happiness index" that yields data with little explanatory power, because it can become contaminated by extraneous factors. For example, learner reports of satisfaction may be due to their expressing pleasure that they were released from work to attend training, or it may mean that they enjoyed the amenities of the setting in which the teaching took place, or it might simply indicate that they enjoyed the opportunity to socialize and meet new friends.

All of these factors can contribute to a haze of positive feelings that develops at the conclusion of a learning experience. This can have the effect of skewing responses to assessment questions that focus on general satisfaction. Feelings of satisfaction may indeed contribute to the achievement of learning outcomes, but such ratings do not necessarily indicate that the stated learning outcomes were in fact achieved. This is the reason why some practitioners prefer to include both a summative evaluation at the end of the event and a follow-up, or "downstream," evaluation at some later date. This downstream evaluation may be described as a postsummative evaluation. It yields important data about the extent to which learning has become internalized and transferred, and it may reveal contextual factors that have influenced reinforcement of what was originally learned.

The practitioner also needs to take into account the type of data required by the various stakeholders in the evaluation process, as well as any practical or ethical constraints on the process. (Are there sufficient resources available to support the proposed evaluation? To what extent can the confidentiality of responses be assured?) Practitioners also need to be conscious of the fact that their own perspectives and attitudes may intrude on the process of gathering and assigning meaning to evaluative data. For example:

> A psychologist conducts an evaluation of a self-help group concerned with weight loss. He concludes that the group was ineffective, because the members eventually regained virtually all of the weight they had lost. Confronted with these findings, the members point out that what they gained from the group was not the loss of weight, but improved self-confidence and a better ability to help other people.

Another consideration is the extent to which learners can be made an integral part of the summative evaluation strategy. To the degree that learners feel some ownership of the evaluative process, they will be more motivated to share assessment data. In due course, this is also likely to further develop the ability of learners to monitor their own learning activities.

In concluding this discussion of formative evaluation, it should be noted that feedback gathered from learners as the process unfolds provides information that is vital to keeping the process on track. Formative data are also some of the most important tools human service professionals can use to continue developing their teaching skills. To the extent he or she can engage learners in the process of continuous teaching improvement, virtually any practitioner can improve his or her teaching skills. This reality further belies the notion that teachers are born and not made. The topic of continuing teaching development is given further attention in Chapter Nine.

Summative Evaluation Strategies

In more structured teaching situations, a simple pen-and-paper survey built on the goals of the learning event provides a practical way to collect evaluative data. Participants can be asked to rate on a continuum the extent to which they were able to achieve each of the stated learning objectives. Similarly, there can be a continuum to rate collective satisfaction with the event, as well as a place for anecdotal comments. For example, learners could be asked to state what they liked best and least about the learning event, or what they would have liked more of or less of in a particular session. In some situations the form may also include a question to gather learners' views on further learning needs. This is important in professional development workshops where the summative evaluation can also yield pre-formative data for future learning events.

Another evaluation approach, goal attainment scaling (Kiresuk and Garwick, 1979), may be used for both formative and summative evaluations. This is a particularly useful strategy, given the kinds of implicit teaching situations that frequently occur in human service practice. It is also a useful approach for assessing progress toward rather diffuse or global objectives that may be relatively difficult to measure (for instance, assessing progress toward the goal of improving the wellness practices of a group of senior citizens, or helping a person with emotional difficulties achieve greater independence).

A goal attainment scale form is illustrated in Figure 8.2. The technique involves the practitioner in teasing out sub-objectives that may contribute to the achievement of a broader learning outcome. In some situations the practitioner may work alone in compiling items for the scale; this may be necessary when there is only an implicit contract between teacher and learner. In other circumstances, where an explicit partnership has been forged between teacher and learner, both parties can work together in completing the goal attainment scale.

Each sub-objective is recorded in the space at the top of each column [A]. The T and L columns in this same cell allow the practitioner and the learners to record their respective ratings of the relative priority of each objective.

The next task is to identify a period of time within which measurable progress can be expected to have been made toward

Figure 8.2. Goal Attainment Scale Form.

	Objective 1 Sample: [A]			Objective 2 Press coverage of seniors' wellness program		
		T	L		T	L
	Rating			Rating	1	X
Less-than-expected outcomes	[D]			less than 20% increase		
Expected outcomes in [B] weeks/months	[C]			50% increase in coverage paper 6 months		
Better-than-expected outcomes	[E]			more than 60% increase		

achieving the learning objective **[B]**. A statement is then developed that outlines the expected and quantified results to be achieved within the specified time period **[C]**. The practitioner, working alone or in partnership with the learners, then develops two further statements. One statement describes less-than-expected results **[D]**, and the other better-than-expected results **[E]**. These two additional statements are entered on the form as indicated.

In order to follow this process, it may be helpful to track a practice example of the use of a goal attainment scale. The selected example assesses progress toward one sub-objective in a program to promote seniors' wellness (see Figure 8.2, Objective 2). An expected result of this program might be a 50 percent increase in the number of column inches devoted to the issue of senior health in a local newspaper. It is expected that this will be achieved within six months of the introduction of a variety of health promotion activities. More-than-expected results would consist of a 60 percent increase in column inches, and less-than-expected results would consist of a less than 20 percent increase. In this example, this outcome is seen to be an implicit objective of the practitioner's; therefore there is no priority recorded for the learning group involved. In another situation a core group of seniors might well be closely involved in this public education thrust; in that case the priority they give to this objective would be recorded in the appropriate slot on the scale.

Although goal attainment scaling retains a fair degree of subjectivity as an approach to evaluating learning outcomes, it does offer several advantages. In many situations it allows teachers and learners to more specifically identify what it is they are trying to accomplish and what sort of results they might expect to see within a certain time frame. Even though less-than-expected results might be achieved, the scale offers important feedback to both parties in the learning enterprise. This data can be used to identify any unanticipated barriers that may have interfered with the learning process, or it may lead to an exploration of why unrealistic expectations were established in the first place. A further benefit is that when learners are actively engaged in the development of goal and outcome statements, they learn to apply a tool that they can use to make their own assessments of their learning progress. This supports the pervasive goal of empowering people to become increasingly active, reflective, and self-directing in the management of their own learning.

Practitioners who use goal attainment scaling in implicit teaching and learning interventions have a way to measure progress in diffuse or complex situations. For example, in more nebulous activities, such as community education and development, the absence of measures of progress can contribute to professional frustration and burnout. Through goal attainment scaling, professionals who engage in these kinds of activities are pushed to clarify sub-objectives and to develop measures of progress.

The evaluation questions in Figure 8.3 may serve as a summary of the overall evaluation issues a practitioner needs to consider in planning an explicit teaching intervention or in taking full advantage of a more implicit learning opportunity.

Not all of the categories in this schema will apply to every teaching intervention. However, this matrix can be used to identify evaluation questions and strategies at each phase of any evaluation process. The information that is gathered may be used to assess learning outcomes, to gather feedback about the practitioner's effectiveness, or to yield data that may be used for both of these purposes.

Transfer of Learning

"Transfer of learning" is the term used to describe the various issues and strategies associated with "assuring that new abilities [that are learned] can be applied when the learner returns to the work [or home] environment" (Fox, 1984, p. 25).

People in the business of promoting continuing learning, including professionals in the human services, have become increasingly

Figure 8.3. Summary of Evaluation Questions.

	Pre-formative	Formative	Summational
Key questions to pose?			
Data needed?			
Whom to collect data from?			
How to collect? Qualitative and quantitative?			
How to collect? Methods?			
How to analyze and share results?			

skeptical about the on-the-job benefits of brief teaching interventions. This includes skepticism about the long-term benefits of a one-hour seminar as well as doubts about the impact of a one-day workshop. Even when such learning events are highly rated by the participants, there may be only limited transfer of the learning into situations in which it might actually be used. Concern with this issue has contributed to the development of a variety of strategies to increase the probability that teaching will result in enduring changes in behavior. Transfer of learning strategies are obviously not something that can only be introduced at the conclusion of a learning event. Rather, the question of transfer should be a consideration during the assessment, design, implementation, and evaluation phases of teaching, and during post-teaching follow-up activities as well. This is particularly evident in human service situations in which clients or patients are confronted with sustaining learning gains over a very long period of time (for example, in the case of the maintenance of long-term employment or life-long sobriety).

Transfer of learning issues during the assessment phase are those that explore the extent to which new learning is likely to fit with the personality of the learner or with the norms of the learner's family or other network. Such networks might include people with whom the person works, a social support network, or the organizational culture of the person's employer. New learning that is markedly at odds with the individual's interpersonal style or with the values and attitudes of his or her social or workplace environment is likely to fade quickly. For example:

A woman who had been assaulted by her husband spends some time in a transition house. During that period she rebuilds some of her self-confidence and learns ways to be more assertive with her partner. However, when she returns home this new behavior is undermined by her mother-in-law and sister and is attacked by her husband. She quickly reverts to her previous position of submission.

These kinds of transfer of learning problems may indicate that teaching is not the appropriate intervention. A more directive, managerial intervention may be necessary in some situations, while in others a more participatory approach may be required. Transfer of learning difficulties will result from an inaccurate assessment that teaching is the required intervention.

A practical way to predict potential transfer of learning hurdles is to use a strategy known as force field analysis, an approach derived from the work of the group dynamics theorist Kurt Lewin (1951). This approach is based on the assumption that the way things are—the status quo—in a given situation represents a balance between the forces for change and the forces against it. Lewin's suggestion is that people who wish to bring about change often attempt to do so by escalating the various pressures that might push a situation in the direction they prefer. Lewin also observes that such demands for change tend to produce resistance, in the form of mounting pressures in the opposite direction, as those who are being pressured struggle to maintain the status quo. For example, a single parent of an adolescent might well respond to the child's pressure for a later curfew by clamping down even more harshly on the existing rules.

Lewin states that it is easier to bring about change by reducing the forces against it than by increasing the forces for it. This, he says, may be accomplished by determining the needs that are threatened by the proposed change and finding ways these may be met even if a change in the status quo is introduced. To return to the previous example, the single parent may feel additional responsibility for the child because she has to carry these duties alone, and she may perceive a potential for additional stigma and guilt if her child gets into trouble. The mother's needs—to feel responsible and to feel some measure of parental control—have to be met if a change in curfew is to become acceptable to her.

The force field analysis approach to problem solving begins by listing the driving and restraining forces that oppose each other to create the status quo in a given situation (see Figure 8.4). The next step is to rate the relative potency of these forces on a five-point scale. In this way it is possible to identify the most influential restraining forces. The final step is to use problem-solving strategies to find ways to meet the needs that are threatened by the proposed changes. These needs underlie the more potent restraining forces. In using this strategy to assess the driving and restraining forces affecting the transfer of a specific piece of learning, it is important that restraining forces not be dismissed with the pejorative label "resistance." Rather, it should be accepted that the restraining forces are present because some felt needs are threatened by the introduction of the new learning.

Figure 8.4 illustrates an assessment of the restraining forces that might confront a person who has completed a course on healthy

Figure 8.4. Force Field Analysis Worksheet.

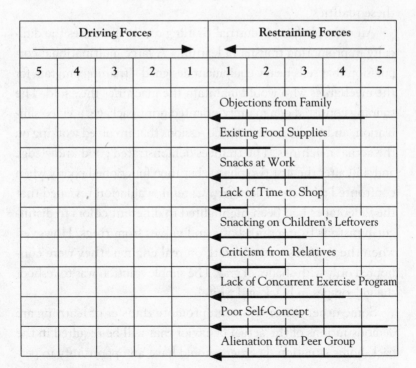

nutrition. The figure reflects some of the factors that might work against this person's being able to change his or her cooking and eating habits within the context of family and home. In this example, the length of the various arrows indicates the estimated potency of the various restraining forces. Here the lack of support from family members and the fragile self-esteem of the learner are important factors that are likely to constrain the transfer of learning from the course on nutrition.

There are several ways in which the probability of transfer of learning can be increased by the manner in which teaching is planned and conducted. First, to the maximum extent possible, the learning environment should reproduce the context in which the new behaviors will be needed. This means that during the assessment phase there should be a careful examination of all facets of the situation in which the new learning will be applied, and there should be practice opportunities that reflect these realities.

An example from industrial training nicely illustrates the difficulty in promoting transfer of learning. A large multinational corporation that sells heavy equipment designed a training program for the mechanics who would maintain the machines they sold. The training consisted of a mastery-oriented print package, a video simulation, and finally some practice sessions that involved working on the actual machines. The trainees demonstrated good knowledge and skill after the first two phases, but then functioned poorly when confronted with the machinery. Careful evaluation revealed that the videotapes had been highlighted in different colors to distinguish pistons from crankshafts and valves from rings. However, when the trainees went to work on real engines, they were confronted only with shades of gray. The simple solution was to reshoot the videotapes in black and white!

Some other factors that can promote transfer of learning are demonstrations of the actual behavior that will be required in the back-home situation. Learners should have an opportunity to perform these behaviors during the learning event. This underscores the need for demonstration and involvement (EDICT) as important elements in teaching.

Summative evaluation may often reveal that what was taught was not in fact learned, and this can point to the need for what has been described as "overteaching." This involves repeated practice of new learnings so that they can be produced fluently in those situations in which they are required. It is all too easy for practitioners to forget how much time and how many errors were involved in arriving at their own current level of performance. One-shot teaching is unlikely to produce embedded learning.

Transfer can also be supported by working with the intact social systems within which the learners will use their new knowledge, skills, or values. These systems include families, work groups, and communities. Fox (1984) notes: "A central problem in the transfer of learning from the workshop environment to the work setting seems to involve the failure to develop a sense within learners of how to integrate new competencies and performances into not only their personality, but also the structure and process that characterize their work environment" (p. 29). Similarly, family therapists have long understood that many difficulties encountered by individual family members can only be addressed through shifts in the behavior of all family members.

Another example serves to illustrate how this kind of difficulty in learning transfer may be successfully overcome:

A plan is developed to have public health nurses learn how to take on different roles and responsibilities within their health unit. In order to increase the chances of transfer of learning, this teaching intervention includes the other human service practitioners who work with the nurses on interprofessional teams.

Another way to support learning transfer during a teaching intervention is to promote conceptual learning, or higher-level learning, rather than informational learning. This enables the learner to act effectively in real-life situations that were not sufficiently approximated by the situations encountered in training. For example:

> A training program for telephone crisis line volunteers helps them learn not just the mechanics of how to respond to certain categories of callers, but also the psychological nature of crisis and some of the dynamics that lead to threats of suicide.

Certain learning activities can help to build bridges between the actual learning event and the back-home application of what has been learned. One such activity is to help learners develop what are known in industrial training as "job aids." These are checklists, slogans, or other reminders that help the learner recall desired behavior once a formal learning event is completed. These might be posted over a workstation or desk, in a meeting room, or even on a refrigerator. Job aids are, in effect, mini mission statements or prescriptions for success; they may be developed from principles generated as a product of experiential and other learning activities. Here are a couple of examples:

> A probation officer is given a one-year assignment to teach in a college program for training new corrections staff. He finds that he tends to relate to his adult students in a somewhat rigid and remote fashion, so he posts a quote from Sam Postlethwaite over his desk: "Students are a lot like people." This provides him with a salutary reminder.

> A practitioner finds the acronym EDICT to be a useful job aid, reminding her of the elements she should consider in planning teaching interventions. Therefore she develops a planning sheet with spaces to record activities associated with each of the five phases of the EDICT planning process.

Many human service professionals would resist suggesting job aids or similar devices to those who come to them for advice. This is interesting in light of the fact that many members of mutual aid groups find such slogans or job aids particularly helpful. Some examples include "One day at a time," "Pin the tail on your own donkey," and "Take it easy." A variation on this approach is to ask learners to write a letter to themselves describing what learnings they expect to have implemented within a specified time period following a learning event. The practitioner collects these "learning transfer contracts" and mails them out to learners at the specified date to serve as a personal reminder of the work to be done. Concept diagrams or idea maps can also be used in the back-home context as a job aid that reminds learners of the interrelationship between various new learnings.

Another way to reinforce transfer of learning is through follow-up teaching sessions that fine-tune the application of prior learnings and troubleshoot implementation difficulties not previously identified through the force field analysis.

Diffusion of Innovations

In the human services there are many situations in which the learning goal is not just to teach a few individuals, but rather to have the new learnings diffuse more generally throughout a community, or beyond. An example is a self-management approach for helping people learn how to cope with arthritis (McGowan, 1990). The Canadian approach to this program involved developing a manual for discussion leaders and recruiting and training people to use the manual in the facilitation of group learning. These facilitators brought together groups of people with arthritis to learn self-management skills through a mutual aid, or self-help, approach. This model spread to over one hundred communities in British Columbia and Yukon, and later to all the other Canadian provinces and several other countries.

This is an important success story, but there are other examples of innovations that were notably slow to be adopted. One classic case was the efforts of the British Navy to control scurvy (Mosteller, 1981). In the fifteenth century, ships on long voyages might return with as few as one-third of their original crew, the rest having succumbed to scurvy. In 1601 an English sea captain in command of four ships sailing to India required each of the crew on the largest vessel to consume a certain quantity of lemon juice each day. The majority of these men remained healthy, while those on the other boats experienced high mortality. However, this experiment was not even replicated until 1747, and the consumption of citrus juice was not made mandatory until 1795—time lags in the adoption process of 146 years and 48 years respectively!

There are numerous other examples of time delays in the adoption-diffusion process; these eventually triggered a whole field of studies of the diffusion process (Rogers, 1983; Rogers and Shoemaker, 1984; Edwards, Tindale, Heath, and Posavac, 1990). The findings from these studies have significance for teaching in the human services, because frequently the aim of a teaching intervention is to spread the results to more people than just those directly involved in the learning event. The aim is not just for gradual contagion through a process of "each one teach one," but rather to embed new practices within the culture of a community. For example, in community education and development the goal may be to teach community leaders, who can in turn influence the knowledge, attitudes, and skills of other members of their community. In this sense the goal is not just for learners to transfer their learning into their back-home behavior, but also for them to transfer or spread their learning to others. Adoption-diffusion studies indicate ways this latter type of transfer occurs and factors that can facilitate this process.

In order to understand how new practices spread throughout a community, it is useful to recognize that there are at least four categories of people who play a part in the process (Rogers, 1983, p. 247): innovators, who initiate the change; pacesetters, who endorse the innovation; the middle majority, who come to accept the new practices; and finally the laggards, who resist changing their present behavior. This process indicates that it may be a very small number of people who are among the first to grasp and implement a new idea. Further, this new learning may not extend very rapidly, or indeed at all, to other people in the community.

Such lags can occur because innovators often tend to be marginal members of mainstream institutions. This situation is noted in an observation by Machiavelli (1961): "There is nothing more difficult to undertake, more dangerous to conduct, or more uncertain of its success than the introduction of a new way of life. The innovator makes enemies of all those who did well under the old order, and he can expect only lukewarm support from those who may prosper under the new partly because they fear the innovator's enemies" (p. 51).

An understanding of how ideas are transmitted and endorsed is particularly useful for practitioners involved in public and community education. Such an understanding can help professionals identify those people who may be able to generate new knowledge or practices. It can also alert the practitioner to the need to identify others who have achieved or been ascribed credibility: these gatekeepers are strategically located to either facilitate or impede the spread of new ideas and practices to the majority of community members. For this reason these people may need to be included in the initial learning event so that they can use their positions of authority to promote the diffusion and adoption of new behaviors. In practice, the adoption-diffusion process might flow in the following way:

A group of people learning to live with AIDS finds that they are able to sustain an optimum level of wellness by following a certain diet protocol [innovators]. Initially this diet is not accepted by the medical establishment. However, some time later a leading heart surgeon [pacesetter] notes how well his own son does by following this protocol, and he begins to champion this approach with other physicians [middle majority].

In developing ways to promote the diffusion of new learning, the practitioner may find it helpful to consider the following five influential factors. The first is the extent to which the new behavior is perceived to be better than the old way of doing things. This is termed *relative advantage*. The key is that other learners, in the community, must be in a position to see that the new practice is indeed more beneficial than the old way of doing things.

A second factor is the extent to which the new behavior is seen as *compatible* with the existing practices, needs, and experience of the social or work-related group it is introduced into. It is important to begin identifying these existing mores during the assessment phase, so that learning outcomes can be developed that are likely to be transferable beyond the learning event.

The third factor is the perceived *complexity* of the new behavior. To the extent that it is perceived to be understandable and easy to adhere to, it will be more likely to be implemented or adopted. A fourth factor has to do with the new behavior's *trialability:* the extent to which it can be experimented with on a limited basis.

Finally, new behaviors will diffuse more quickly if they are visible to others in the social network: thus the fifth factor is the *observability* of the innovation. Observability ensures that the positive outcomes are visible to others, who can also learn from the modeled behavior. The following are some examples of how failure to take into account these five factors might adversely effect the transfer and diffusion of newly learned behavior:

Relative advantage: A social worker teaches a course in budgeting skills to a number of single parents in the same low-income housing complex. The participants are able to improve their financial management skills; however, their practices are not adopted by the other residents, who feel that any savings they accumulate could easily be "ripped off." They also see no advantage to postponing the gratification of instant spending.

Compatibility: A school teacher in a remote northern island community is appalled to find that his mixed-grade students spend their recess time hunting and killing songbirds with slingshots. He tries to help them explore some of the ethical issues connected with this pastime and to learn some different behaviors. Shortly thereafter, a delegation of fathers arrives to denounce this teaching intervention, pointing out that the kids were "only learning how to hunt birds"—a valued skill on the island, where seabirds are a staple of the diet.

Complexity: The nurses in an extended care facility are taught how to use computers to keep track of client records. However, some nurses, particularly those who have been in practice for more than twenty years, are intimidated by the new technology, which they find complicated and confusing.

Trialability: Staff members in a government human service department learn some new ways to run their departmental meetings. They hope that these new approaches will be tested in a single department, but they resist when asked to implement these procedures as a general practice.

Observability: Trainees in a sheltered workshop learn procedures for packing a line of products into shipping cartons. However, their performance varies widely. The vocational counselor determines that part of the problem is that the work stations are arranged in such a way that those who are performing poorly are unable to observe how the high performers do their job.

In each of these examples, an understanding of some of the factors that can influence the diffusion of new learning might have enabled the practitioner to achieve a wider adoption of the new practices.

In order to promote the spread of learning to larger populations, it can be helpful for practitioners to understand the various stages in the adoption-diffusion process. The first stage, *awareness*, is achieved when the targeted group of learners develops general knowledge regarding an innovative practice. This is followed by *interest*, which is manifested by the request for more detailed information about the practice. In the third stage learners become involved in mental trials or testing of the new idea, in order to arrive at an *evaluation* of its potential value. In the event that this mental trial is positive, then the stage is set for experimentation, or actual *trial*. Finally, if this too is judged to be satisfactory, this leads to continued use, or *adoption*, of the practice.

This model can provide a useful structure around which to build a public education program. For example, many of the educational programs designed to promote safer sex practices, including the use of condoms, exemplify this sequence of activities.

An alternative way to think about the challenges involved in transferring learning is to consider the position of various people who may be affected by the new behaviors. A model developed by Peter Block (1987), illustrated in Figure 8.5, can help both the practitioner and the learner think through the position of a range of stakeholders. Block suggests that in seeking to ensure that new learning does translate into innovative behavior, it is helpful to consider the position of various stakeholders along the dimensions of trust and agreement. Those persons in the learner's social or workplace environment that the learner trusts and who agree with the introduction of new behaviors are characterized as allies. They will tend to support the proposed innovation. However, there will also be those who are trusted by the learner, but who do not agree with the proposed changes. These people are termed opponents. They can be a valuable source of information about the nature of the resistance that may be encountered, and they can help the practitioner refine innovations in ways that make them more acceptable to pacesetters and the middle majority. (In effect, opponents can

Figure 8.5. Allies and Adversaries: Block's Model of Innovation.

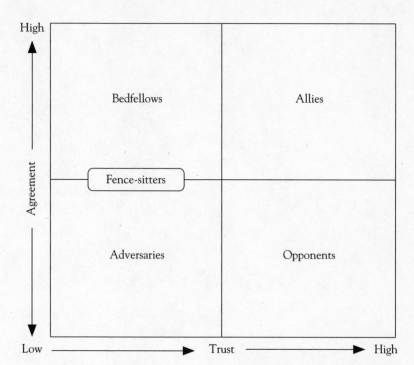

identify the forces against change that should be addressed in a force field analysis. See Figure 8.4.)

Block identifies three other kinds of players in the innovation process: bedfellows, fence-sitters, and adversaries. Bedfellows indicate agreement with the proposed change but cannot be relied upon. Fence-sitters are also untrustworthy, and they are reluctant to take a position on whether they agree or disagree with the innovation. Adversaries are both untrustworthy and opposed to the proposed change.

To conclude, this chapter has briefly touched on some basic considerations in the evaluation of teaching, some principles to consider in promoting the transfer of learning back to the real world, and some strategies for diffusing learning to a broader audience beyond the learners who are directly involved in a teaching intervention.

9

Helping Through Teaching: Enhancing Professional Practice

This chapter reviews some of the themes covered earlier in the book and addresses some of the ways human service professionals can meet the career-long challenge of improving their teaching skills. The discussion includes an examination of topics currently of interest to both human service professionals and adult educators, followed by a selective review of the innovations in educational technology that will influence teaching and learning in the human services in the immediate future.

The Place of Teaching in the Human Services

The argument was made at the outset of this book that much of the day-to-day practice of helping professionals involves teaching interventions and the facilitation of learning. Further, many teaching activities are embedded in the other work of human service professionals. These activities include intake, assessment, negotiation of client and practitioner roles, definition of goals, and evaluation of outcomes. Many practitioners are inadequately prepared to perform these multiple teaching tasks with the wide range of people they serve. Targets for teaching in human service practices range from individual clients, patients, and colleagues to families, other small groups, and the larger community. Such a wide and varied client base would pose a challenge to an adult education specialist, let alone a professional who has been given little or no preparation for his or her teaching responsibilities.

Fortunately, the close parallels between the traditional helping professions and the field of adult education mean that human service professionals already have many of the understandings, skills, and values that contribute to effective teaching. For example, many individuals come to the human service professions with excellent skills in communication and relationship building. Such individuals need only to modestly reframe their existing repertoire of professional skills so they more directly address teaching and learning, while adding some of the additional teaching competencies discussed in this book. The most important attitude practitioners can bring to this exercise is a strong belief that effective teaching is more than just an innate talent. Teaching is a skill that can be learned and improved, and even practitioners who are innately gifted as teachers can continue to develop this skill.

A key element of teaching improvement is a critical awareness of the assumptions and skills that drive teaching interventions—and the impact these have on learners. Increasing awareness of one's innate teaching style, coupled with the conscientious study of emerging understanding of adult learning processes, can lead to continuous teaching improvement.

In summary, the message of this book is that practitioners are teachers *and* learners; the ability to teach is not just a gift from God; there are tangible ways for any professional to improve his or her teaching; and lifelong, critically reflective, self-directed learning is an important activity for professionals, as well as for the people they work with.

Continuing Teaching Improvement

Human service professionals who invest time and effort in the continuous development of their teaching skills tend to have the following characteristics:

- They readily accept the parallels between teaching and the other ways they promote growth and change in their clients' lives.

- They have a keen eye for spotting teaching and learning opportunities, and they respond to these in a timely way.

- They take the time to clarify their own assumptions about how learning takes place and about how this should influence their teaching.

- They know how to plan teaching interventions based on an assessment of needs, a coherent design, and systems for formative and summative evaluation. They are likewise able to cultivate and facilitate learning in situations that call for emergent design or emancipatory learning.

- They know and use ways to transfer, reinforce, and, in some situations, diffuse learning in the back-home environment.

- They believe that people are learners—that people have learned, are learning, and will continue to learn in the future.

- Finally, they tend to be creative, flexible, resourceful, and proactive in the pursuit of their own continuing learning projects.

These qualities may be augmented in the following way: practitioners will be more effective facilitators of learning to the extent that they bring flexibility and responsiveness (Brookfield, 1990) to their teaching practice, are aware of their teaching styles (Heimlich and Norland, 1994) and are clear about the beliefs and assumptions they bring to their teaching (King and Kitchener, 1994).

Flexibility and Responsiveness

Practitioners who embrace their role as teachers and facilitators of learning will find that they become increasingly adroit at identifying and anticipating teaching opportunities. This makes it possible to develop more effective teaching interventions that can target a range of learners.

A growing enthusiasm for teaching can carry certain dangers, however. For instance, there is the possibility that as professionals become increasingly enamored with teaching as a potent practice intervention they may become correspondingly more rigid or doctrinaire in their use of teaching strategies. It is therefore important to stress that there is no cookbook approach to teaching that accommodates the teaching style of all professionals and is suitable for all learners and contexts. Rather, each practitioner brings to his or her teaching activities a unique personal style, individual strengths and perspectives, and specific content expertise. And in turn, these need to be tailored to the unique characteristics of individual learners and the particular context of each teaching intervention.

Teaching Philosophy

Human service professionals may be concerned by the call to develop and articulate a philosophy to base their teaching on. To allay these fears, it should be understood that the aim is not to start with a well-crafted, fully coherent statement. Rather, the goal is to surface and set down the attitudes and assumptions a practitioner already brings to teaching. This becomes the baseline for continuing reflection and teaching development.

In this connection, Brookfield (1990) urges those who teach to be aware of their purpose and philosophy for teaching: "Develop a theory of practice, a critical rationale for why you are doing what you are doing. . . . Without a personal organizing vision we are rudderless vessels tossed around on the waves and currents of whatever political whims and fashions are prevalent at the time. Our practice may win us career advancement, but it will be lacking in the innate meaning that transforms teaching from a function into a passion" (p. 195).

Another key to effective, responsive teaching is for the professional to be constantly alert to opportunities that offer a chance to learn more about their own particular identity as a teacher. These situations should promote consideration of how the teacher's interpersonal style influences his or her learners and the learning process. For example, many people have certain expectations, developed from their early schooling experience, of the role of teacher. These often include a belief that teachers should always be in full control of the learning and that they should be the source of answers for every question. Self-limiting beliefs of this kind can cramp the development of optimum and flexible learning. The goal is not for the practitioner to become a standard-brand, bionic teacher, but rather that he or she develop a stance of constantly probing to expand awareness of his or her style of teaching and personal assumptions about learning. This ongoing process of reflection can contribute to a fresh appreciation for alternative teaching approaches. The ability to remain flexible and creative in responding to each new teaching opportunity is of paramount importance in the process of continuing teaching improvement.

Together with teaching skills, there are certain value stances and personality traits that are characteristic of effective practitioners. The first of these is exemplified by the helping professional who believes that he or she should control personal ego needs throughout the duration of the teaching or learning experience. To the extent that a practitioner has a need to take credit for being the sole influence on what someone else has learned, he or she detracts from the accomplishment of the learner. It is the learner who learns, and the learner who takes action on the basis of that learning. Effective teachers can let go of any need to own these accomplishments.

(And this is equally true of the other helping relationships that characterize human service practice.)

It is also desirable for practitioners to remain aware of their own belief systems and the way these personal paradigms influence the way they teach. This is of particular importance when there are subtle but important differences between the teacher's and the learner's frames of reference. It is often easier for practitioners to recognize these differences when there is a wide discrepancy between their own paradigms and those of the learners. But these differences become much more difficult to recognize when the shadings between the perspective of practitioner and learner are more subtle. In such situations the professional, from a position of power, may perceive that the learner's narrowly *differing* interpretation of a situation constitutes a narrowly *incorrect* perspective. The influential position of helping professionals makes it possible for them to colonize learners into accepting their—the dominant party's—belief system. This potential for a "tyranny of ideology" was neatly captured by the author Doris Lessing (1972) in a warning she gives to students in formal systems of education:

> You are in the process of being indoctrinated. We have not yet evolved a system of education that is not a system of indoctrination. We are sorry, but it is the best we can do. What you are now being taught here is an amalgam of prejudices and the choices of this particular culture. The slightest look at history will show you how impermanent these must be. You are being taught by people who have been able to accommodate themselves to a regime of thought laid down by their predecessors. It is a self-perpetuating system. Those of you who are more robust and individual than others will be encouraged to leave and find ways of educating yourselves—educating your own judgement. Those of you who stay must remember, always and at all times, that you are

being molded to fit into the narrow and particular needs
of this particular society" [pp. xv–xvi].

The same observation might be made for those who become
consumers of the formal network of human services—the Lessing
quote might carry a salutary warning for those who are becoming
patients or clients (Illich, 1987).

Brookfield (1986) expresses a related concern with the following observation: "Effective facilitation is present when adults come
to appreciate the relative, provisional and contextual nature of public and private knowledge and when they come to understand that
the belief system, value frameworks and moral codes informing their
conduct are culturally constructed" (p. 283).

Brookfield is speaking primarily of adult learners, but this same
observation could apply equally to professionals who teach in the
human services.

The two preceding quotations underscore that teaching can never
be values-free. Human service professionals have the position, the
power, and the access to powerful new communication technologies
that give them the opportunity to shape—or overdetermine—the
learning process. In the past, teaching in practice was often so casually
undertaken that there was little chance of impinging on learners'
rights to self-determination. Today, however, skillfully designed but
unethical teaching interventions have the real potential to limit the
free will of individuals, groups, and communities. This is apparent in
the considerable power of the advertising industry in shaping public
opinion and manipulating consumer needs. It is also evident in the
use of highly structured and coercive training methods to prepare
impressionable adolescents for jobs in the fast-food industry. This
training can be so influential that these young people become pro-
grammed as smiling, robotic extensions of the touch-sensitive key-
board. Similar kinds of indoctrination are found in some of the more
coercive and manipulative training and workfare programs required
of those in need of financial and other forms of public assistance. Each

of these situations poses the question of whether such indoctrination represents an unfair intrusion upon personal rights or the legitimate right of interest groups to shape the behavior of others.

There is no simple formula to resolve each of the ethical and value dilemmas that can arise for human service practitioners. However, professionals whose practice involves teaching should maintain a scrupulous and continuing inventory of their beliefs and the other frames of reference they bring to this work. A useful strategy is for the practitioner to develop the kind of brief written statement outlining his or her personal teaching philosophy that was discussed earlier. Such a statement makes the practitioner's philosophy more accessible for discussion by peers, and perhaps learners, and it also provides a baseline for making periodic comparisons of the values proclaimed and those practiced.

A few specific value dilemmas that tend to recur in human service teaching include the following:

- Should a teaching intervention be based primarily on the felt needs of the learners, the perceived needs identified by the professional or his or her employer, or by some combination of felt and perceived needs?

- Under what conditions is it acceptable for the professional to engage in implicit teaching if the learner is not able to fully comprehend what is taking place?

- Is it acceptable to teach to involuntary learners? If so, under what conditions? What about quasi-involuntary learners, who must participate in the teaching session if they are to receive a needed service?

- Who should decide what is to be taught: learners, practitioners, or those who hire or fund the professionals?

- Teaching certain knowledge and skills to one group of learners may thereby disadvantage others who do not have access to the same learning opportunities. How should these kinds of dilemmas be resolved?

- What should a practitioner do if colleagues feel that the content of his or her teaching infringes on their professional territory? What information should *not* be shared with consumers?

- What guidelines cover the confidentiality of the interactions that take place during teaching and learning sessions?

- Do certain teaching programs have the effect of cooling off legitimate dissent (Freire's "education for domestication")?

- How potent should the teaching strategy be? Is it acceptable if it infringes on self-determination? What rewards and reinforcements are acceptable?

Other useful guidelines to ensure ethical teaching practices may be found in the codes of ethics for various human service professions. These codes may be reviewed, particularly from the perspective of what they suggest about ethical teaching practices and the rights of clients as learners.

Those who wish to further explore the ethical issues related to teaching interventions might use the preceding questions to create a values clarification exercise. These questions could then be used a tool to enable a group of professionals to identify ethical issues and practice guidelines for teaching in their particular profession or setting.

Continuous Professional Development

It was noted in Chapter Eight that one of the most effective ways for practitioners to improve their teaching is by learning from learners. The development of a partnership relationship between practitioner and learner has been recommended as one means to foster learners' capacity to be increasingly self-directed (Vella, 1994). These learning partnerships also offer practitioners a rich source of information on ways to improve their teaching, by providing continuous formative evaluation about the teaching process from the learner's perspective.

Data from learners, from peer observers, and from video recordings can be used to identify areas for further teaching improvement. In order to support this process, three competency profiles have been included in this book (see Resources). These checklists cover teaching and facilitation skills, group facilitation skills, and self-directed continuing professional development. These three assessment profiles have been included to help the practitioner assemble data for a personal plan of ongoing teaching improvement. Skills for which these checklists indicate there is a need for improvement may be plotted on a goal attainment scale (see Figure 8.2) so that teaching improvement may be tracked over a specified period of time. For example, a practitioner might decide that he or she needs to improve skills in eliciting learning needs from learners. An expected outcome over a period of six months might be for the practitioner to have moved from soliciting learning needs in less than one-third of interventions to making these assessments two-thirds of the time. An example of the diverse teaching and teaching improvement methods of human service professionals is evident in the following example:

A consulting psychologist employed by a federal law enforcement agency engages in the following diverse range of teaching activities as part of his practice. On a regular basis he is involved in individual and group debriefing sessions to help line officers learn how to manage stress triggered by traumatic events. He is also frequently involved in helping witnesses learn how to present evidence effectively and in helping officers learn to deal with personal and family

difficulties. In addition, he is a standing member of the public education committee of an organization that explains police activities to
community groups. For each of these activities, the psychologist
uses a wide variety of methods to gather information about the
effectiveness of his teaching, and on this basis he establishes annual
teaching improvement goals.

Future Trends and Challenges

It is always hazardous to suggest what the future may hold during
times of social, economic, political, and technological turbulence,
but it seems safe to predict that the links between the adult education and human service professions will continue to grow. In part
this is likely to occur because teaching and learning are increasingly
recognized as integral to so much of the practice of helping professionals. The synergy that already exists between teaching and
human service practice is likely to be further strengthened by the
growing understanding of the process of learning and its facilitation.
The future of the relationship between adult education and the
human services remains opaque, but it does seem that two existing
developments are likely to gain, or at least sustain, momentum.
These are a growing attention to (1) learner-centered learning that
emphasizes self-direction; active, collaborative learning; and critical, constructivist thinking; and (2) transformative learning. A further catalyst for continuing developments in these areas is likely to
come from the advent of increasingly potent and accessible educational technologies.

Lifelong and Self-Directed Learning

The term "lifelong learning" began to gain currency following the
publication of the influential UNESCO report *Learning to Be*
(Faure, 1972). In the intervening years, recurrent lifelong learning has been afforded increased attention with growing public

recognition of accelerating changes in the job market. These changes have generated the need for frequent retraining to meet the shifting demands of new jobs and alternative career paths. At the same time, the world has experienced an exponential growth in all types of knowledge—continuous learning has become a necessity for people to remain current in their understanding of themselves and their world.

It has been noted that human service practitioners need to be involved in a process of lifelong learning in order to upgrade their disciplinary and teaching abilities. This learning should include both formal professional development programs and workplace learning that is an outgrowth of reflective practice (Baskett and Marsick, 1992). Lifelong learning is likewise important for social service consumers, who are also experiencing the impact of socio-economic, political, and technological change. Given these realities, it is important for teaching interventions to be conducted in a way that increases the ability of human service consumers to become lifelong learners. In effect, a subtext in all practice teaching should be a commitment by the professional not just to teaching, but to enabling the learner to increasingly direct his or her own continuing learning activities (Grow, 1991).

This overarching goal can be realized by first helping learners recognize and value the full range of their past and present formal and informal learning activities. Self-confidence is vital to optimum continuing learning, and practitioners can help build self-esteem by enabling learners to reframe and reclaim some of their past learning achievements. In this way these people can build the confidence necessary to take full advantage of both formal and informal learning opportunities in the future.

The ability to assume increasing responsibility for lifelong learning has become an even more central life skill, given the factors mentioned above. For example, being able to take full advantage of dynamic new communication technologies to support continuing learning is a valuable survival skill. In the parlance of the day, everybody needs to know how to drive on the information superhigh-way—and how to bushwhack their own side roads as they pursue their learning journeys.

Practitioners have a vitally important role to play in helping to rehabilitate people who, while they may not have experienced much success as students, can become excellent lifelong and self-directed learners. In effect, this position suggests that the way in which teaching is conducted may be as important as the content that is taught. It follows that one of the important questions to ask about any teaching encounter is the extent to which it serves to enhance or diminish the learner's ability to engage in lifelong, self-guided learning.

Cooperative Learning

Cooperative or collaborative learning is learning that is accom-plished by groups of learners; it is rooted in the belief that learn-ing is inherently social and that inquiry is a basic learning process (Whipple, 1987). Cooperative learning strategies grow from the understanding that learners have accumulated life experiences that can be an important learning resource when shared with others, and an appreciation that teaching is one of the more powerful means of learning. Cooperative learning may be defined in the fol-lowing way: "Cooperative Learning [is] a learner-centered instruc-tional process in which small, intentionally selected groups of 3–5 [learners] work interdependently on a well-defined learning task" (Cuseo, 1992, p. 4).

The assumptions behind cooperative learning are that learning is an active, constructive process; it depends on providing rich and challenging contexts to the learner; learners are diverse; and learn-ing is inherently social (Smith and MacGregor, 1992). The inter-esting aspect to this approach is that it is essentially an application of group work, which has for a very long time been a cornerstone of many forms of human service practice. In this respect cooperative, collaborative learning is a contribution to the discipline of adult education that has been pioneered and developed within the context of the human service professions.

Explicit cooperative learning strategies are presently used for the most part in the education of human service professionals, but implicit group strategies are very much part of the daily facilitation of learning by practitioners. This is evident in the majority of the examples of group teaching given in earlier chapters. In the future, self-aware, proactive learners will be able to take advantage of innovative communication technologies to forge new learning alliances.

Critical Thinking and Transformational Learning

Critical thinking was mentioned in earlier chapters. It is the general term used to describe the efforts of teachers who are working to help themselves and learners develop skills in critical reflection. Critical reflection does include higher-order thinking skills such as analysis, synthesis, and evaluation; but it also embraces the capacity to blend action and reflection (praxis), creativity, and a zest for ambiguity. Meyers (1986) stresses "the ability to make sense of new [and complex] experiences and to envision possibilities outside one's own immediate experiences" (p. 26).

Brookfield (1987) underscores the need to examine internal processes that may act to limit the meanings ascribed to new experiences: "Critical thinking comprises two inter-related processes: identifying and challenging assumptions and imagining and exploring alternatives" (p. 229).

There are two reasons why it is important for those who teach in the human services to help people develop their critical thinking abilities. First, one of the distinguishing characteristics of a connoisseur, or excellent practitioner, is his or her ability to be constantly engaged in a cycle of action and reflection. These premier professionals tend to be constantly monitoring and connecting all the qualitative and quantitative data available to them. They use this data to construct theories to modify their subsequent actions, and then they again observe their results (Benner, 1983, 1984; Brookfield, 1993). In this way there is an intimate link between the ability to engage in critical thinking and the ability to engage in self-directed learning. Together, critical reflection and self-direction characterize practitioners who develop the highest levels of expert professional performance.

The second reason to foster an ability to engage in critical reflection is that clients and patients who are consumers of human services may tend to be, or become, trapped by self-limiting beliefs about themselves or their social circumstances. A lack of critical consciousness can leave people fenced in by the assumptions they have made about themselves or about the reality and potential of their social situations. Learners may also become immobilized if they are unable to find a simple, prescriptive way to approach the social, physical, or psychological challenges they confront. Those who are more dualistic in their thinking may prefer simple rote memorization of a series of action steps, but these concrete steps may not be helpful given the unique and ephemeral nature of many real-life challenges. For example:

In a support group for women who had undergone mastectomies, a professional teaches a structured version of the grieving process and discusses only one way to deal with the reactions of family and friends. The learners find that this standardized approach does little to help them deal with the realities of their unique physical and social situations.

A training course for social workers responsible for investigating alleged child abuse attempts to teach a standard investigatory approach. However, learners who already have a good deal of practice experience find that this prescriptive model does not take into account the complex contextual factors that tend to give each investigation a unique character.

Professionals who find themselves in these kinds of teaching situations may find that consumers have been socialized to expect them, as "experts," to provide concrete solutions to complex issues. In our answer-oriented culture, which takes its cues from the world of formal education, it is all too easy for the practitioner to fall into the trap of trying to meet these kinds of learner expectations. In order to avoid this pitfall, professionals can use the assessment phase to tease out those learning needs that are not satisfied by formulaic responses. These are the kinds of needs that can only be addressed by learners who have the ability and the opportunity to engage in critical thinking and problem solving. In our previous examples this goal might be fostered by restructuring the approach as follows:

> In a support group for women who have undergone mastectomies, the practitioner makes sure that the group includes both women who have just experienced surgery and women who have been living with the condition for some time. Members are encouraged to share their own response to their condition as well as the reactions of family and friends. They also share coping strategies that have been more and less successful for them, and later these are incorporated into a handbook for those living with the condition.

> In a training course for social workers responsible for investigating alleged child abuse, there is a heavy emphasis on experiential methods. These include case studies, print and video accounts of critical incidents, and role-playing. The experiential knowledge generated from the participants is combined with professional know-how from the practitioner. Together this forms the data upon which the learners generate a series of job aids, including a personalized list of questions to consider in approaching their daily work.

Practitioners work not only with individuals to promote their ability to engage in critical reflection, they also do this with groups and communities. In many situations the goal is to enable learners to function with greater autonomy and for them to be capable of exercising influence over factors that affect their well-being. It is not always easy to promote this kind of critical awareness in people who have been systematically taught to discount their own thoughts and feelings or to distort and deny their own experience.

The process of empowerment through critical reflection may involve the learner in a process of incremental change, or it may lead to more profound, second-order changes. These kind of transformations in perspective are said to have been accomplished through a process of "conscientization" (Freire, 1970a), perspective transformation (Mezirow, 1991), emancipatory learning (Habermas, 1979), or transformational learning (Clark, 1993; Cranton, 1994). These terms are used to describe situations in which learners make fundamental changes in the way they view themselves, their communities, and their place in the world. Incremental, or first-order, changes result from critical thinking triggered by less potent situations—situations that do not profoundly dislodge the learner's present equilibrium. Transformational learning experiences are particularly important in the human services, where incremental learning may not produce the profound shifts in perspective that are necessary to achieve fundamental and lasting change. This is particularly evident in the kinds of objectives addressed by popular education methods, which may involve broad and basic changes in employment or public health practices.

The promise of this line of inquiry is that it may yield important insights into how practitioners can design conditions that can predictably stimulate such dramatic growth and change. The challenge to critical thinking in replacing one meaning perspective with another is captured by Thomas Kuhn (1970): "The decision to accept one paradigm is always simultaneously the decision to reject another, and the judgement leading to that decision involves the comparison of both paradigms with nature and with each other" (p. 77).

New Educational Technologies

Another factor that is likely to add impetus to these other trends is the rapid evolution of an array of new communications technologies. These include educational media such as the Internet, multimedia, and video conferencing, to name only a few. All of these technologies are already having an impact on teaching and learning in practice. The challenge is for human service professionals to maintain a current understanding of these emerging technologies and develop creative ways to harness them to provide humane, responsive support and services.

Internet

The Internet represents a transformational change in people's ability to communicate with other people and resources. It offers access to electronic mail, databases, libraries, and electronic bulletin boards—technologies that are all now used to support continuing professional development in the human services. The Internet also increases the ability of consumers to communicate with one another and with service providers as they take the initiative in their pursuit of social and physical well-being.

People who might previously have been designated as consumers can now access bulletin boards that offer them a powerful way to connect with peers. For example, not so long ago people might have placed a notice in the personals column of their local newspaper in an effort to locate others with shared concerns. The goal might have been simply to gather advice or, in other cases, to contact peers willing to be part of a self-help group. Today people are able to browse through several hundred bulletin boards covering a wide range of mostly health-related interests (White and Madara, 1992). In some instances the Internet is also being used for actual online group meetings. This is particularly helpful for people who are homebound because of physical difficulties or caregiving responsibilities. The Internet is also used by the American Self-Help Clearinghouse to link people who wish to establish new face-to-face mutual aid groups, bulletin boards, or online meetings (Madara, 1993). This kind of proactive involvement transforms people into producers of their own continuing learning.

Multimedia

The potential of multimedia was explored in Chapter Seven. At this point it is sufficient to note that the sophistication of this integrated technology is likely to increase rapidly. This technology is already stimulating development of a wide array of learning and self-diagnostic software programs. One example is a self-diagnosis package used by the student health service at the University of Washington. Students are able to feed in data about their health status and receive a provisional diagnosis and directions for further action. Similar software is likely to become available in other human service settings, including multimedia software accessible in office waiting rooms.

Video Conferencing

The ability of professionals to consult with specialists using interactive video conferencing is already well established. In the future it is probable that this technology will also be used extensively by practitioners to support learning at a distance. It remains to be seen exactly how this technology will be used in this way, but it offers a range of exciting possibilities.

Expert Systems

A great deal of research and development activity is now focused on the development of so-called expert systems. These involve taking computers to a new level of sophistication, where they are capable of artificial intelligence. This would make it possible for a learner to directly consult with and learn from a computer capable of responding in a manner akin to a human practitioner—for example, in arriving at a diagnosis of an illness. There will still be a need for the critical thinking skills of the helping professional, but expert systems promise to offer a powerful adjunct to skillful professional practice.

Instructional media are likely to become increasingly potent with the further integration of telephones, televisions, computers, and home entertainment systems. For this reason it is hazardous to predict where emerging technologies will take teaching and learning in the human services. Certainly some of the innovations that have been described in this book are likely to have been superseded in a very few years. Faced with this accelerating pace of technological change, it will be important for helping professionals to remain as technologically literate as possible in order to harness these resources for effective teaching and learning.

Conclusion

Notwithstanding the impact of these changes, teaching and the facilitation of learning will remain central to the practice of most human service professionals. In the future these activities are likely to expand, in fact, becoming an increasingly visible, effective, and satisfying aspect of a career in the human services. This book presents just the tip of the iceberg of the literature of adult learning—a feast of further learning awaits the reader. To get you started on the next stage of that journey, this introduction to teaching in practice will now return to the situations that launched it.

What would be the best way to approach the teaching challenges presented at the start of Chapter One? What kinds of teaching relationships should be developed in each of these situations? What forms of influence should be exercised? What would be the most effective teaching plan? What learning resources will this plan require? How can the learning process and outcomes be assessed? Consider again the following situations:

The scene is a hospital. A nurse is helping a young woman recently diagnosed with diabetes learn the intricacies of correctly filling a syringe in order to inject herself with insulin.

The scene is a community hall in a low-income neighborhood within a large city. A community worker is helping a group of people who live in public housing sort out ways they might take some of their grievances to the appropriate authorities.

The scene is the office of a family physician. She is helping two generations of a family understand what the alternative care options may be for their aging parent and grandparent, who has suffered a disabling stroke and is no longer able to care for himself in his own home.

The scene is a drop-in shelter for street youth. A young social worker is chatting informally with a group of teens. In subtle ways he is posing questions that encourage them to exchange ideas about how they might defuse situations that carry the potential for confrontation.

Resource A

. . . .

Self Assessment of Teaching/ Facilitating Skills

Self-Assessment of Teaching/Facilitating Skills for the Practitioner/ Teacher (P/T). (Developed by Andy Farquharson and Sharon Styve, University of Victoria.)

Promoting Purposeful Interaction

	Very Poor	Poor	Average	Good	Very Good
Preteaching Preparation	P/T is preoccupied *and* unprepared with available background on learner.	P/T is preoccupied *or* unprepared.	P/T seems ready to attend to learner.	P/T is responsive to learner *or* well prepared.	P/T is responsive to learner *and* well prepared.
Meeting, Greeting, Seating	P/T fails to establish personal contact *and* makes learner more anxious.	P/T fails to establish personal contact *or* makes learner more anxious.	P/T greets learner and attempts to help learner attend.	P/T makes contact *or* helps learner to attend.	P/T makes personal contact *and* helps learner attend.
Exploring Learner Needs	P/T does not discuss learner's range of needs *and* does not discuss learner's priorities.	P/T does not discuss learner's range of needs *or* does not discuss learner's priorities.	P/T discusses both the range and priority of learner's needs in a minimal way.	P/T explores the range of learner needs *or* establishes learner's priorities.	P/T explores the range of learner needs *and* establishes priorities.
Establishing P/T and Agency Resources and Learner Expectations	P/T does not discuss role/resources *and* ignores learner expectations.	P/T does not discuss role/resources *or* ignores learner expectations.	P/T identifies self and acknowledges some of learner's expectations.	P/T explores role and resources *or* explores learner expectations.	P/T explores role and resources *and* explores learner expectations.

	Very Poor	Poor	Average	Good	Very Good
Establishing Objectives and Activities for Teaching Episode	P/T does not discuss objectives and does not discuss activities.	P/T does not discuss objectives or does not discuss activities.	P/T discusses objectives and activities in a minimal way.	P/T and learner establish clear objectives or clear activities.	P/T and learner establish clear objectives and clear activities.
Exploring Resources	P/T ignores the range of resources and does not attempt to prioritize resources.	P/T ignores the range of resources or does not attempt to prioritize them.	P/T discusses some resources and attempts to prioritize them in a minimal way.	P/T explores the range of resources appropriate to learner needs or engages learner in prioritizing them.	P/T explores the range of resources and engages learner in prioritizing them.
Establishing Favorable Outcomes	P/T does not discuss outcomes with the learner.	P/T does not check out unrealistic and unspecific goals.	P/T engages learner in developing favorable outcomes that are minimally specific and realistic.	P/T and learner develop very specific or very realistic goals.	P/T and learner develop very specific and very realistic goals.
Developing Action Plan	P/T does not discuss alternatives and does not engage the learner in selecting a plan.	P/T does not discuss alternatives or does not engage learner in selecting a plan.	P/T explores a few alternatives and engages learner in selecting a plan.	P/T and learner explore many alternatives or worker and learner systematically select a plan.	P/T and learner explore many alternatives and select a plan.

	Very Poor	Poor	Average	Good	Very Good
Assigning Tasks and Establishing a Time Frame	P/T does not discuss tasks or time frame.	P/T discusses tasks or time frame.	P/T discusses tasks and time frame in a minimal way.	P/T and learner assign clear tasks or establish time frame.	P/T and learner assign tasks and establish time frame.
Evaluation and Termination	P/T does not check if agenda was met and does not review progress or feelings regarding termination.	P/T does not check if agenda was met or does not review progress or feelings regarding termination.	P/T checks whether agenda was met and discusses overall progress in a minimal way.	P/T explores extent to which agenda was met or explores progress or feelings regarding termination.	P/T explores extent to which agenda was met and explores progress or feelings regarding termination.

Purposeful Use of Self

	Very Poor	Poor	Average	Good	Very Good
Communicating Understanding	P/T ignores/misses both the content and feelings learner expresses.	P/T ignores/misses the content or feelings learner expresses.	P/T acknowledges the content and feelings learner expresses in a minimal way.	P/T adds to the content or feelings learner expresses.	P/T adds to both the content and feelings learner expresses.
Fostering Learner Specificity	P/T encourages learner to remain vague and impersonal.	P/T encourages learner to remain vague or impersonal.	P/T is willing for learner to be specific and personal.	P/T helps the learner be more specific or more personal.	P/T helps the learner be more specific and more personal.

	Very Poor	Poor	Average	Good	Very Good
Speaking Clearly	P/T's communication is vague and filled with jargon.	P/T's communication is vague or filled with jargon.	P/T uses little jargon and is at least minimally specific.	P/T uses no jargon or is very specific.	P/T uses no jargon and is very specific.
Being Genuine	P/T is not congruent and appears to be "playing a role."	P/T is not congruent or appears to be "playing a role."	P/T does not seem "phony."	P/T is clearly congruent or is clearly being him/her self.	P/T is clearly congruent and is being him/her self.
Attending	The physical setting is distracting and the P/T is distracted from the learner.	The physical setting is distracting or the P/T is distracted from the learner.	The physical setting has no negative effects and the P/T is ready to attend.	The physical setting is conducive to the interview or the P/T is clearly focused on learner.	The physical setting is conducive to the interview and the P/T is clearly focused on learner.
Respecting the Learner	P/T downgrades learner's strengths and weaknesses and rejects the learner.	P/T downgrades the learner or rejects the learner.	P/T minimally acknowledges learner strengths and seems willing to accept learner.	P/T recognizes strengths and potential or accepts learner in the "here and now" situation.	P/T recognizes strengths and potential and accepts learner in the "here and now" situation.

	Very Poor	Poor	Average	Good	Very Good
Disclosing	P/T disclosure is absent or inappropriate *and* worker promotes inappropriate learner disclosure.	P/T disclosure is absent or inappropriate *or* worker promotes inappropriate learner disclosure.	P/T is willing to disclose self and is open to learner disclosure.	P/T uses self-disclosure constructively *or* facilitates appropriate learner disclosure.	P/T uses self-disclosure constructively *and* facilitates appropriate learner disclosure.
Giving Feedback	P/T has no capacity for giving relevant, nonevaluative feedback.	P/T gives irrelevant *or* evaluative feedback.	P/T is willing to give useful and relevant nonevaluative feedback.	P/T gives particularly relevant *or* nonevaluative feedback.	P/T gives very relevant *and* nonevaluative feedback.
Using Summary Statements	Summary statements are vague *and* inappropriately timed.	Summary statements are vague *or* inappropriately timed.	Summary statements are minimally clear and appropriately timed.	Summary statements are very clear *or* are very well timed.	Summary statements are very clear *and* very well timed.
Giving Information	P/T gives too little/too much information *and* the information is given inappropriately.	P/T gives too little/too much *or* inappropriate information.	P/T usually gives adequate and appropriate information.	P/T always gives adequate *or* appropriate information.	P/T always gives adequate *and* appropriate information.

	Very Poor	Poor	Average	Good	Very Good
Controlling Personal Needs	P/T is unaware of personal needs *and* these interfere with work situation.	P/T is aware of personal needs but is unable to prevent them from interfering in his/her work.	P/T is aware of personal needs but these sometimes interfere in the work situation.	P/T is aware of personal needs and is usually able to prevent them from interfering in his/her work.	P/T is aware of personal needs and these never interfere in the work situation.
Asking Appropriate Questions	P/T asks vague *and* irrelevant questions.	P/T asks vague *or* irrelevant questions.	P/T's questions are minimally specific and meaningful to the learner.	P/T's questions are very specific *or* very meaningful to the learner.	P/T's questions are very specific *and* very meaningful to learner.
Generic Skills					
Timing the Teaching/ Learning Process	The pace is inappropriate to the learner *and* many steps are omitted.	The pace is inappropriate to the learner *or* many steps are omitted.	The pace is usually appropriate to the learner and all steps are touched upon.	The P/T and learner establish an appropriate pace *or* explore each step thoroughly.	The P/T and learner establish an appropriate pace *and* explore each step thoroughly.

	Very Poor	Poor	Average	Good	Very Good
Achieving Mutuality	P/T ignores the limits of mutuality *and* does not share responsibility with the learner.	P/T ignores the limits of mutuality *or* does not share responsibility with the learner.	P/T recognizes the limits of mutuality and attempts to share some responsibility with the learner.	P/T and learner clearly define the limits of mutuality *or* worker shares responsibility with learner as possible.	P/T and learner clearly define the limits of mutuality *and* share responsibility whenever possible.
Integrating Interpersonal and Process Skills	P/T displays insufficient interpersonal *and* process skills.	P/T displays insufficient interpersonal *or* process skills.	P/T displays adequate interpersonal and process skills.	P/T displays excellent interpersonal *or* process skills *and* some spontaneity.	P/T displays excellent interpersonal *and* process skills *and* spontaneity.

Resource B

Self-Assessment of Group
Facilitation Competencies

Self-Assessment of Learning Group Facilitation Competencies for the Practitioner/Teacher. (Developed by Andy Farquharson and Sharon Styve, University of Victoria.)

Function[1]	Very Poor	Poor	Average	Good	Very Good
Initiating	Never offers new ideas *and* discourages others from contributing anything new.	Seldom offers new ideas *or* seldom encourages others to do so.	Offers some new ideas and sometimes encourages others.	Offers many new ideas *or* actively encourages others to do so.	Offers many new ideas *and* actively encourages others.
Seeking Information	Never clarifies information *and* never seeks clarification from others.	Seldom clarifies information when asked *or* seldom seeks clarification from others.	Clarifies when asked and seeks clarification from others.	Clarifies when asked *and* seeks clarification occasionally.	Always clarifies information *or* always seeks clarification from others.
Seeking Opinions	Never offers own opinion *and* discourages other members from giving opinions.	Seldom offers own opinion *or* discourages others from giving opinions.	Occasionally offers opinions and asks for other members' opinions.	Offers own opinion whenever appropriate *or* always seeks others' opinions.	Offers own opinion whenever appropriate *and* encourages other members to offer their opinion.
Coordinating	Never draws different suggestions together *and* discourages others from doing so.	Seldom draws different suggestions together *or* discourages others from doing so.	Occasionally draws different suggestions together.	Is usually able to draw different suggestions together.	Is always able to draw different suggestions together.

[1]Role categories adapted from J. William Pfeiffer and John E. Jones (eds.). *Annual Handbook for Group Facilitators*. La Jolla, Calif.: University Associates, 1976, pp. 136–137.

Function	Very Poor	Poor	Average	Good	Very Good
Summarizing	Never summarizes the group's thoughts and activities *and* discourages others from doing so.	Seldom summarizes group thoughts and activities *or* discourages others from doing so.	Is able to summarize for the group.	Summarizes group thoughts and activities whenever appropriate.	Summarizes for the group whenever appropriate and encourages others to do so.
Checking Feasibility	Never checks the feasibility of alternatives *and* discourages others from doing so.	Seldom checks the feasibility of alternatives *or* discourages others from doing so.	Occasionally checks feasibility of alternatives and does not interfere when other members do so.	Checks feasibility of alternatives whenever appropriate.	Checks feasibility of alternatives when appropriate and encourages others to do so.
Maintenance Roles					
Encouraging	Never encourages or supports others *and* actively discourages other members from doing so.	Never encourages or supports others *or* actively discourages others from doing so.	Occasionally supports and encourages others and does not interfere with others' doing so.	Is usually supportive and encouraging to other members.	Is always supportive and encouraging to other members.

Function	Very Poor	Poor	Average	Good	Very Good
Gatekeeping	Always discourages contributions from other members.	Usually discourages contributions from other members.	Is open to contributions from all members.	Usually attempts to get all members' contributions.	Actively seeks to make opportunities for all members to make contributions.
Setting Standards	Does not contribute to the setting of group standards *and* actively discourages group from setting standards.	Does not contribute to the setting of standards *or* actively discourages group from setting standards.	Is open to setting standards in the group.	Contributes to setting standards *or* encourages the group to set standards.	Contributes to setting standards *and* encourages the group to set standards.
Following	Never accepts group decisions *and* actively opposes the ideas of other members.	Never accepts group decisions *or* actively opposes ideas of other members.	Is usually able to accept group decisions or the ideas of other members.	Is always able to accept group decisions or the ideas of other members.	Is always able to accept group decisions *and* the ideas of other members.
Expressing Group Feelings	Ignores group feelings *and* discourages others from expressing them.	Ignores group feelings *or* discourages others from expressing them.	Is open to expressions of group feelings.	Expresses group feelings whenever appropriate *or* actively encourages others to do so.	Expresses group feelings *and* encourages others to do so.

Function	Very Poor	Poor	Average	Good	Very Good
Fostering Group Identity and Humor	Never attempts to solidify the group *and* discourages others from doing so.	Never attempts to solidify the group *or* discourages others from doing so.	Makes occasional attempts to solidify the group and is open to others' efforts.	Actively attempts to solidify the group *or* actively encourages others to do so.	Actively attempts to solidify the group *and* actively encourages others to do so.

Roles Involving Both Task and Maintenance Activities

Function	Very Poor	Poor	Average	Good	Very Good
Evaluating	Never assesses group progress *and* discourages others from doing so.	Never assesses group progress *or* discourages others from doing so.	Is open to assessing group progress.	Assesses group progress appropriately *or* encourages others to do so.	Assesses group progress *and* encourages others to do so.
Assessing Needs	Ignores difficulties and needs of the group *and* discourages others from assessing them.	Ignores difficulties and needs of the group *or* discourages others from assessing them.	Is open to assessing the difficulties and needs of the group.	Assesses needs and difficulties of the group whenever appropriate *or* encourages others to do so.	Assesses needs and difficulties of the group whenever appropriate *and* encourages others to do so.

Function	Very Poor	Poor	Average	Good	Very Good
Checking Consensus	Never checks for group consensus *and* actively disrupts consensus.	Never checks for group consensus *or* actively disrupts consensus.	Occasionally checks group consensus and does not impede the development of consensus.	Frequently checks for group consensus *or* facilitates development toward consensus.	Frequently checks for group consensus *and* facilitates development toward consensus.
Mediating	Promotes conflict in the group *and* refuses to compromise personally.	Promotes group conflict *or* refuses to compromise personally.	Usually attempts to resolve conflict and is usually open to compromise.	Always attempts to resolve conflict *or* is always open to compromises.	Always attempts to resolve conflict *and* is open to compromises.
Goal Setting	Discourages the group from setting group goals *and* has no personal goals.	Discourages the group from setting group goals *or* has no personal goals.	Is open to setting group and personal goals.	Has clear personal goals *or* facilities the group in setting goals.	Has clear personal goals *and* facilities the group in setting goals.
Pursuing Goals	Makes no effort toward achievement of personal goals *and* interferes in the achievement of group goals and goals of other members.	Makes no effort toward achievement of personal goals *or* interferes in the achievement of group goals and goals of other members.	Makes some minimal effort toward achievement of personal goals and cooperates toward the achievement of group goals and goals of others.	Actively works toward personal goals *or* actively works toward group goals and goals of other members.	Actively works toward personal goals *and* actively works toward group goals and goals of other members.

Function	Very Poor	Poor	Average	Good	Very Good
Using Resources	Does not offer personal resources to the group *and* interferes in the use of other members' resources.	Does not offer personal resources to the group *or* interferes in the use of other members' resources.	Occasionally offers own resources to the group and is open to using the resources of other members.	Offers own resources whenever appropriate *or* actively develops and uses the resources of other members.	Offers own resources whenever appropriate *and* actively develops and uses the resources of other members.

Resource C

· ·

Skills for Learner-Managed Learning

Self-Directed Continuing Professional Development for the Practitioner/Teacher. (Developed by Andy Farquharson.)

A Personal Skills Checklist

Skills for Learner-Managed Learning (check self-assessment of competence)

		Competence		
Major Domain	*Constituent Skills*	Good	Weak	Fair
Learning Styles	Describes personal learning styles			
	Uses system of categories to describe learning events			
	Manages system for continuous monitoring of learning style changes			
Learning Needs	Generates input from clients/patients			
	Generates input from the profession			
	Monitors the profession: practice and knowledge base			

· · · · · · · · · · · · ·

Adapted from: Andy Farquharson. "Competencies for Continuing Learning in the Professions." *Canadian Journal of University Continuing Education*, 1983, 9(2), pp. 120–125.

Major Domain	Constituent Skills	Good	Weak	Fair
Resource Identification	Knows range of learning resources Demonstrates skill in accessing nonhuman learning resources Demonstrates skill in mobilizing human learning resources			
Program Development	Translates generalized needs into specific learning objectives Selects mode and sequence of learning activities Seeks appropriate consultation			
Program Implementation	Manages time effectively Maximizes learnable moments Demonstrates flexibility in linking learnings			
Evaluation	Implements pre-formative/ formative/summative systems to evaluate personal learning Implements systems to evaluate utility of learning resources Monitors subjective responses to life events			
Intuition	Values nonlinear approaches to learning/problem solving Demonstrates skill in using creative ways of knowing Demonstrates ability to postpone judgment			

References

Abt, C. *Serious Games*. New York: Viking Penguin, 1970.

Angelo, T., and Cross, P. *Classroom Assessment Techniques: A Handbook for College Teachers*. San Francisco: Jossey-Bass, 1993.

Apps, J. *The Adult Learner on Campus: A Guide for Instructors and Administrators*. New York: Cambridge Books, 1981.

Arnold, R., and Burke, B. *A Popular Education Handbook*. Toronto: CUSO/O.I.S.E. Publications, 1983.

Arnold, R., Barndt, D., and Burke, B. *A New Weave*. Toronto: CUSO/O.I.S.E. Publications, n.d.

Ausubel, D. "The Use of Advance Organizers in the Learning and Retention of Meaningful Verbal Material." *Journal of Educational Psychology*, 1960, *51*, 267–272.

Babcock, D., and Miller, M. *Client Education: Theory and Practice*. St. Louis, Mo.: Mosby, 1994.

Bales, R. *Interaction Process Analysis: A Method for the Study of Small Groups*. Reading, Mass.: Addison-Wesley, 1950.

Bandura, A. "Self-efficacy: Toward a Unifying Theory of Behavioral Change." *Psychological Review*, 1977a, *84*, 191–215.

Bandura, A. *Social Learning Theory*. Englewood Cliffs, N.J.: Prentice-Hall, 1977b.

Barnsley, J., and Ellis, D. *Research for Change*. Vancouver, B.C.: Women's Research Centre, 1992.

Baskett, M., and Marsick, J. (eds.). *Professionals' Ways of Knowing: New Findings on How to Improve Professional Education*. New Directions for Higher and Adult Education, no. 55. San Francisco: Jossey-Bass, 1992.

Bateman, W. *Open to Question: The Art of Teaching and Learning by Inquiry*. San Francisco: Jossey-Bass. 1990.

Bates, T., Harrington, R., Gilmore, D., and van Soest, C. "Compressed Video and Video-Conferencing in Open and Distance Learning: A Guide to Current Developments." In D. Black (ed.), *Distance Education in B.C.: Selected Papers and Case Studies*. Vancouver: Open Learning Agency, 1993, 117–139.

Becker, M. "The Health Belief Model and Sick Role Behavior." *Nursing Digest*, 1974, *2*, 54–71.

Belenky, M., Clinchy, B., Goldberger, N., and Tarule, J. *Women's Ways of Knowing*. New York: Basic Books, 1986.

Benner, P. "Uncovering the Knowledge Embedded in Clinical Practice." *The Journal of Nursing Scholarship*, 1983, 5(2), 36–41.

Benner, P. *From Novice to Expert: Excellence and Power in Clinical Nursing Practice*. Reading, Mass.: Addison-Wesley, 1984.

Bennis, W., Benne, K., and Sheets, P. "Functional Roles and Group Members." *Journal of Social Issues*, 1948, 4(2), 41–49.

Bergevin, P., and McKinley, J. *Participation Training for Adult Education*. St. Louis, Mo.: Bethany Press, 1970.

Block, P. *The Empowered Manager: Positive Political Skills at Work*. San Francisco: Jossey-Bass. 1987.

Bloom, B., and others (eds.). *Taxonomy of Educational Objectives: Cognitive Domain*. White Plains, N.Y.: Longman, 1977.

Bloomwell, A. "47 Tips for Flip-chart Users." *Training*, June 1983, 35–38.

Borkman, T. "Experiential Knowledge: A New Concept for the Analysis of Self-Help Groups." *Social Service Review*, 1976, 50, 444–456.

Broad, M. "Management Actions to Support Transfer of Training." *Training and Development Journal*, 1982, 6(5), 124–128.

Brookfield, S. (ed.). *Self-Directed Learning: From Theory to Practice*. New Directions for Continuing Education, no. 25. San Francisco: Jossey-Bass, 1985.

Brookfield, S. *Understanding and Facilitating Adult Learning: A Comprehensive Analysis of Principles and Effective Practices*. San Francisco: Jossey-Bass, 1986.

Brookfield, S. *Developing Critical Thinkers: Challenging Adults to Explore Alternative Ways of Thinking and Acting*. San Francisco: Jossey-Bass, 1987.

Brookfield, S. *The Skillful Teacher: On Technique, Trust, and Responsiveness in the Classroom*. San Francisco: Jossey-Bass, 1990.

Brookfield, S. "On Impostership, Cultural Suicide, and Other Dangers: How Nurses Learn Critical Thinking." *The Journal of Continuing Education in Nursing*, 1993, 24(5), 197–205.

Brundage, D., and MacKeracher, D. *Adult Learning Principles and Their Application to Program Planning*. Toronto: Ministry of Education, 1980.

Bunning, R. "The Delphi Technique: A Tool for Serious Inquiry." *The Annual Handbook for Group Facilitatiors*. La Jolla, Calif.: University Associates, 1979, 174–181.

Butler, K. *Learning and Teaching Style in Theory and Practice*. Columbia, Conn.: The Learner's Dimension, 1986.

Candy, P. "Constructivism and the Study of Self-direction in Adult Learning." *Studies in the Education of Adults*, 1989, *21*, 95–116.

Candy, P. *Self-Direction for Lifelong Learning: A Comprehensive Guide to Theory and Practice*. San Francisco: Jossey-Bass, 1991.

Cantor, J. *Delivering Instruction for Adult Learners*. Toronto: Wall & Emerson, 1992.

Cardinal, T., and Farquharson, A. *The Self-Help Resource Kit*. Victoria, B.C.: University of Victoria, 1991.

Cervero, R. "Evaluating Workshop Implementation and Outcomes." In T. Sork (ed.), *Designing and Implementing Effective Workshops*. San Francisco: Jossey-Bass, 1984.

Clark, C. "Transformational Learning." In S. Merriam (ed.), *An Update on Adult Learning Theory*. San Francisco: Jossey-Bass, 1993, 47–56.

Cochran, M. "The Parental Empowerment Process: Building on Family Strengths." In J. Harris (ed.). *Child Psychology in Action: Linking Theory and Practice*. London: Croom Helm, 1985, 12–33

Conger, J., and Kanungo, R. "The Empowerment Process: Integrating Theory and Practice." *Academy of Management Review*, 1988, *13*(3), 471–482.

Corey, G. *Theory and Practice of Counseling and Psychotherapy*. Pacific Grove, Calif.: Wadsworth, 1991.

Cossom, J. "Teaching from Cases: Education for Critical Thinking." *Journal of Teaching in Social Work*, 1991, *5*(1), 139–155.

Covey, S. *The Seven Habits of Highly Effective People*. New York: Simon & Schuster, 1989.

Cranton, P. *Planning Instruction for Adult Learners*. Toronto: Wall & Emerson, 1989.

Cranton, P. *Working with Adult Learners*. Toronto: Wall & Emerson, 1992.

Cranton, P. *Understanding and Promoting Transformative Learning*. San Francisco: Jossey-Bass, 1994.

Cuseo, J. "Cooperative Learning vs. Small Group Discussions and Group Projects: The Critical Differences." *Cooperative Learning and College Teaching*, 1992, *2*(3), 4–8.

Daloz, L. *Effective Teaching and Mentoring: Realizing the Transformational Power of Adult Learning Experiences*. San Francisco: Jossey-Bass, 1986.

de Bono, E. *The CORT Thinking Skills Program*. Elmsford, N.Y.: Pergamon Press, 1984.

De Geyndt, W., Zhao, X., and Liu, S. *From Barefoot Doctor to Village Doctor in Rural China*. (World Bank Technical Paper No. 187). Washington, D.C.: World Bank, 1992.

Denis, M., and Richter, I. "Learning About Intuitive Learning: Moose-Hunting Techniques." In D. Boud and V. Griffin (eds.), *Appreciating Adults Learning*. London: Kogan Page, 1987, 25–36.

Deshler, D. "Conceptual Mapping: Drawing Charts of the Mind." In J. Mezirow, (ed.), *Fostering Critical Reflection Adulthood: A Guide to Transformative and Emancipatory Learning*. San Francisco: Jossey-Bass, 1990, 336–353.

Deutsch, M. "The Effects of Cooperation and Competition upon Group Process." In D. Cartwright and A. Zander (eds.), *Group Dynamics: Theory and Research*. Evanston, Ill.: Row Peterson & Co., 1960.

Draves, W. *How to Teach Adults*. Manhatten, Kans.: Learning Resources Network, 1984.

Duffy, T., and Jonassen, D. "Constructivism: New Implications for Instructional Technology." *Educational Technology*, 1991, *31*(5), 7–12.

Edwards, J., Tindale, R., Heath, L., and Posavac, E. (eds.). *Social Influence Processes and Education*. New York: Plenum, 1990.

Egan, G. *Change Agent Skills in Helping and Human Services Settings*. Pacific Grove, Calif.: Brooks/Cole, 1985.

Egan, G. *The Skilled Helper*. Pacific Grove, Calif.: Brooks/Cole, 1990.

Elbow, P. *Embracing Contraries: Explorations in Learning and Teaching*. New York: Oxford University Press, 1986.

Epp, J. *Achieving Health for All: A Framework for Health Promotion*. Ottawa: Ministry of Supply and Services, 1986.

Epp, J. *Mental Health for Canadians: Striking a Balance*. Ottawa: Ministry of Supply and Services, 1988.

Farquharson, A. "Peers as Helpers: Personal Change in Members of Self-Help Groups." Unpublished doctoral dissertation, University of Toronto, 1975.

Farquharson, A. "Planning Need Assessment Activities." *Canadian Journal of University Continuing Education*, 1978, *4*(2), 13–16.

Farquharson, A. "Competencies for Continuing Learning in the Professions." *Canadian Journal of University Continuing Education*, 1983, *9*(2), 38–47.

Farquharson, A. "Learning Through Teaching Among Undergraduate Social Work Students." In M. Knowles (ed.). *Andragogy in Action: Applying Modern Principles of Adult Learning*. San Francisco: Jossey-Bass, 1985, 265–272.

Farquharson, A. *Critical Incidents: A Videotape*. Victoria, B.C.: University of Victoria, 1993.

Faure, E. *Learning to Be: The World of Education Today and Tomorrow*. Paris: UNESCO, 1972.

Ford, D. "Nominal Group Technique: An Applied Group Problem-Solving Activity." In J. Jones and J. Pfeiffer (eds.), *The 1975 Annual Handbook for Group Facilitators*. La Jolla, Calif.: University Associates, 1975, 179–182.

Fox, R. "Fostering Transfer of Learning to Work Environments." In T. Sork (ed.), *Designing and Implementing Effective Workshops*. San Francisco: Jossey-Bass, 1984.

Franklin, J. "Toward the Style of the Community Change Educator." In W. Bennis, K. Benne, R. Chin, and K. Corey (eds.), *The Planning of Change*. Troy, Mo.: Holt, Rinehart & Winston, 1976, 352–358.

Freire, P. *Cultural Action for Freedom*. Monograph Series no. 1. Cambridge, Mass.: Harvard Educational Review and Center for the Study of Development and Social Change, 1970a.

Freire, P. *Pedagogy of the Oppressed*. New York: Seabury Press, 1970b.

Freire, P. *Education for Critical Consciousness*. New York: Seabury Press, 1973.

Frew, J. "The Functions and Patterns of Individual Contact Styles During the Developmental Phase of the Gestalt Group." *The Gestalt Journal*. 1986, 9(1), 55–70.

Gagné, R. *The Conditions of Learning*. (4th ed.) Troy, Mo.: Holt, Rinehart & Winston, 1985.

Gagné, R., and Driscoll, M. *Essentials of Learning for Instruction*. Englewood Cliffs, N.J.: Prentice-Hall, 1988.

Gartner, A., Greer, C., and Reissman, F. *Consumer Education in the Human Services*. Elmsford, N.Y.: Pergamon Press, 1979.

GATT-Fly. *Ah-Hah! A New Approach to Popular Education*. Toronto: Between the Lines, 1983.

Gelfand, B. *The Creative Practitioner*. New York: Haworth, 1988.

Glanz, K., Lewis, F., and Rimer, B. *Health Behavior and Health Education: Theory, Research, and Practice*. San Francisco: Jossey-Bass, 1990.

Goad, T. *Delivering Effective Training*. San Diego: University Associates, 1982.

Gordon, J. "The Woo Woo Factor." *Training*, May 1985, 26–42.

Gordon, R. *Interviewing: Strategy, Techniques and Tactics*. Belmont, Calif.: Dorsey Press, 1980.

Gottleib, B. "Social Networks and Social Support: An Overview of Research, Practice and Policy Implications." *Health Education Quarterly*, 1985, 12(1), 5–22.

Gregorc, A. *An Adult's Guide to Style*. Maynard, Mass.: Gabriel Systems, 1982.

Grow, G. "Teaching Learners to Be Self-Directed." *Adult Education Quarterly*, 1991, *41*(3), 125–149.

Guba, E., and Lincoln, Y. *Fourth Generation Evaluation*. Newbury Park, Calif.: Sage, 1989.

Habermas, J. *Communication and the Evolution of Society*. Boston: Beacon Press, 1979.

Haggard, A. *Handbook of Patient Education*. Rockville, Md.: Aspen Publishers, 1989.

Harrow, A. *A Taxonomy of the Psychomotor Domain*. New York: McKay, 1972.

Havighurst, R. *Developmental Tasks and Education*. New York: McKay, 1970.

Health and Welfare Canada. *Knowledge Development for Health Promotion*. Ottawa: Ministry of Supply and Services, March 1989.

Heimlich, J., and Norland, K. *Developing Teaching Styles in Adult Education*. San Francisco: Jossey-Bass, 1994.

Hepworth, D., and Larsen, J. *Direct Social Work Practice*. Belmont, Calif.: Wadsworth, 1990.

Hersey, P., and Blanchard, K. *The Management of Organization Behavior: Utilizing Human Resources*. (6th. ed.) Englewood Cliffs, N.J.: Prentice-Hall, 1988.

Houle, C. *Continuing Learning in the Professions*. San Francisco: Jossey-Bass, 1980.

Illich, I. *Disabling Professions*. New York: Marian Boyars, 1987.

Ingham, J., and Dunn, R. "The Dunn and Dunn Model of Learning Styles: Addressing Learner Diversity." *The 1993 Annual: Developing Human Resources*. La Jolla, Calif.: University Associates, 1993, 181–192.

Isaksen, S., and Treffinger, D. *Creative Problem-Solving: The Basic Course*. Buffalo: Bearly Ltd., 1985.

Ivey, A. *Intentional Interviewing and Counseling*. (2nd ed.) Pacific Grove, Calif.: Brooks/Cole, 1988.

Johnson, D., and Johnson, F. *Joining Together*. Englewood Cliffs, N.J.: Prentice-Hall, 1982.

Jones, J. "A Model of Group Development." In J. Jones and J. Pfeiffer (eds.), *The 1973 Annual Handbook for Group Facilitators*. La Jolla, Calif.: University Associates, 1973, 127–129.

Joyce, B., and Weil, M. *Models of Teaching*. (3rd. ed.) Englewood Cliffs, N.J.: Prentice-Hall, 1986.

Keller, F., and Sherman, J. (eds.). *The Keller Plan Handbook*. Menlo Park, Calif.: Benjamin-Cummings, 1974.

Kemp, J. *The Instructional Design Process*. New York: HarperCollins, 1985.

King, P., and Kitchener, K. *Developing Reflective Judgment: Understanding and Promoting Intellectual Growth and Critical Thinking in Adolescents and Adults*. San Francisco: Jossey-Bass, 1994.

Kiresuk, T. and Garwick, G. Basic Goal Attainment Scaling Procedures. In B. Compton and B. Galaway (eds.). *Social Work Processes*. Homewood, Ill.: The Dorsey Press, 1979. 412–421.

Knowles, M. *Self-Directed Learning: A Guide for Learners and Teachers*. Chicago: Follett, 1975.

Knowles, M., and Associates (eds.). *Andragogy in Action: Applying Modern Principles of Adult Learning*. San Francisco: Jossey-Bass, 1985.

Knox, A. *Adult Development and Learning: A Handbook on Individual Growth and Competence in the Adult Years*. San Francisco: Jossey-Bass, 1977.

Knox, A. *Helping Adults Learn: A Guide to Planning, Implementing, and Conducting Programs*. San Francisco: Jossey-Bass, 1990.

Kolb, D. *Experiential Learning*. Englewood Cliffs, N.J.: Prentice-Hall, 1984.

Kolb, D. *Learning Style Inventory*. Boston: McBer and Co., 1985.

Kozma, R., and Johnson, J. "The Technological Revolution Comes to the Classroom." *Change*, Jan.–Feb. 1991, 10–23

Krathwohl, D. *A Taxonomy of Educational Objectives: Affective Domain*. New York: Longman, 1969.

Kreuger, R. *Focus Groups*. Newbury Park, Calif.: Sage, 1988.

Kuhn, T. *The Structure of Scientific Revolutions*. (2nd ed.) Chicago: University of Chicago Press, 1970.

Kurfiss, J. *Critical Thinking*. Washington. D.C.: Association for the Study of Higher Education, 1988.

Labonte, R. "Developing a Community Health Development Approach to Addressing Heart Health Inequalities." *Report of the Second Workshop on Heart Health Inequalities*. Ottawa: Health and Welfare Canada, 1988, 7–17.

Labonte, R. "Community Empowerment: The Need for Political Analysis." *Canadian Journal of Public Health*, 1989, 80, 87–88.

Lessing, D. *The Golden Notebook*. London: Michael Joseph, 1972.

Levin, L. "Patient Education and Self-Care Care: How Do They Differ?" *Nursing Outlook*, 1978, 3, 170–176.

Lewin, K. *Field Theory in Social Science*. New York: HarperCollins, 1951.

Lewis, L. (ed.). *Experiential and Simulation Techniques for Teaching Adults*. San Francisco: Jossey Bass, 1986.

Long, L., Paradise, L., and Long, T. *Questioning: Skills for the Helping Process*. Pacific Grove, Calif.: Brooks/Cole, 1981.

Lovelock, C. "Teaching with Cases." In L. Lewis (ed.), *Experiential and Simulation Techniques for Teaching Adults*. San Francisco: Jossey Bass, 1986, 25–35.

Luft, J. *Of Human Interaction*. Palo Alto, Calif.: National Press Books, 1969.

McGowan, P. *The ABC Project: Providing Active Participation in Responsible Health Care*. Vancouver: Arthritis Society, 1990.

Machiavelli, N. *The Prince*, trans. G. Bull. Baltimore: Penguin Books, 1961.

Madara, E. "Using High Tech to Find and Form Self-Help Groups for Better Health." Paper presented at the Healthy Cities Summit Conference, San Francisco, December 1993.

Mager, R. *Preparing Instructional Objectives*. Belmont, Ca.: Lake Publishers, 1984.

Maluccio, A. *Learning from Clients*. New York: Free Press, 1979.

Mann, K. "The Client Educator." In M. Stewart (ed.), *Community Health Nursing in Canada*. Toronto: Gage, 1985, 203–221

Mayer, J., and Timms, N. "Clash in Perspective between Worker and Client." *Social Casework*, 1969, *50*, 32–40.

Meyers, C. *Teaching Students to Think Critically: A Guide for Faculty in All Disciplines*. San Francisco: Jossey-Bass, 1986.

Meyers, C., and Jones, T. *Promoting Active Learning: Strategies for the College Classroom*. San Francisco: Jossey-Bass, 1993.

Mezirow, J. "A Critical Theory of Self-Directed Learning." In S. Brookfield (ed.), *Self-Directed Learning: From Theory to Practice*. New Directions for Continuing Education, no. 25. San Francisco: Jossey-Bass, 1985.

Mezirow, J. (ed.). *Fostering Critical Reflection in Adulthood: A Guide to Transformative and Emancipatory Learning*. San Francisco: Jossey-Bass, 1990.

Mezirow, J. (ed.). *Transformative Dimensions of Adult Learning*. San Francisco: Jossey-Bass, 1991.

Monette, M. "The Concept of Educational Need: An Analysis of Selected Literature." *Adult Education* (U.S.A.), 1977, *27*(2), 116–127.

Moore, D. "Assessing the Needs of Adults for Continuing Education: A Model." In F. Pennington (ed.), *Assessing Educational Needs of Adults*. New Directions for Continuing Education, no. 7. San Francisco: Jossey-Bass, 1980.

Mosteller, F. "Innovation and Evaluation." *Science*, 1981, *211*, 881–886.

Mullaly, R. *Structural Social Work*. Toronto: McClelland and Stewart, 1993.

Myers, I., and Myers P. *Gifts Differing*. Palo Alto, Calif.: Consulting Psychologists Press, 1980.

Naftulin, H., Ware, J., and Donnelly, F. "The Dr. Fox Lecture: A Paradigm of Educational Seduction." *Journal of Medical Education*, 1973, *48*, 630–635.

Narayan, U. "Working Together Across Difference." In B. Compton and B. Galaway (eds.), *Social Work Processes*. Belmont, Calif.: Wadsworth, 1989, 317–328.

Neufeld, V., and Barrows, H. "Preparing Medical Students for Lifelong Learning." In M. Knowles (ed.), *Andragogy in Action: Applying Modern Principles
of Adult Learning*. San Francisco: Jossey-Bass, 1985, 207–226.

Nored, A., and Shelton, E. "Competency-Based Adult Education." In C.
Klevens (ed.), *Materials and Methods in Adult and Continuing Education*.
Los Angeles: Levens Publications, 1982, 74–81.

Nylen, D., Mitchell, J., and Stout, A. "Role Functions in a Group." In J. Pfeiffer
and J. Jones. (eds.), *The 1976 Annual Handbook for Group Facilitators*. La
Jolla, Calif.: University Associates, 1976, 136–138.

Parnes, S. *The Magic of Your Mind*. Buffalo, N.Y.: The Creative Education Foundation, 1981.

Paul, R. *Critical Thinking*. Santa Rosa, Calif.: The Foundation for Critical
Thinking, 1992.

Percival, A. *Practicing Theory*. Saskatoon, Sask.: University Extension Press,
1993.

Perry, W. *Forms of Intellectual and Ethical Development in the College Years: A
Scheme*. Troy, Mo.: Holt, Rinehart & Winston, 1970.

Perry, W. "Cognitive and Ethical Growth: The Making of Meaning." In A.
Chickering and Associates (eds.), *The Modern American College: Respond-
ing to the New Realities of Diverse Students and a Changing Society*. San
Francisco: Jossey-Bass, 1981.

Pfeiffer, J., and Jones, J. (eds.). *The 1980 Annual Handbook for Group Facilitators*.
La Jolla, Calif.: University Associates, 1980.

Pfeiffer, W. (ed.) *The Encyclopedia of Icebreakers*. La Jolla, Calif.: University
Associates, 1991.

Postman, N., and Weingartner, C. *Teaching as a Subversive Activity*. New York:
Dell, 1969.

Powell, T. *Self-Help Organizations and Professional Practice*. Silver Spring, Md.:
National Association of Social Workers, 1987.

Rankin, S., and Stallings, K. *Patient Education: Issues, Principles and Practices*.
(2nd. ed.) Philadelphia: Lippincott, 1990.

Rappaport, J. "Studies in Empowerment: Introduction to the Issue." *Prevention in
Human Services*, 1984, 3, 1–7.

Redman, B. *The Process of Patient Education*. (7th. ed.) St. Louis, Mo.: Mosby, 1993.

Reilley, D. *How to Produce Your Own Press Release*. Victoria, B.C.: Integrate Publishing, 1985.

Reissman, F. "The 'Helper Therapy' Principle." *Social Work*, 1965, 10(2), 276–32.

Renner, P. *The Instructor's Survival Kit*. Vancouver: Training Associates, 1983.

Renner, P. *The Quick Instructional Planner*. Vancouver: PFR Training Associates,
1988.

Richardson, A. *Participation*. New York: Routledge & Kegan Paul, 1982.

Ricks, F. "If You Care You Count: Canadian Trends in Child and Family Services." *Proceedings: National Child Care Workers Conference*. Victoria: University of Victoria, 1981.

Rogers, E. *Diffusion of Innovations*. (3rd ed.) New York: Seabury Press, 1983.

Rogers, E., and Shoemaker, F. "Diffusion of Innovations." In C. Lovelock and C. Weinberg (eds.), *Public and Non-Profit Marketing*. Palo Alto: Scientific Press, 1984.

Sarason, S. *The Creation of Settings and the Future Societies*. San Francisco: Jossey-Bass, 1972.

Satir, V. *Peoplemaking*. Palo Alto, Calif.: Science and Behavior Books, 1972.

Schmidt, J., and Davidson, M. "Helping Students Think." *The Personnel and Guidance Journal*, 1983, *61*(9), 563–569.

Schön, D. *The Reflective Practitioner*. New York: Basic Books, 1983.

Schwarz, R. *The Skilled Facilitator: Practical Wisdom for Developing Effective Groups*. San Francisco: Jossey-Bass, 1994.

Senge, P. *The Fifth Discipline*. New York: Doubleday, 1990.

Shor, I. *Empowering Education*. Chicago: University of Chicago Press, 1992.

Shor, I., and Freire, P. *A Pedagogy for Liberation*. Granby, Mass.: Bergin and Garvey, 1987.

Smith, B., and MacGregor, J. "What Is Collaborative Learning?" In A. Goodsell, M. Maher, and V. Tinto (eds.), *Collaborative Learning: A Sourcebook for Higher Education*. University Park, Penn.: National Center on Postsecondary Teaching, Learning, and Assessment, 1992, 9–22.

Smith, R. *Learning How to Learn*. New York: Cambridge University Press, 1982.

Sork, T. (ed.). *Designing and Implementing Effective Workshops*. San Francisco: Jossey-Bass, 1984.

Squyres, W. (ed.). *Patient Education: An Inquiry into the State of the Art*. New York: Springer, 1980.

Stanley, M. "Literacy: The Crisis of a Conventional Wisdom." In S. Grabowski (ed.), *Paulo Freire: A Revolutionary Dilemma for the Adult Educator*. Syracuse, N.Y.: Syracuse University Publications in Continuing Education, 1972, 36–54.

Stice, J. (ed.). *Developing Critical Thinking and Problem-Solving Abilities*. New Directions for Teaching and Learning, no. 30. San Francisco: Jossey-Bass, 1987.

Suessmith, P. "A List of Learning Transfer Techniques." *Training Ideas*. Aug.–Sept. 1985, 48–53.

Thomas, A. "Studentship and Membership: A Study of Roles in Learning." *The Journal of Educational Thought*, 1967, *1*(2), 65–76.

Tiberius, R. *Small Group Teaching: A Trouble-Shooting Guide*. Toronto: Ontario Institute for Studies in Education, 1990.

Timpson, J., and others. "Depression in a Native Canadian in Northwestern Ontario: Sadness, Grief or Spiritual Illness?" *Canada's Mental Health*, June/Sept. 1988, 5–8.

Tough, A. *The Adult's Learning Projects*. Toronto: Ontario Institute for Studies in Education, 1979.

Tough, A. *Intentional Changes*. Chicago: Follett, 1982.

Tuckman, B. "Developmental Sequence in Small Groups." *Psychological Bulletin*, 1965, *63*, 384–399.

Van Ments, M. *The Effective Use of Role Play: A Handbook For Teachers and Trainers*. (2nd. ed.) New York: Nichols, 1989.

Vella, J. *Learning to Listen, Learning to Teach: The Power of Dialogue in Educating Adults*. San Francisco: Jossey-Bass, 1994.

Verderber, R. *The Challenge of Effective Public Speaking*. (7th ed.). New York: Wadsworth, 1988.

von Oech, R. *A Kick in the Seat of the Pants*. New York: HarperCollins, 1986

Weimer, M. "Characteristics of Effective Teachers." Unpublished presentation, Pacific Institute for Faculty Development. Victoria, B.C., 1991.

Whipple, W. "Collaborative Learning: Recognizing It When We See It." *American Association for Higher Education Bulletin*, 1987, *40*(2), 3–5.

White, B., and Madara, E. *The Self-Help Sourcebook*. Denville, N.J.: American Self-Help Clearinghouse, 1992.

Whitman, N. *Peer Teaching*. ASHE-ERIC Higher Education Report No. 4. Washington, D.C.: Association for the Study of Higher Education, 1988.

Whitman, N. "A Review of Constructivism: Understanding and Using a Relatively New Theory." *Family Medicine*, 1993, *25*(9), 517–521.

Whitman, N., Graham, B., Gleit, C., and Boyd, M. *Teaching in Nursing Practice*. East Norwalk, Conn.: Appleton & Lange, 1992.

Willis, S., Dubin, S., and Associates. *Maintaining Professional Competence: Approaches to Career Enhancement, Vitality, and Success Throughout a Work Life*. San Francisco: Jossey-Bass, 1990.

Wlodkowski, R. *Enhancing Adult Motivation to Learn: A Guide to Improving Instruction and Increasing Learner Achievement*. San Francisco: Jossey-Bass, 1991.

Women's Self-Help Network. *Working Together for Change*. Vol. 1. Campbell River, B.C.: Ptarmigan Press, 1984.

Zastrow, C. *Social Work with Groups*. Chicago: Nelson-Hall, 1985.

Index